Assessment and testing

Assessment and testing

A survey of research commissioned by the University of Cambridge Local Examinations Syndicate

Robert Wood

CAMBRIDGE
UNIVERSITY PRESS

Published by the Press Syndicate of the University of Cambridge
The Pitt Building, Trumpington Street, Cambridge CB2 1RP
40 West 20th Street, New York, NY 10011–4211, USA
10 Stamford Road, Oakleigh, Melbourne 3166, Australia

First published 1991
First paperback edition 1993
Reprinted 1995

Printed in Great Britain by Athenaeum Press Ltd, Newcastle upon Tyne.

British Library cataloguing in publication data

University of Cambridge, Local Examinations Syndicate
Assessment and testing: a survey of research.
1. Education. Assessment 2. Education. Tests. Setting
I. Title
379.154

The author and publisher gratefully acknowledge the College Entrance Examinations Board, New York, for permission to reproduce the diagram on p. 88, and the *Journal of Occupational Psychology* for permission to reproduce the table on p. 154.

ISBN 0 521 44997 9 paperback

Contents

Foreword

For more than 50 years assessment of educational attainment has been recognised as a subject for research and extensive investigations have been undertaken on it for perhaps half that time. It seems sensible to ask now what has been learnt from this activity: what is known now that was not known before, has it been put into practice, and where should one go from here?

Although one could with some objectivity catalogue the projects and reports that have been completed over the years, it is unlikely that such a list would give much guidance for the future. Nevertheless the questions posed still need to be answered, and they press upon nobody with such urgency as they do upon the examining bodies, such as the University of Cambridge Local Examinations Syndicate, which are the practitioners of assessment.

In 1987 the Syndicate set up a Research Advisory Committee who then invited Dr Robert Wood to undertake a survey of research in assessment, wide in scope (wider indeed than the Syndicate's activities) and personal in approach. It follows that the Syndicate does not necessarily agree with every position adopted or every view expressed in this report. It has however become plain during its preparation that Dr Wood has made an interesting and significant contribution which has relevance far beyond the purposes of the original commission.

This book is accordingly commended as a resource for the researcher and as a reference for the examiner. Those whose principal concern in education does not lie in assessment will also find it instructive and readable.

Richard M. Laws

RICHARD M. LAWS
Chairman, University of Cambridge Local Examinations Syndicate

Members of the Research Advisory Committee
Miss S. J. Browne
Professor N. J. Macintosh
Professor D. Nuttall
Mr J. L. Reddaway
Dr D. J. Shoesmith
Dr R. R. McLone (Secretary)

Preface

This survey occupied me for 18 months in varying degrees of intensity. The model for the enterprise, following a suggestion by John Reddaway, the Secretary of the University of Cambridge Local Examinations Syndicate, was R. H. Thouless' *Map of Educational Research.* Thouless had various helpers or correspondents who submitted material to him, whereas I had none, but the idea was the same – an informed and experienced individual (although Thouless was vastly my superior in both respects) taking a look at research in a large field and writing a synoptic and inevitably idiosyncratic account of what he found. Just as Thouless did, I have laced the reporting of results with evaluation and commentary; there seemed to be little point in writing a non-evaluative review. I have not myself engaged in meta-analysis, although I have used the results of others where available. To have attempted meta-analysis on all the many issues I have addressed would have been to turn the project into a life's work.

Thouless had for his audience the educational research community. I have had to tailor my presentation to what I perceived the Syndicate would want, although naturally I hope that the survey can be read with profit by anyone interested in the field. At the outset I was encouraged to go beyond examinations into psychological testing, and certain chapters (12, 14, 17 and 18) show that I managed to do this some of the time. But inevitably I kept coming back to examinations, which largely means British examinations.

I can hardly claim that the survey is exhaustive, although I have surveyed 80 or so journals and picked up odd references in others. Evidently there are references leading out from my references. I have been concerned to summarise directionally from the beginning to now. What I hope is that anyone who wishes to focus on a particular area or issue has the wherewithal in the references to do so.

Various individuals have assisted me by offering comments on chapters, or by feeding me leads or points of view. Members of the research committee steered me with the lightest of touches. They wanted my own voice to emerge and I am grateful for that. Nick Macintosh stimulated me to reshape chapter 14, and David Shoesmith prodded me to think again about some of the things I was saying in chapter 11. Needless to say, neither is responsible for what has appeared. Desmond Nuttall, a good friend since we were colleagues at the NFER over 20 years ago, was supportive throughout. As secretary to the committee, Ron McLone saw to it that the project proceeded at a steady pace.

At the start of the project I visited Professors Emeritus Lee Cronbach at Stanford and Bill Coffman at the University of Iowa. Both helped me to think through the shape of the survey and to put it in historical perspective. In this last respect Bill was particularly giving of his time, and I could not have gone to anyone better. Right at the end of the project I returned to the US, to the University of Pittsburgh where stimulating discussions with Bob Glaser helped improve chapter 8, and to Boston College where George Madaus offered last-minute thoughts and materials.

I would also like to thank John Johnson of the National Oracy Project, Andrew Harrison and John Foulkes for help in connection with chapter 19, Simon French for bringing me up to date on the DAATE project, and my colleague Charles Johnson for a critical reading of several of the chapters. On the production side, I am grateful, as ever, to Vera Preston for preparation and assembly of the document.

ROBERT WOOD

1 Preparing specifications for achievement tests

To construct an assessment procedure, it is necessary to have specifications. These specifications should state what it is hoped to measure, and by what methods. Ideally, the specifications should go so far as to state how individual questions or items are to be derived and how reward is to be assigned, and for what reasons. If a mix of methods is proposed, weights for each method should be stated and defended.

Specifications will have different characteristics according to whether the assessment is of aptitude or achievement. With aptitude tests, the object of interest is a blend of skills and abilities which, for instance, it is thought the budding law student should have, as in the Law School Admissions Test (LSAT), or which Executive Officers in the Civil Service will need to do their work well and to advance, as in the Civil Service Qualifying Test (EOQT). With achievement tests or school-based assessments, the object of interest is the performance students can be expected to produce having followed a prescribed course of instruction and learning.

Aptitude test specifications ought to vary considerably according to the sphere of application but, in practice, certain traditional categories tend to be imposed, notably the verbal versus non-verbal reasoning dichotomy, which goes back to the twenties, and, beyond that, various kinds of reasoning, such as analytical, logical and so on. Specifications for the LSAT, the EOQT, and now the Academic Aptitude Profiles (AAP), to be introduced by UCLES, all partake of these categories to a greater or lesser extent.

With achievement testing there has been a similar press towards standardisation, the agent this time being the so-called Bloom's *Taxonomy of Educational Objectives*, which has had such a profound impact since its publication in 1956 (Bloom *et al.* 1956), but particularly in Britain since 1965 or so. Many achievement test specifications, notably those for examinations, bear the marks of its influence, and this has had a standardising effect within and across subjects. The International GCSE (IGCSE) syllabuses may talk about domains rather than categories, but the classifications and the terminology are recognisable progeny of the

Taxonomy. The Economics syllabus, for instance, states four domains – (A) Knowledge and understanding, (B) Analysis, (C) Judgement and decision-making and (D) Investigation. Of these, (A) and (B) feature directly in the *Taxonomy*, although (B) also takes in Application, (C) is a version of Evaluation while (D) is a bit of a hotch-potch but certainly involves Comprehension and Evaluation (UCLES 1988).

From 1966 onwards, the examination boards began to incorporate *Taxonomy* categories into their syllabus requirements as research workers adapted the *Taxonomy* to specific subject areas. Twenty years on we would expect to see somewhat sophisticated versions of those rather primitive efforts, for it is quite obvious that the educational objectives movement has not been replaced by some new orthodoxy, even if it is unfashionable to acknowledge the fact. Perhaps we are in a neo-*Taxonomy* phase, as witness the IGCSE example. Certainly the hierarchical nature is played down in that particular case, in that (D) (Investigation) would presumably sit alongside (B) and (C), and not subsume them.

The research interest here is the veridicality in practice of the *Taxonomy* and the variations it has spawned. This takes us into matters of validity (chapter 12). Specifically, it is construct validity which is under scrutiny when claims are made that assessment instruments are eliciting samples of Analysis or Application or whatever it is. To the extent that test constructors have abandoned hierarchically organised schemes, the validation burden on them is lessened. Abandonment is, in any case, a wise move because all the evidence to date concerning hierarchical organisation is negative.

Once the *Taxonomy* had been rumbled as ad hoc and psychologically naïve, and even before, it was the standard defence to say that the chief virtue of deploying it lay in the signals it sent to examiners and teachers that there was more to learning, teaching and assessing than knowledge of facts. It might not be possible to differentiate these named higher order skills very well, and validation of the classification might never arrive, but adherence to the *Taxonomy* was worth it if teachers and examiners started to raise their sights and be more ambitious in what they taught and then asked of students. No doubt we have seen those benefits in improved syllabus design and better, more searching questions. Blueprints do have structuring and clarifying properties, but then so would any algorithm for converting syllabus requirements into tests where none existed before. What strikes the detached observer now, as then (1966), is the massive assumption that there is (and was) a tight correspondence between what the examiners say students should exhibit and what is developing and being developed in those students. Perhaps, after 20 years of syllabus requirements couched in *Taxonomy* terms, there is input to resemble the hoped-for output. The way behavioural objectives were seized upon provides an unmistakable example of assessment driving the curriculum, but has the curriculum ever responded in the way it was meant to?

Reference to input should not be taken to mean that analysis, evaluation and so on, are expected to be cultivated directly as if they were self-standing entities. Reification was always the greatest crime of uncritical *Taxonomy* users and, of course, the *Taxonomy* has more than a whiff of nineteenth-century faculty psychology about it – for memory and imagination read analysis and application. It is disappointing to find Heyneman (1987), in the course of a discourse directed at developing countries, writing of the *Taxonomy* as if it were a cast-iron reality – 'In each testing situation there exists a hierarchy of skills which tests wish to measure. Most simple are (i) knowledge and vocabulary awareness skills (ii) comprehension (iii) application', and so on. It is hard to disagree with Travers (1980) when he argues that taxonomies such as Bloom's *Taxonomy* are more a means of inventorying items than understanding behaviour.

Now the more sophisticated examining board might say that it too does not believe in some entity called Judgement and Decision-making. A term like that happens to be a convenient label when packaging a syllabus. It is the actual competences detailed under that head, and the others, which matter, for example recognising that economic theory is subject to various limitations and uncertainties. If a board were to take this kind of line then the onus on it shifts away from a classic construct validation exercise towards the kind of exercise described elsewhere (chapter 4) and associated with the name of Robert Gagné (1970). His question was the fundamental one – 'Is this item measuring what the constructors say it is measuring and not something else instead, or as well?' It is, in any case, a validation task the boards could hardly expect to escape, but there are no signs in the research literature, published or fugitive, of any activity in this direction. Assertions are made that questions A, B and C test competences X, Y or Z, but there never seem to be any logical and empirical checks that this might be so. It is not as if the *Taxonomy* categories and subcategories were founded on any sort of post-hoc empirical analysis such as factor analysis would supply, however dubious that method. Nothing can be taken for granted.

An early attempt at validating the hierarchical structure of the *Taxonomy* in fact used factor analysis or, more precisely, principal components analysis (Madaus, Woods & Nuttall 1973). The effect of introducing a *g* factor into the causal flow of the taxonomic structure was to weaken the strength of all lower level linkages (Knowledge → Comprehension and so on) and to split off the highest level categories, that is Synthesis and Evaluation, completely. Performance on tests purporting to tap these categories was so highly dependent on *g* that the only conclusion was that they were measuring general mental ability rather than knowledge or specific attributes. Blumberg, Alschuler & Rezmovic (1982) reported that the results of their study were consistent with those of Madaus *et al.*

A causal flow model is one way of checking the *Taxonomy*; another is to analyse expected correlation structures. If the *Taxonomy* is truly hierarchical and cumulative from bottom to top then measures of the various levels should correlate in a certain, predictable way; in fact, what is known as a **radex**. Seddon and colleagues (Seddon, Chokotho & Merritt 1981) have studied departures from the idealised pattern. They concluded that evidence to support the existence of a radex requires that the inter-item correlations should never be less than 0·3, and some should be of the order of 0·8–0·9. Since it is extremely uncommon to find pairs of items satisfying the last condition, it seems unlikely that many examples of positive evidence of a radex will be found in practice. Consequently, the Bloom *Taxonomy* structure is found wanting in terms of empirical validation. Seddon's (1978) conclusions have not been overturned. It is hard to argue with the view that 'perhaps Bloom's scheme should be used only for research purposes and not for designing examination blueprints' (Blumberg *et al.* 1982, p. 6). Accepting a compromise position where the *Taxonomy* is essentially two-category (Synthesis and Evaluation vs. the rest), as Solman & Rosen (1986) do, is hardly helpful to modern test developers. It is just the knowledge, higher order skills distinction all over again, and it is surely no longer necessary to chivvy item writers into going beyond knowledge, that is knowledge as bits and pieces to memorise, whatever schema is driving their efforts.

After content–process specifications for tests have been laid down through a blueprint, and priorities assigned, the test developer is customarily left to write items to fill quotas for each cell in the blueprint. However, the item writer is rarely given explicit rules that specify the content and form of the items. S/he is left to sample in a largely intuitive way from the very large number of items which s/he could prepare. This very loose procedure, commonly employed in test development work, provides very little guidance for the test constructor. Anderson (1972) captured the item writer's predicament when he asked, 'Which of the innumerable things said to students shall they be tested on?' (He did not even mention how the predicament is compounded massively by the many idiosyncratic interpretations of syllabus requirements, all unknown to the item writer.)

A table of specifications can help a test maker avoid asking too many questions about some topics, and too few about others, or too many questions that can be answered from verbatim memory and too few which require thinking. A table of specifications is a kind of worksheet, a reasonable intermediate step in test construction. It is not, said Anderson, a systematic solution to the problem of which questions to ask any more than a ledger sheet is a system of accounting.

Rather less loose, but not much, are the criterion-referenced approaches, exemplified first by objectives-based techniques and later by domain referencing. The objective becomes the target of assessment, and test items are generated to match the conditions specified, such as in IGCSE Economics, 'All students should be able to define retail price index and its simple calculation'. The probability that items produced by two writers will correspond is higher for objectives-based approaches than for content–process schemes, but the unavoidability of having to exercise discretion, leading to divergence between item writers, is still there. In the face of such irreducible slippage, there has been an urge, especially among American workers, to outlaw 'subjectivity' altogether by constructing a person-proof system, as it were. Thus the talk about a 'science of item writing' (Roid & Haladyna 1982). Rules are specified to generate a 'universe' or 'domain' of every possible test item of interest in a field of knowledge. To form a test, items are sampled from the universe in random or quasi-random fashion. The proportion of items in a sample a person gets correct is an estimate of the proportion he would get correct if he answered every item in the universe. Because all items are the product of explicit generative rules, ambiguity is (or should be) minimal or non-existent. Among these rule-based approaches are the 'linguistic transformations' approach, discussed by Anderson, and the 'item forms' approach (Hively *et al.* 1973). One or more sets of rules may operate in item generation, for example reading comprehension items may demand one set of rules for passage selection, another for answer generation and another for scoring.

As is the way, item forms analysis was applied to elementary mathematics and little else. The problems of dealing with domains of knowledge expressed in a natural language are of a quite different order, and the most deadly criticism of the 'linguistic transformations' approach is that it produces far too many trivial or nonsensical items.

An ambitious attempt to deal with achievement across subjects is 'facet design', originated by the late Louis Guttman (Guttman 1969). The idea is to treat achievement as multidimensional and to locate those facets which contribute to that achievement. A domain of items is then created by permuting systematically, and perhaps even exhaustively, those facets so as to produce, through their combination, single items from whose aggregate sampling can take place, again according to rules. Peled's (1984) work with verbal comprehension items provides an example. Facet design remains promising, but has yet to be taken up by examining authorities. Occasionally, constructors of psychological tests have put it to use (Blinkhorn 1985), although they may not have called it such or even formalised what they were doing. All of the items in the test known as Raven's Matrices eventuated as a result of permuting three or four basic manipulations of figural material.

It will be apparent that it is necessary to tread a fine line between over- and under-specification of tests, given that under-specification has been, and still is, the norm. This topic is taken up further in chapter 5 (*Essay questions*) when stimuli for writing answers are discussed. These stimuli are very much part of an examination specification. Are students told, for example, how long they should write, or if they are to describe, narrate or reflect?

Popham (1980), having pondered the results of over-specification or, as he called it, 'amplified objectives', thought that a limited-focus strategy was desirable. Measurement should be limited to a smaller number of assessed behaviours, but these behaviours should be conceptualised so that they are large-scale, important behaviours that subsume en route lesser behaviours (Popham, p. 21). He proposed that a test specification should consist of (1) a short general description, and (2) a sample item. These would give the item writer a general idea of what the test might contain, and would be followed by (3) a detailed specification of the stimulus attributes and (4) response attributes including specification of the correct answer, and, in the case of multiple choice items, of the reasons for the various distractors. A practical example of this kind of approach, in the medical context, is given by Laduca *et al.* (1986).

The point to notice about Popham's proposal is that it is in many respects a regression to the anti-analytic, holistic ways Gagné set out to challenge. Let us say that a big behaviour is Creativity (which it certainly is). The question is how shall we ever know that we have succeeded in measuring it, that is in isolating it, or whether we have measured something else, or something else as well?

Discussion

Educational researchers do not seem to be following anyone's advice about test construction... Procedures currently in use for constructing and describing achievement tests are in a mess. Conclusions about methods, variables or procedures can hardly be taken seriously when you don't know what the test measures.

That was Anderson in 1972. He had analysed 130 achievement tests and the results were grim. In 90% of cases no description of empirical test development procedures was given. In 67% of cases there was no indication of how questions had been selected. Reliability estimates were supplied in only 21% of cases. When it came to stating how test items were related to instruction, there was no information in 51% of cases. Hall's (1985) later survey was hardly more promising. Of 37 published achievement tests scrutinised, 11 (30%) reported no reliability data at all. Barely more than half reported on the procedures for deriving their skill domains and those that did typically limited that information to two or three brief perfunctory sentences. In addition, 54% only reported any information on how items were selected. When it came to avowedly criterion-referenced tests, of which there were nine, none, or virtually none, provided data on their item selection procedures or on reliability, and none reported any type of validation data other than content validation (chapter 7).

Anderson judged, and this is the acid test, that it would be impossible for an independent investigator to construct an equivalent test based on what was reported.

Against this rather abject record, it is a little heartening that an exercise in systematic test construction from carefully designed specifications, carried out in a medical context (Laduca *et al.* 1986), should report that knowledgeable non-doctors were able to write acceptable items directly from approved specifications. Preparing specifications may be as time-consuming as writing individual items in the conventional manner, thought the authors of the study. This illustrates the first law of sound assessment – put in most effort at the front end. If most effort has gone in at the back end, that is in marking and adjustment, then something has gone wrong.

Examinations differ crucially from tests in that the obligation to produce a manual is not present, simply because examinations self-destruct, whereas tests have a 'shelf-life'. Thus it seems pointless to produce a manual per examination, or even one for a particular year's examinations. This is highly convenient because it is certain that any single examination in this country, taken at random, would fail to satisfy even moderately pitched desiderata, not only those identified by Anderson, but others like reliability not mentioned there. There is no evidence that what is claimed to be measured is measured and no idea how reliably what **is** being measured, is measured. It is no longer possible to suppress the question, 'Why are the boards allowed to get away with producing no technical data?' This is not a matter of yearly manuals but of producing a compendium of technical data which bears on whole series of examinations, either in particular subjects over the years or on collections of cognate examinations. There is no reason at all why boards should not take on such a task, either singly or in concert. A model is to hand in the technical manual produced by the American College Testing Program (ACT). 'Its principal purpose', says ACT, 'is to document the Program's technical adequacy for serving its intended purposes' (ACT 1988). Presumably the British examination boards would wish to do no less.

References

ACT (1988) *ACT Assessment Program: Technical Manual.* Iowa City, IA: American College Testing Program.

Anderson R. C. (1972) How to construct achievement tests to assess comprehension. *Review of Educational Research*, **42**, 145–70.

Blinkhorn S. F. (1985) *Graduate and Managerial Assessment: Verbal, Numerical, Abstract.* Windsor: NFER-Nelson.

Bloom B. S. *et al.* (1956) *Taxonomy of Educational Objectives, Handbook 1: The Cognitive Domain.* New York: McKay.

Blumberg P., Alschuler M. D. & Rezmovic V. (1982) Should taxonomic levels be considered in developing examinations? *Educational and Psychological Measurement*, **42**, 1–7.

Gagné R. (1970) Instructional variables and learning outcomes. In Wittrock M. C. & Wiley D. E. (eds.) *The Evaluation of Instruction.* New York: Holt, Rinehart & Winston.

Guttman L. (1969) Integration of test design and analysis. In *Proceedings of the 1969 Invitational Conference on Testing Problems.* Princeton, NJ: Educational Testing Service.

Hall B. W. (1985) Survey of the technical characteristics of published educational achievement tests. *Educational Measurement: Issues and Practice,* **4**, 6–14.

Heyneman S. (1987) Uses of examinations in developing countries: Selection research in education sector management. *International Journal of Educational Development*, **7**, 251–63.

Hively W. *et al.* (1987) *Domain-referenced Curriculum Evaluation: A Technical Handbook and a Case Study from the Minnemast Project.* CSE Monograph Series in Evaluation No. 1. Los Angeles, CA: Center for the Study of Evaluation.

Laduca R. *et al.* (1986) Item modelling procedure for constructing content-equivalent multiple-choice questions. *Medical Education*, **20**, 53–6.

Madaus G. F., Woods E. M. & Nuttall R. L. (1973) A causal model analysis of Bloom's taxonomy. *American Educational Research Journal*, **10**, 253–62.

Peled Z. (1984) The multidimensional structure of verbal comprehension test items. *Educational and Psychological Measurement*, **44**, 67–83.

Popham W. J. (1980) Domain specification strategies. In Berk R. A. (ed.) *Criterion Referenced Measurement: The State of the Art.* Baltimore, MD: Johns Hopkins University Press.

Roid G. & Haladyna T. (1982) *A Technology for Test-Item Writing.* New York: Academic Press.

Seddon G. M. (1978) The properties of Bloom's taxonomy of educational objectives for the cognitive domain. *Review of Educational Research*, **48**, 303–23.

Seddon G. M., Chokotho N. C. J. & Merritt R. (1981) The identification of radex properties in objective test items. *Journal of Educational Measurement*, **18**, 155–70.

Solman R. & Rosen G. (1986) Bloom's six cognitive levels represent two levels of performance. *Educational Psychologist*, **6**, 243–63.

Travers R. M. W. (1980) Taxonomies of educational objectives and theories of classification. *Education and Evaluation Policy Analysis*, **2**, 5–24.

UCLES (1988) *IGCSE Economics Syllabus*. Cambridge: University of Cambridge Local Examinations Syndicate.

2 Selecting and ordering of questions and question choice

Selecting items and questions

The purpose of item analysis (chapter 9) goes beyond the weeding out of defective items and the identification of items which need further work. Through the calibration of items information is generated which can assist materially in the shaping of outcomes, whether the intention is to discriminate between individuals, or else to discriminate at some threshold, as in mastery testing. The fact that item statistics and test statistics are functionally related makes it possible, in principle, to engineer or forecast score distributions. In so doing, it is necessary to assume that the test population will behave much the same as the pre-test sample(s), which makes the choice of the latter important.

These possibilities of control are restricted to multiple choice testing and there is a modest literature on the subject: see for example Stanley (1971) and Scott (1972). Whatever control is exercised over the distribution of essay test scores, or of school-based assessments, is done through marking schemes and instructions to markers through moderation (scaling). In the nature of things such control is bound to be weak, especially if the push for discrimination is tempered by demands that 'positive achievement' be sought and rewarded (chapter 13). Since the incidence of positive achievement is (or ought to be) unpredictable, and since it is revealed most authentically by free response or open-ended enquiry and not by multiple choice, the examination planner who is using a mix of assessment methods can really only exercise control over the multiple choice component. What effect this has on the overall mark distributions will depend on the intercorrelations of the components and which steps are taken to adjust for these when aggregating (chapter 10), but the judgement must be that precision engineering is somewhat wasted against a background of uncontrolled outcomes. The introduction of criterion-referencing ideologies into examinations has resulted in a degree of ambivalence towards shaping outcomes which is liable to appear as inaction, let the chips fall where they may.

Such a policy of non-intervention might just be tolerable for some thoroughly criterion-referenced regime, if the concept of differentiation had not also been introduced. Whatever else differentiation is, it must be intended as an instrument of control. It is explicitly so at the point of entry where, for differentiation to work, it is necessary that outcomes behave in a more or less predictable way. This was presumably the intention behind the short-lived 'performance matrices' enterprise, sponsored by the Secondary Examinations Council in 1986–7. The notion of targeting questions (chapter 13) is just another way of saying that score distributions need to be engineered. With discrimination meant to coexist with differentiation **and with** the expression of positive achievement, the basic rule of psychometrics comes into play; the most efficient way of separating people is to administer items/questions of 50% difficulty for them. With large, fully-distributed, test populations this prescription is necessarily sub-optimal because it neglects those at the near and far extremes. On this neglect hinges the rationale for differentiation and ultimately for individualised adaptive testing where individuals are always meant to be faced with items of 50% difficulty for them. But if there is to be differentiation, then it follows that steps must be taken to translate the 50% rule into practice at as many levels (grades) as have been decided upon. If such steps are not taken simultaneously across all components (thereby raising problems hitherto not tackled), then differentiation becomes a dead letter, for the outcomes will ostensibly be no better or fairer than if differentiation had never been attempted.

There are indeed problems not hitherto tackled, and it seems likely that they never will be. The practice of attempting to engineer score or mark distributions pre-GCSE was never common in what now seem relatively straightforward conditions. In the new situation incoherent system requirements mean that conflicting signals are being sent to examination planners. Allowing people to differentiate themselves by their own responses is obviously to abandon control, yet discrimination is also demanded. Moving ultimately to individualised adaptive testing still seems the only honest solution to what remains a major societal sorting task, however it is dressed up.

Whatever the fate of item selection procedures in the GCSE, it is worth noting that not only may items be chosen to discriminate between individuals, but also between groups of individuals. The principal importance of such a measure lies in the evaluation of teaching programmes or instructional success. Suppose a number of classes within a school have been taught the same material, and it is desired to set all class members a test to find out which class has learnt the most. The items which differentiate within classes will not necessarily register differences between classes (Lewy 1973). This is what would be expected, given that the basic units of observation, the individual score and the class average, are so different. For item selection to differentiate between classes, the appropriate discrimination index is the within-class correlation. Using indices like the biserial will most likely result in tests which are not sensitive to differences between class performance. (Critics of the American studies, which claimed that school makes little or no difference to achievement, made much of this point.)

It will be evident that there are other possibilities once the distinction between unit of observation and unit of analysis is observed. Interest may lie in maximising discrimination among students within particular classes or, more generally, in differentiating between individuals within their respective sub-groups rather than among all of them.

Personal experience with within-class correlation on item response data from achievement tests has been that the highest values occur with items on topics that are either new to the syllabus or are controversial. If, as seems likely, these topics are taken up by only some teachers, the effect will be to create a possibly spurious impression of greater between-school variability than really exists.

Ordering items and questions and the effect of context

In conventional group testing there is an issue concerning the ordering of items in terms of difficulty. The received opinion is that items should be ordered from easy to hard (E–H), the reasoning being that the anxiety induced by encountering difficult items early in the test interferes with performance on easier items later in the test. The GCE boards would appear to favour E–H ordering (Hodson 1987). JMB multiple choice papers include a few easy questions at the start in order to encourage the candidates. Similarly, the London board states that at the beginning of a test '...some easy items may be put in to encourage the less able candidates'. Whether strict E–H sequencing continues thereafter is not known.

There is also an issue over whether item performance is affected by context; specifically whether success is affected by the immediate company an item keeps. There are two aspects to this, over and above any effects deriving from order-difficulty relationships. The company can be any company, or cognate company. For a pre-test, an item may appear (indeed is likely to appear) in a particular position and among certain company. In deciding where it should go in the operational test it would be good to know that the pre-test (or, as the Americans would say, pre-equating) statistics can be trusted for any position and any company.

Recent work indicates that such an assumption should never be made lightly.

Then there are the non-discrete items which always appear with cognate items, usually because they draw on the same stimulus material. These will always be pre-tested and tested in the same blocks if not the same position, more or less; an odd item in the set might be deleted or altered. Here it would be useful to know if performance on one item influences performance on another. Admittedly, this is more of a problem for item response theory (IRT) calibrators who rely heavily on the local independence assumption holding up. Indeed the whole business of what happens when you decontextualise items is crucial to the success of item banking strategies, whether or not conducted along IRT lines, and of computerised adaptive testing arrangements.

Running through both issues is the possibility that there might be interactions between item position (and ordering) and candidate characteristics. Any E–H arrangement or incline of difficulty is only good for a group on average, not even for the average candidate who is defined differently, and variation in individual inclines of difficulty is to be expected even if it cannot be accommodated in group testing arrangements.

The early work on E–H sequencing (pre-1970) generally converged on the view that item and test characteristics were little affected by rearranging items from E–H to random to H–E, and might even be slightly inferior under E–H sequencing. Perhaps the most thorough enquiry of the period was that by Munz & Jacobs (1971). They concluded that while an E–H arrangement did not appear to improve test performance or reduce test-taking anxiety, as compared to an H–E arrangement, it did leave students with a more positive feeling about the test afterwards ('easier and fairer') than did the H–E arrangement. Whether such feelings mean anything very much is another matter. Munz & Jacobs took the view that arranging items according to candidates' perception of item difficulty, that is subjective item difficulty, constitutes the only justification for the E–H arrangement. The snag with that, of course, is that the subjective difficulty of any item will vary with the candidate.

The foregoing remarks apply to power (unspeeded) tests. It will be apparent that E–H sequencing is always preferable for speeded tests where slower and weaker candidates might not attempt the easier items located towards the end of the test. Incidentally, there is a suggestion that aptitude tests, which will often be a little more speeded than achievement tests, are more subject to variation in candidate performance (Leary & Doran 1985).

There has now been a British study using O and A level Chemistry items (Hodson 1987). Providing, says Hodson, that the H–E sequence is avoided (as if there might be any merit in deliberately choosing it), there is no persuasive evidence to justify taking the trouble to produce an E–H sequence. Some American work (Plake 1981; Plake, Thompson & Lowry 1981) tends to bear this out. The argument goes as follows. If the test so constructed is no more discriminatory or reliable than another constructed by some other method, it confers no advantage in a norm-referenced assessment scheme. The fact that multiple choice tests are usually less discriminating than free response tests (Wood 1977), which are certainly not arranged in any particular sequence except perhaps for gentle starters, is something to be borne in mind. Perhaps the GCE boards who advise a gentle start have got it right on balance, however the rest of the test or paper is organised. There is no harm in it, and it might do some good.

So much for sequencing by difficulty without reference to any other factors. More recent work has gone further. Lane *et al.* (1987) looked not only at E–H sequencing but at what happens when students have foreknowledge of the way items are sequenced, and also at the effect of ordering items in terms of cognitive difficulty, as opposed to statistical difficulty. They also investigated whether there were differential results by gender.

The first thing to bear in mind is that cognitive difficulty was defined in terms of Bloom's *Taxonomy* categories, and we know how problematic those are (chapter 1). That said, these investigators found that when items were explicitly labelled with such categories, average performance improved, regardless of the order in which items were arranged. This is the foreknowledge just referred to. The suggestion is that when students are told to expect, say, an Application item, 'they may activate more appropriate and correct response sets and cognitive processes' than when items are sequenced simply on statistical item difficulty. As we might say colloquially, they tend to raise their game. Naturally, this procedure presupposes acquaintance with *Taxonomy* categories, something we would not expect of British students. It appears that some students were frustrated when their interpretation of what the item was demanding did not match the label on the item. We might be inclined to put this down to a strongly suspected elasticity in category definition and attribution.

Turning to gender effects, the Lane *et al.* study had something to report, to add to the Plake *et al.* (1982) study, which found that for a mathematics test male students made significant gains on tests sequenced E–H, whilst females did not. In another study (Plake & Ansorge 1984) involving non-quantitative content no significant gender differences were observed. What the Lane *et al.* study showed was an interaction of gender on performances with labels. Specifically, males' scores increased dramatically (their word) when labels were used. This suggests that males had underperformed females on this particular test. It follows, say the investigators, that labels may lessen gender differences on test performance. Given doubts about the provenance of the labels (*Taxonomy* categories), such a finding should not be taken too seriously. There is a deeper point here about the cueing it is permissible to give candidates (chapter 3).

Does the positioning of an item affect the stability of item parameter estimates? This is the question raised earlier, now expressed directly in item response theory language. The literature, as reviewed by Leary & Dorans (1985), reveals evidence of context effects but, so they claim, has not demonstrated that the effects are so strong as to invalidate test theory or practice that is dependent on an assumption of item parameter invariance. This is a strong claim. It says that it is possible to go on believing that the statistics associated with any test item, notably difficulty and discrimination, remain constant more or less regardless of the ability of the examinees or the position of the item in the test (leaving aside, of course, harebrained notions like embedding a discrete item in an alien cluster, although even that might work).

All the same, context effects have been reported. Take the matter of repositioning intact test sections. An issue here is how context effects are item-type dependent; that is to say, where the same item type crops up more than once, how much does the practice gained on the first or first and second sets improve performance on the later set(s)? Several studies (see Leary & Dorans) found at least one item type that exhibited sensitivity to material that preceded it in the testing sequence. In the most serious case, Educational Testing Service (ETS) took the step of eliminating the two suspect item types from the GRE General Test. Further analysis of these item types (Analysis of explanations and Logical diagrams) suggested that the adverse results were at least partially a consequence of the complexity and novelty of these item types; in other words, there was so much to be learned that practice effects were bound to occur.

Another area where palpable context effects have been observed is reading comprehension. A number of studies (see Leary & Dorans) have found that reading passage items are generally found to be more difficult when they appear at the end of a test or section than when they appear near the beginning. This, say Leary & Dorans, raises questions about what is being measured by reading comprehension items. Is the item measuring complex processing that is fatiguing to candidates? Is it the complexity of the item that makes it difficult? Might there be a change in cognitive processing between reading passages and responding to comprehension questions that is slower or more difficult for some candidates than for others? Leary & Dorans are right to say that understanding what makes an item difficult is still something we know too little about. An item may be difficult because it is complex or because it is obscure.

It may be that the ETS staffers were too sanguine about the effects of context on performance. Some recent Australian work (Bell, Pattison & Withers 1988) using the premier Australian aptitude test (the ASST) has demonstrated that not only was there marked dependence between items within a cluster drawing on the same stimulus material, which is perhaps to be expected, but that there were also, more worryingly, dependencies between items positioned in quite separated places within the test. These latter dependencies were associated more with mathematical than verbal material. Moreover, the extent of dependency increased with total score on the test. The local independence assumption simply did not hold. The item response model used was Rasch (chapter 9) and the test was an aptitude test, for which Rasch is ostensibly better conditioned. How much more would local independence be breached with an achievement test?

The Australian work is important not just for what it says about the efficacy of item response models and the procedures which ride on them, notably adaptive testing, but for what it says about ordinary test construction practice. It is, generally speaking, not good practice to make success on an item dependent on another. A test construction paradigm which is based on item sampling stands to be undermined if, running through the domain, there is a chain of dependencies.

Everything that has been said so far about ordering applies to multiple choice items only. We know nothing about ordering applied to free response tests. That is perhaps why the foregoing is more relevant to aptitude tests than to examinations.

Choice of questions

The very opposite of the last sentiment applies to question choice. Here is a phenomenon only encountered with free response tests. It may be noted that the allowing of question choice is a way of individualising measurement, where the routeing is self-routeing. But it is not efficient. The choice is usually based on syllabus coverage and personal taste and has little to do with measurement characteristics; at least there is no evidence that it does (Wood 1973). By 'individualising' group tests is meant the idea of contriving person–question encounters so that persons spend most of their time working on questions just within or at the threshold of their ability. Question choice does not do that.

Modularisation is merely question choice writ large. It exists to accommodate personal taste and to make syllabus coverage manageable. Like question choice, it creates vexatious marking and scaling problems. The less popular options or questions cannot possibly be marked as accurately as the well subscribed ones simply because there is not the same opportunity to establish a feel for the whole range of achievement. There is a suggestion in the literature that examiners discriminate better as time goes on (Farrell & Gilbert 1960; Sandon 1961).

Early work (Wiseman & Wrigley 1958) suggested that allowing students to select a topic had little impact on errors in marking. Later, rather more thorough work (Willmott & Hall 1975), indicates that allowing question choice does have a deleterious effect on test and examination reliability, as the consequences of uneven coverage would imply. Nor can it be said to improve validity. The many examinations within an examination which the permutations throw up would not be so much of an objection if a coherent method for arriving at comparable scores had been formulated. All are agreed that if there is a solution it will come from item response modelling procedures or else the ANOVA methods developed by Backhouse (1972) – Willmott & Hall (p. 84) note the equivalence between the Rasch model and ANOVA in this application – but that the assumptions needed for the solution to go through are far from holding up in practice.

In earlier school examinations question choice was generous, and no doubt examples can still be found. More recently, attempts have been made to curb out-and-out choice by sectionalising free response papers. Stipulating *x* questions from section A, *y* from section B and so on has the effect of reducing the number of permutations, sometimes quite drastically. This in turn means that the numbers attempting each question are more nearly equalised, with consequent gains in marking reliability.

An intriguing, if under-researched, issue is whether candidates are the best judges of the questions on which they can perform best or whether, in some sense, they are their own worst enemies. The Taylor & Nuttall study (1974) investigated the issue by asking candidates taking a CSE examination to answer the questions they omitted to answer on a separate occasion following the actual examination. In spite of the arguments concerning the lack of motivation of candidates and the fact that the majority of candidates did perform less well on the omitted questions (for whatever reasons), Taylor & Nuttall discovered that about 25% of candidates actually showed an improvement in final marks; candidates are therefore not necessarily able to choose in advance the questions on which they will score most highly. Two studies with university-level students, now rather venerable (Meyer 1939; Gowan 1972), also reported that about 25% of students in their respective samples were unable to select for assessment their best four questions from a total of five questions actually answered; specifically they scored higher marks on the one question upon which they chose not to be assessed than on at least one of the four questions upon which they chose to be assessed.

Thus a fair proportion of candidates are seen, in differing circumstances, not only to be unable to select their best questions when presented with a choice, but to be unable to assess their performance even after the event. Godshalk *et al.* (1966) observe, 'In the first place, there is no evidence that the average student is able to judge which topic will give him the advantage. In the second place, the variability in topics...would be introducing error at the same time that students might be eliminating error by choosing the topic on which they were most adequately prepared' (pp. 13–14). Naturally, the problem is exacerbated if the alternative topics are not carefully matched, and no examination board has ever pretended that it is able to do this, probably because it is impossible given individual tastes and interests.

The effects of question choice on candidates' chances were investigated in some detail by Willmott & Hall (1975). Their conclusion (p. 87) remains unsettling:

> Candidates have been penalised for attempting some questions and rewarded for answering others in all of the twenty-nine examinations analysed; such penalties and rewards are surely undue. Should it be assumed, for a moment, that this is not the case, the consequent implication is strange indeed – that the ability of candidates to pick the easier questions (avoid the harder questions) is to be rewarded and vice versa. Could this be said to be part of the purpose of examining? The view of many of the subject panels with whom the project team have had contact was that it was certainly not in the spirit of examining but that little else could be done, as a choice of questions had come to be expected by boards, teachers and pupils alike.

Apart from the unwanted equity deficits it introduces, the permitting of question choice only aids and abets that fragmentation and disarticulation of what is learnt, and which is discussed elsewhere (chapter 13). But pick-and-mix is very much in vogue.

References

Backhouse J. K. (1972) Reliability of GCE examinations: A theoretical and empirical approach. In Nuttall D. L. & Willmott A. S. *British Examinations: Techniques of Analysis*. Slough: NFER Publishing Co.

Bell R. C., Pattison P. E. & Withers G. P. (1988) Conditional independence in a clustered item test. *Applied Psychological Measurement*, **12**, 15–26.

Farrell M. J. & Gilbert N. (1960) A type of bias in marking examination scripts. *British Journal of Educational Psychology*, **30**, 47–52.

Godshalk F., Swineford F. & Coffman W. E. (1966) The measurement of writing ability. *College Board Research Monographs*, No. 6.

Gowan J. (1972) Is freedom of choice in examinations such an advantage? *The Technical Journal*, February, 31.

Hodson D. (1987) How important is question sequence? *Education in Chemistry*, **24**, 11–12.

Lane D. S. *et al.* (1987) The effects of knowledge of item arrangement, gender, and statistical and cognitive item difficulty on test performance. *Educational and Psychological Measurement*, **47**, 865–79.

Leary L. F. & Dorans N. J. (1985) Implications for altering the context in which test items appear: A historical perspective on an immediate concern. *Review of Educational Research*, **55**, 387–413.

Lewy A. (1973) Discrimination among individuals vs. discrimination among groups. *Journal of Educational Measurement*, **10**, 19–24.

Meyer G. (1939) The choice of questions in essay examinations. *Journal of Educational Psychology*, **30**, 161–71.

Munz D. C. & Jacobs P. D. (1971) An evaluation of perceived item-difficulty sequencing in academic testing. *British Journal of Educational Psychology*, **41**, 195–205.

Plake B. S. (1981) Item arrangement and knowledge of arrangement on test scores. *Journal of Experimental Education*, **49**, 56–8.

Plake B. S. & Ansorge C. J. (1984) Effects of item arrangement, sex of the subject, and test anxiety on cognitive and self perception scores in a non-quantitative content area. *Educational and Psychological Measurement*, **44**, 423–30.

Plake B. S., Ansorge C. J., Parker C. S. & Lowry S. R. (1982) Effects of item arrangement, knowledge of arrangement, test anxiety and sex on test performance. *Journal of Educational Measurement*, **19**, 49–57.

Plake B. S., Thompson P. A. & Lowry S. (1981) Effect of item arrangement, knowledge of arrangement and test anxiety on two scoring methods. *Journal of Experimental Education*, **49**, 214–19.

Sandon F. (1961) Contribution to Discussion of Lindley D. V. (1961) An experiment in the marking of an examination. *Royal Statistical Society, Series A*, **124**, 285–312.

Scott W. A. (1972) The distribution of test scores. *Educational and Psychological Measurement*, **32**, 725–35.

Stanley J. C. (1971) Reliability. In Thorndike R. L. (ed.) *Educational Measurement* (2nd edition). Washington, DC: American Council on Education.

Taylor E. C. & Nuttall D. L. (1974) Question choice in examinations: An experiment in geography and science. *Educational Research*, **16**, 143–50.

Willmott A. S. & Hall C. G. W. (1975) *O-level Examined: The Effects of Question Choice*. London: Schools Council.

Wiseman S. & Wrigley J. (1958) Essay reliability: The effect of choice of essay title. *Educational and Psychological Measurement*, **18**, 129–38.

Wood R. (1973) Response-contingent testing. *Review of Educational Research*, **43**, 529–44.

Wood R. (1977) Multiple choice: A state of the art report. *Evaluation in Education*, **1**, 191–280.

3 Administrative issues

Emphasis here is on those aspects of administration which are directly open to research. Even so, these are not topics which have received a great deal of attention. There has, for example, been next to no work done on rubrics and very little on a related topic, the wording of questions. Some work on readability of questions and instructions is beginning to emerge, however, and there is concrete evidence that in the 1988 examinations, UCLES itself (and perhaps other boards) took steps to monitor layout, question wording and instructions. The topic of question wording is dealt with in chapter 5.

The topics considered in this chapter are:

- design of rubrics;
- setting appropriate time limits, including the needs of the disabled;
- training for test-taking, including test-wiseness;
- open book examinations.

The plan was to have a section on the use of electronic calculators but there was nothing remotely like *research* in the literature, although plenty of rhetoric.

Design of rubrics

In chapter 4 the point is made that the choice of wording for telling candidates how to take multiple choice tests is determined by the view taken on how appropriate response behaviour is to be induced. It is noted that, in principle, this might mean quite sophisticated rubrics but that, in practice, if instructions are not simple, clear and concise, some candidates will behave in ways which impair their chances; for an illustration in the context of the multiple completion item type see Wright (1975).

The same principle applies to other kinds of assessment, notably essay papers. The complicating factor there has been the growth of sectioning coupled with the provision of choice within sections. The results used to be some hideously convoluted rubrics which only those with Boolean algebra could unravel. That tricky operator 'Not more than' was particularly troublesome. Now the more twisted rubrics are less evident, suggesting that the examination boards have been giving attention to making the 'rules of the game' clearer.

This is certainly the case with UCLES. A survey of the whole range of question papers from the 1988 examination (UCLES 1988/89) found that the instructions to candidates are adequately clear and consistent. Even so, certain recommendations were made, of which the most significant are:

> the straightforward, plain imperative alone should be used, that is 'Answer xxx questions' or 'Answer questions 1 and 2 and three other questions';
> likewise, all instructions should be in the second person and in the active voice, for example 'Write your answer' **not** 'Candidates are advised to write their answers';
> on the basis that candidates cannot be told too often what to do, specific requirements for sections should be repeated below the headings for sections;
> information about marks should be separated from instructions;
> italics are the least readable of type faces and yet are over-used (the same point is made by the DIME researcher, 1988); upper and lower case, roman and bold type should be used in preference.

To draw together all its recommendations, the UCLES survey produced an example of a rubric embodying good practice. Interestingly, it is rather similar to the one offered by Mobley (1987, p. 30) as an improvement on an actual O level Physics paper rubric. In the Mobley version, the contrast in clarity between 'before' and 'after' is really quite striking.

Time limits

It is hard to understand why there is so little British research on time limits. Chapter 17 contains a discussion of **speededness** in the context of aptitude tests, but it is of general application. The distinction is made between speeded tests and unspeeded or **power** tests, such as the LSAT or most, if not all, examinations. Of course, every test or examination is subject to a degree of speededness, unless candidates are allowed to spend as long as they like. Chapter 17 mentions an operational benchmark for unspeeded tests, which is that at least 75% of persons who take the test

Mark values per time allowed

Paper	Time (min.)	Number of questions	Mark value	MV/per min.
1	60	28	42	1·43
2	90	21	60	1·50
3	75	7	48	1·57
4	90	8	60	1·50
5	45	5	30	1·50
6	60	4	40	1·50

*Taken from specimen papers, UCLES 1988*a.

should be able to finish 95% or more of the questions on the test. This can always be checked, but with multiple choice items there is no guarantee that this objective is being achieved given that candidates are encouraged to guess at items they are unable to answer.

Concerning time limits for multiple choice tests, more than one rule-of-thumb has been proposed. It used to be reckoned (such as in the University of London GCE board) that 90 seconds per item was a fair allowance, and multiple choice papers would be timed accordingly. A Schools Council survey (1973) started with the premise that each item presents candidates with a different situation so that they are required to switch their thoughts rapidly from one to another. The survey concluded that this introduces a fatigue element into objective tests. Just how many items it takes before fatigue becomes significant for most candidates is unknown. The survey suggests that a fairly common rule-of-thumb is to assume that each true/false item will take the candidate half a minute to answer and all other types will take one minute.

Where free response questions are concerned, there appear to be no rules-of-thumb, another illustration of the way multiple choice is girt about with rules and requirements which free response manages to escape. Naturally, it is more difficult to set limits where demands posed by questions are so much more variable, but it should not be impossible. A comparison of the time limits proposed by UCLES for its IGCSE Mathematics offerings is instructive, especially when set alongside the mark values attached to each paper, and the maximum mark value per minute spent (see table).

The Paper 1 and 2 questions are, of course, short answer; the others are deeper, meatier questions. The mark value gainable per minute spent, which is the statistic to look at, is reasonably consistent, with 1·5 marks emerging as the modal value. This is interesting in that it carries the suggestion that the payoff from free response questions is better than for multiple choice, with its 1 mark per minute tariff (assuming the favoured rule-of-thumb).

In deciding upon realistic time limits for a test containing a number of different item or question types, it is necessary to take a view on what the more elaborate types might demand. One minute per item may not be enough. A complicating factor is the presence of recognisable minority groups who, for whatever reason, may take longer to finish, on the whole, than the majority group. Several ETS studies (such as Dorans, Schmitt & Curley 1988) found that Black students appear to need more time to complete the Scholastic Aptitude Test (SAT) verbal sections than White students with comparable total SAT verbal scores. Hartigan & Wigdor (1989) reported along the same lines for a much larger data set. They noted (p. 108) that Blacks 'were at a relative disadvantage in the range of the test at which the influence of time limits was most keenly felt'.

Supporting evidence in this country comes from my own study with young quite poorly educated ethnic minority groups (Wood 1990) and from the Civil Service Commission (CSC) study (Bethell-Fox 1988, p. 29) where ethnic minority candidates were in trouble with a verbal test after item 12 of a 30-item test. For them, this test had become progressively speeded (as it had also for the majority group, although with less marked acceleration). Whether this was as a result of trying to cope with novel formats, of struggling with a lot of dense reading material, or simply of poor time management is not known. The CSC study was chary about interpreting the minority results but did suggest that their 'tending to lack strong reading and comprehension skills' (p. 37) might have something to do with it! I was inclined to be more forthright, pointing to the historical record of known poor reading attainment among Black groups and thus the almost inevitability of impaired performance on any tests which require reading and comprehension – and at speed.

A study involving Hispanics indicated that they would do as well as Anglos if given extra time. Llabre & Froman (1987) compared Hispanic and Anglo college students with respect to the amount of time allocated to items on a reasoning test administered via microcomputer. Their results revealed that the Hispanic examinees consistently spent more time than the Anglo examinees on the test items; it would take them 30 minutes longer to complete a 100-item test, but, if they were allowed the extra time, they would do as well.

Failing to answer questions can be due to believing that guessing is frowned upon (often quite mistakenly) or to running out of time. Grandy (1987) found that the tendency to leave items blank on the GRE General test was most evident among women and non-Whites (particularly Blacks and resident aliens). It is a pity she was unable to separate the two causes of omitting. However, she did find that, for the verbal test, ethnicity was the second best predictor of omissiveness, after total GRE score.

The literature in this area is still somewhat incoherent. To set against the studies which say that certain groups need more time, there are studies which say that extending time limits will not differentially increase scores of groups defined by race, sex or years out of school (Evans & Reilly 1972; Wild, Durso & Rubin 1982). This last study observes that the impact of timing on test score by ability level is not well understood, and this seems fair comment.

Time limits and the disabled

Whether students with disabilities might benefit from more time, and how much, are issues which a series of ETS studies has begun to open up (Willingham *et al.* 1988). Packer (1987) reported that the type of disability individuals had, and the version of the test taken (braille, cassette, larger type or regular print), was related to the amount of time that students took on average. Disabled students, on average, used much more time than the routinely expected $2\frac{1}{2}$ hours to complete five sections of the SAT. Some groups averaged almost two-and-a-half times the standard and many individuals, particularly visually impaired individuals who took braille or cassette versions, took well over three times the standard. For hearing impaired students, who took the least time of any of the disability groups, vocabulary and English reading appeared to be the most serious problems, and an increase in time does not appear to fully compensate. Besides, there are no ready formulas for arriving at suitable extensions.

Packer stresses the importance of recognising the existence of individual variation in all disability groups. If specific guidelines are set for the amount of time that disabled students can take, there should be some mechanism for students to be considered individually if they have an impairment that makes the time limits unreasonable for them. How difficult it is, though, to judge how bad a handicap is.

Packer's was not an experimental study and so she was unable to interpret causally the relationship between SAT scores and testing time. Why, for instance, did verbal scores for visually impaired students taking braille exams tend to be lower for students who took more time to complete the verbal sections? Is it that the brighter students work faster? Is it that slower readers become more fatigued during the test because they are working longer, and therefore get lower scores? Or is it that poor braille readers are taking longer, and are also not doing as well, simply because they do not read braille well?

That manipulating time alone may be irrelevant in helping the disabled is borne out by work undertaken by the Recruitment Research Unit (RRU) in the Civil Service Commission (Johnson, personal communication). For some kinds of test format braille is a poorly conditioned medium. In the first place text takes more space to represent in braille. This automatically slows down braille readers. Lengthy word problems and tables (which usually extend across two braille pages) may be more difficult to process because information takes longer to encode and must, therefore, be kept in short-term memory longer. Another result is that figure labels (such as angle measurements) cannot be unambiguously placed unless the figure is substantially larger than the printed model (Bennett, Rock & Novatkoski 1989).

Sometimes, says Johnson, alleged solutions borne of conventional wisdom actually make matters worse. An example is where copies are enlarged to help visually impaired candidates. The real issue here is the quality of contrast – what is actually wanted are manageable documents with excellent contrasts. Thus time is something of a red herring when what disabled candidates really need is a fundamental rejig. For instance, Johnson reports that candidates using braille could not cope at all with flow diagrams; when these were recast as truth tables, their performance improved.

When efforts are made to create helpful braille versions, and time limits are modified appropriately, it appears that, for SAT-M at any rate, the results for visually handicapped and non-handicapped are comparable (Willingham *et al.* 1988). That said, there have been instances of differentially functioning items (Bennett, Rock & Novatkoski 1989).

Training for test-taking including training for test-wiseness

There is evidence that giving people prior familiarisation with the material they are likely to encounter in tests and examinations is helpful to most people. It is a step on the road to becoming test-wise, which means using all the information available in the testing experience so as to boost test score. School candidates taking public examinations are usually privy to formats and kinds of questions and may even be given extensive practice in dealing with these. But for out-of-school candidates, and for those taking tests for entry into public service, it is not so easy. One way of avoiding people taking tests cold is to send them a description of the test and examples of questions beforehand. The Civil Service Commission does this for its EO Qualifying Test (reproduced in Bethell-Fox 1988). The material describes the three different tests and offers sample questions, all of which is useful. What it does not do is to help candidates get test-wise.

Nowhere is there any indication of how much time should be given to the sample questions, or what the real test might demand in terms of time management.

The Civil Service Commission also produces a leaflet for Administrative Grade applicants taking the Short Answer Test. The trouble here is that apart from being light on examples (only one is given), the leaflet will not necessarily find its way into the hands of those who most need it. A further problem is that in the test itself there is an unusual item format for which the candidate receives no familiarisation at all and literally has to do from cold. That this may be the most difficult section, anyway, only aggravates the problem.

Whatever the value to the individual of prior familiarisation material, it is quite conceivable that many people, with and without such material, would find it of greatest help to be able to ask a few questions, and in general to fathom the rules of the game. Such questions are not allowed in traditional settings, but they could be. Granted, to allow questions would require careful handling so as not to compromise the standard administration procedures applying to psychometric tests, although these too are not enshrined forever. A limit would have to be placed on the total number of questions or on the time allowed for questions and answers, and all answers (and questions) would have to be relayed clearly to all candidates. It is worth noting that the American *Standards for Educational and Psychological Testing* (APA 1985) recommends (Standard 13.1) that in some group testing situations where many test-takers typically come from a particular linguistic minority, the test administration might profitably be conducted by personnel specially trained to interact with members of that group. There is, of course, no reason at all why, in order to lighten the reading load and increase confidence, written instructions on the test booklet should not be read out **as well** (which is actually quite common), or better still played from a tape, as is done for instance in US armed forces testing programmes (Wigdor & Green 1986).

Test-wiseness was analysed by Cole (1982) into the following elements:

utilising test construction flaws or cues – a gross example (and a good check on item soundness) would be the ability to answer questions on a passage without reading that passage (see for example Pyrczak 1972, 1974 and FairTest 1989);
being careful;
following directions;
guessing effectively (chapter 4);
using time well;
marking answers with care.

To which might be added:

> reviewing answers and changing them if necessary – something always worth doing (Wood 1977).

All of these elements are said to be susceptible to training, some more than others. In a meta-analysis of the evidence to date, Samson (1985) concluded that training programmes in test-taking skills were effective, especially those which continue for five weeks or longer. Dreisbach & Keogh (1982) studied young Mexican-American children and found that training in test-wiseness was an important influence on test performance on a school readiness test. Working with older Hispanics, Maspons & Llabre (1985) demonstrated improved test performance as a consequence of training in test-taking skills.

Evidently there is a distinction, an important one, between on the one hand training in test-wiseness and on the other practice in answering questions similar to those which may occur where there may be no special instruction or assistance, such as in the EO Qualifying Test booklet. There is also a distinction between test-coaching and test-wiseness. Test-coaching is specific to the content being examined, whereas test-wiseness is applicable across a range of content areas (Ritter & Idol-Maestas 1986) and is essentially a meta-construct, like an executive skill.

In a comprehensive evaluation of the evidence on coaching and practice, Bond (1989) makes the point that the only situation in which extensive instruction in test-taking per se can yield a substantial payoff in terms of increased test performance (note substantial) is when the test is poorly constructed or administered, or when clues to correct answers are contained in the items themselves or implied by the test administrator. Pyrczak (1972) identified two strategies used by persons who scored better than chance, one making use of interrelationships among the items accompanying a given passage, the other involving the tendency to select alternatives that state general principles rather than specific facts. (Prior knowledge and general verbal ability are also importantly related to this skill.)

A study by Powers (1987) suggests that, when offered the same relevant pre-examination experience, various subgroups, even those that differ dramatically with respect to initial test scores, can achieve similar improvements on tests that are susceptible to special test preparation. So, to that extent, nobody benefits most. What, though, about groups that Powers did not study? His results do not cover those anxious about test-taking, or those with slow but deliberate styles of working, or those with little experience of standardised tests.

To summarise: being test-wise does help, and it is not difficult to acquire the necessary nous. As Bond says (p. 432), some elements of test-wiseness are little more than a set of rules that any individual can, with minimal practice, apply with profit. The fact that the gains are likely to be modest on the whole and perhaps also quite uniform is not, of course, a reason for belittling training in test-taking. Some gains are bound to be large, as when the confidence which comes with effective training enables the individual to mobilise what s/he knows and understands so that competence is, as it were, **actualised** (Wood & Power 1987).

Open book examinations

Reviewing the pre-1982 literature (a rather thin literature) Francis (1982) interpreted the findings as showing that under open book conditions, students rely less on memorising facts and their anxiety about the examination is reduced. This, he said, seems to help weaker candidates more than stronger candidates. Francis then carried out his own study and found just the opposite. For A level English Literature examinations set in open book and traditional formats, candidates who gained grade B on the open book examination were judged to have achieved significantly higher levels of achievement compared with those given grade B on the traditional examination. For grade E candidates the differences were hard to spot.

What distinguishes Francis' study from others is the decision to frame quite different questions, as in this example:

Traditional syllabus	**Alternative syllabus**
Twelfth Night	Shakespeare, *Measure for Measure*
'For the rain it raineth every day' Consider the element of melancholy and human sadness in **Twelfth Night**.	Read Act II, scene iv, lines 30–187 from Isabella's entrance to the end. How well do you think Isabella and Angelo understand each other in this scene?

Most teachers, questioned by Francis, said that they were able to concentrate to a far greater extent on developing candidates' literary skills through, for example, the detailed study of text. The evidence from UCLES' involvement with the Plain Texts scheme (UCLES 1988*b*) bears this out. It would seem to be the biggest single advantage of open book examinations.

The other kind of study found in the literature looks at what happens when candidates are allowed to use books to help them answer questions like that on *Twelfth Night*. In these circumstances, time spent consulting notes and books turns out to be a critical variable. Boniface (1985) found that weaker candidates made more use of notes and obtained lower marks on the open book examination. Stronger candidates made less use of notes and texts and obtained higher scores. Certain candidates devoted more than the average amount of time to consulting notes and texts and seemed to have changed their strategy in this respect around two-thirds of the way through the examination (Boniface had them signal by way of bleepers under the desk whenever they went into open book mode).

Boniface urged that students be trained in taking open book examinations, but this is to miss the point as long as the examinations are traditionally conceived. Training is needed, but of a different kind, so as to facilitate the handling of texts in relation to appropriately framed questions.

If the books have to be opened to deal with questions assuming, as in the example, that no one memorises 158 lines of text, then the trade-off between the number of questions and the time which must be spent searching and reading must be delicately gauged. According to Francis, candidates felt it was still important to memorise quotations, or their location; there being insufficient time in the examination to search for these.

The issue of cutting out search time was addressed by Trigwell (1987). His idea was to get students to work up their own crib cards ahead of time. The cards contain a limited amount of material, they do not usually contain material unfamiliar to the student, and the student usually knows where items of information can be found. The very familiarity of the cards' contents would seem to be their undoing. Because the card closely reflects what they already know, the content is of little use to students in the examination given, says Trigwell, that few students seem capable of answering questions that they are unfamiliar with, even though the card may contain much of the information needed to answer the question. In common with other commentators, Trigwell finds the card (or the open book) to have security blanket value in decreasing anxiety among candidates.

References

American Psychological Association (1985) *Standards for Educational and Psychological Testing*. Washington: APA/NCME/AERA.

Bennett R. E., Rock D. A. & Novatkoski I. (1989) Differential item functioning on the SAT-M braille edition. *Journal of Educational Measurement*, **26**, 67–79.

Bethell-Fox C. E. (1988) *Fairness in selection: Adverse impact and the Civil Service Commission's Executive Officer Qualifying Test: Part I: Evidence of bias.* Recruitment Research Unit Report No. 35.

Bond L. (1989) The effects of special preparation on measures of scholastic ability. In Linn R. L. (ed.) *Educational Measurement* (3rd edition). London: Collier-Macmillan.

Boniface D. (1985) Candidates' use of notes and text books during an open-book examination. *Educational Research*, **27**, 201–9.

Cole, N. S. (1982) The implications of coaching for ability testing. In Wigdor A. K. & Garner W. R. (eds.) *Ability Testing: Uses, Consequences and Controversies*. Washington, DC: National Academy Press.

DIME (1988) Some factors which may affect the candidates' understanding of examination questions. *Report No. 2, Differentiation in MEG Examinations Project*. Midland Examining Group.

Dorans N. J., Schmitt A. P. & Curley W. E. (1988) Differential speededness: Some items have DIF because of where they are, not what they are. Paper presented at the National Council on Measurement in Education. New Orleans.

Dreisbach M. & Keogh B. K. (1982) Testwiseness as a factor in readiness test performance of young Mexican-American children. *Journal of Educational Psychology*, **74**, 224–9.

Evans F. R. & Reilly R. R. (1972) A study of speededness as a source of test bias. *Journal of Educational Measurement*, **9**, 123–31.

FairTest (1989) SAT-Verbal measures test wiseness. *FairTest EXAMINER*, Spring, p. 9.

Francis J. (1982) A case for open-book examinations. *Educational Review*, **34**, 13–26.

Grandy, J. (1987) Characteristics of examinees who leave questions unanswered on the GRE general test under rights-only scoring. *ETS Research Report*, 87-38.

Hartigan J. A. & Wigdor A. K. (eds.) (1989) *Fairness in Employment Testing*. Washington, DC: National Academy Press.

Llabre M. M. & Froman T. W. (1987) Allocation of time to test items: A study of ethnic difference. *Journal of Experimental Education*, **55**, 137–40.

Maspons M. M. & Llabre M. M. (1985) The influence of training Hispanics in test taking on the psychometric properties of a test. *Journal for Research in Mathematics Education*, **16**, 177–83.

Mobley M. (1987) Making ourselves clearer: Readability in the GCSE. *Working Paper No. 5*. Secondary Examinations Council, London.

Packer J. (1987) SAT testing time for students with disabilities. Unpublished paper, Educational Testing Service.

Powers D. E. (1987) Who benefits most from preparing for a 'coachable' admissions test? *Journal of Educational Measurement*, **24**, 247–62.

Pyrczak F. (1972) Objective evaluation of the quality of multiple-choice test items to measure comprehension in reading passages. *Reading Research Quarterly*, **8**, 62–71.

Pyrczak F. (1974) Passage-dependence of items designed to measure the ability to identify the main ideas of paragraphs: Implications for validity. *Educational and Psychological Measurement*, **34**, 343–8.

Ritter S. & Idol-Maestas L. (1986) Teaching middle school students to use a test-taking strategy. *Journal of Educational Research*, **79**, 350–7.

Samson G. E. (1985) Effects of training test-taking skills on achievement test performance: A quantitative synthesis. *Journal of Educational Research*, **78**, 261–6.

Schools Council (1973) Objective test survey. Unpublished document.

Trigwell K. (1987) The crib card examination system. *Assessment and Evaluation in Higher Education*, **12**, 56–65.

University of Cambridge Local Examinations Syndicate (undated, but 1988 or 1989) *Clarity and Consistency of Instructions to Candidates*. Cambridge: UCLES.

University of Cambridge Local Examinations Syndicate (1988*a*) *International General Certificate of Secondary Education: Mathematics* (specimen syllabus). Cambridge: UCLES.

University of Cambridge Local Examinations Syndicate (1988*b*) *O level Literature Plain Texts Scheme 1966–1987* (ed. J. Ogborn). Cambridge: UCLES.

Wigdor A. K. & Green B. F. (eds.) (1986) *Assessing the Performance of Enlisted Personnel*. Washington, DC: National Academy Press.

Wild C. L., Durso R. & Rubin D. B. (1982) Effect of increased test-taking time on test scores by ethnic group, years out of school and sex. *Journal of Educational Measurement*, **19**, 19–29.

Willingham W. W. *et al.* (1988) *Testing Handicapped People*. Boston, MA: Allyn & Bacon.

Wood R. (1977) Multiple choice: A state of the art report. *Evaluation in Education: International Progress*, **1**, 191–280.

Wood R. (1990) *Ethnic Minorities and Ability Tests*. London: Commission for Racial Equality.

Wood R. & Power C. N. (1987) Aspects of the competence–performance distinction: Educational, psychological and measurement issues. *Journal of Curriculum Studies*, **19**, 409–24.

Wright P. (1975) Presenting people with choices: The effect of format on the comprehension of examination rubrics. *Progress in Learning and Educational Technology*, **12**, 109–14.

4 Multiple choice testing

No assessment technique has been rubbished quite like multiple choice, unless it be graphology.

The Orangoutang score is that score on a standardised reading test that can be obtained by a well-trained Orangoutang under these special conditions. A slightly hungry Orangoutang is placed in a small cage that has an oblong window and four buttons. The Orangoutang has been trained that every time the reading teacher places a neatly typed multiple choice item from a reading test in the oblong window, all that he (the Orangoutang) has to do to get a bit of banana is to press a button, any of these buttons, which, incidentally, are labelled A, B, C and D. (Fry 1971)

If this sort of snidery is the low road, Banesh Hoffman tried to take the high road. In his various onslaughts on multiple choice (see for example Hoffman 1967), he insisted that multiple choice 'favours the picker of choices rather than the doer', and that students he variously called 'gifted', 'profound', 'deep', 'subtle' and 'first rate' are liable to see more in a question than the questioner intended, a habit which, he claimed, does not work to their advantage. Hoffman was never able to substantiate these charges and there have been surprisingly few attempts by others to do so. His polemic was, of course, motivated by the exclusive use (at the time) of multiple choice testing in the USA. For him, it was a matter of 'picking' **or** 'doing', whereas we can see that students can be asked to 'pick' **and** 'do'.

When justifying multiple choice (or MCQ) it is necessary to insist that it is a technique which does a particular job and no more; that it should not be judged against criteria which would not be applied to other techniques; and that the job it does – making students read and think (hopefully) but **not** write – is well worth doing. It is, in any case, only good assessment practice to insist on multiple methods, and multiple modalities. Mathews (1967) reckoned that students who are not fluent in writing skills, which is most students, might, with alternative suggestions before them to choose from, be encouraged to think further about a problem met in class or laboratory situations, where an open-ended question, with the demand of more complex thinking, may actively discourage a response.

It has been the practice of critics of multiple choice to apply double standards. Dudley (1973), for instance, writing in the medical context, criticised multiple choice on the grounds that it fails to test adequately all aspects of an individual's competence. This is about as fair as complaining about a stethoscope because it cannot be used to examine eyes and ears.

It is said about multiple choice that it favours and promotes **convergent** thinking. But the people who frame MCQ are, by and large, the same people who frame and mark (or have framed and marked) essay questions. If their thinking is convergent, it will show in both cases. Vernon (1964) may have had this in mind when he remarked that it is by no means certain that conventional examinations are capable of eliciting what are often called the 'higher qualities', which include **divergent** thinking. He observed, quite correctly, that the typical examination answer, at least at age 15 or 16, tends to be marked more for accuracy and number of facts than for organisation, originality and so on, not least because this tends to produce acceptable levels of reliability.

Multiple choice is castigated because it gives the impression that there are unequivocally correct answers to questions. This in turn arises from MCQ being a realisation of what Ravetz (1971), writing about science, called **vulgarised knowledge**, and what Kuhn (1962) more kindly called **normal science** – that kind of degraded knowledge which arises from progressive banalisation and displacement of teaching from contact with research and high class scientific debate. Again, it is necessary to get perspective. It is not PhD scientists who are being tested, but 15–16 or even 18 year olds. In general, it seems inevitable that most young students will be equipped only with received knowledge and ideas which for the time being, and for some always, amount to an outdated view of the physical world.

It seems pointless to deny that MCQ embodies standardised knowledge. If that is what is taught, then all examining techniques will deal in it. More than anything else, examinations serve to codify what at any time passes as 'approved' knowledge, ideas and constructions. Through the items they set, MCQ examiners make bare their view of the world, and are exposed in doing so. Essay examiners, by contrast, can conceal their views behind questions like 'It is often said that Britain has an unwritten constitution. Discuss.', a question for which only standardised knowledge will do.

MCQ is too simple-minded and trivial, say the critics. What they mean is that it is perfectly obvious what the candidate has to do. There is none of that guesswork, trying to work out what the examiner wants. So transparent is MCQ that the gifted, creative, non-conformist mind is apt to see more than was intended, and ends up uncertain, perplexed and wrong, or so Hoffman believed. Again, some perspective is necessary. Superior intellect can take apart questions in ways the average 16 or 18 year old would not dream of. Whether or not 'gifted' 16 or 18 year olds find these ambiguities in the examination room is very much an open question. The best study to date (Alker, Carlson & Hermann 1969) concluded that 'first-rate' students were not, in general, upset and penalised by MCQ. They found that characteristics of both superficial and deep thinking were associated with doing well on MCQ. There the matter rests until more evidence comes along. A further study along the lines of the one just discussed would be worth doing.

A perennial research question is whether, and to what extent, MCQ succeeds in measuring distinctly different elements of performance from other techniques. That there is more commonality than might be supposed from a priori reasoning, and from surface inspection, is borne out by the good prediction secured by well-made aptitude tests like the SAT, and also by some empirical work. In general, these findings should not be taken to mean that MCQ is coming up with richer measures than might be expected, but rather that the other forms of testing, notably essays, are less rich than they might be. Ultimately, however, interpretation of correlations depends on what view one takes of the distribution of within- and between-individual differences at certain ages. The ubiquity of the so-called **positive manifold** indicates that within-individual distributions of skills and abilities are quite restricted and truncated at the ages we are talking about, and perhaps also into early adulthood.

Studies by Bracht & Hopkins (1970) and Huxham & Lipton (1974) and Breland (1977) are more recent examples of a line of enquiry which began with an article by D. G. Patterson in 1926 entitled 'Do new and old type examinations measure different mental functions?'; 'new', of course, meaning MCQ and 'old' essay. It is a line of enquiry which generalises into relationships between all types of measures, a topic which is more properly dealt with under **construct validity** (chapter 12).

The research question concerns the uniqueness of the information provided by each type of measure when it is designed to capitalise on its purported advantages. The Bracht & Hopkins study found that neither measure added much at all to the other; operational decisions based on either would have been much the same, once allowance was made for errors of measurement. An extensive literature search pointed in the same direction. Vernon (1962), for instance, noticed very high correlations among reading tests in such diverse fields as social studies, science and literature and he wondered if they might be due to the fact that all were multiple choice tests. He designed a study aimed at distinguishing between content and format factors in vocabulary and reading tests. Parallel forms of several tests were developed in both multiple choice and free response formats. To Vernon's surprise, he found no evidence of format factors; the intercorrelations among the free response forms and among the multiple choice forms were no higher than the correlations between the two formats. This was a particularly careful piece of work.

Reviewing the research on the assessment of writing ability, Cooper (1984) found enough evidence to justify the conclusion that multiple choice and essay tests of writing ability both contribute unique information to an overall assessment. Indirect assessment (MCQ) generally focuses on word and sentence level characteristics, such as mechanics, diction, usage, syntax and modification, whereas direct assessment (essay) often centres on higher order or discourse level characteristics, such as statement of thesis, clarity, organisation, development and rhetorical strategy (Cooper, p. 40). Cooper concluded that the best form of writing assessment should contain an essay as well as a multiple choice section.

Summing up the results to date, Frederiksen (1984) concluded that for the kinds of tests studied, format at most makes a small difference. The qualifier 'kinds of tests' was the key to explaining this outcome, he thought. If the multiple choice format tends to exclude items that measure higher level processes, it would be desirable also to make comparisons in which the multiple choice tests are adaptations of free response tests intended to measure complex cognitive skills. The only work of that nature, as far as he was concerned, made use of tests that elicit problem-solving behaviour in life-like situations. For a test called Formulating Hypotheses, correlations between corresponding scores for the two formats were found to be very low.

Was Frederiksen saying that MCQ can never measure higher level processes? Not necessarily, but he was sure that it is much easier to write factual items than items that require inference, analysis, interpretation or application of a principle. This, of course, is a general observation. Multiple choice does best when it checks out factual knowledge quickly. Claims are made that it can do more and item types have been constructed which appear to elicit particular higher order skills, such as data sufficiency, yet there is still uneasiness about the supporting evidence. Frederiksen maintained that he knew of only two studies which spoke to this issue. In one, Bowman & Peng (see, for reference, Frederiksen) asked five psychologists to judge which one of four cognitive abilities was predominantly involved in answering each item in four forms of the GRE Advanced Psychology Test. The four abilities were named memory, comprehension, analytic thinking and evaluation. The consensus of the judges was that 70% were memory items, 15% measured comprehension primarily, 12% required analytic thinking, and only 3% involved evaluation. Thus, Frederiksen concluded, even a professionally made test that is widely used for admission to graduate schools was found to be primarily a measure of factual knowledge. The result also prompts the thought that Popham's (1980) proposal to test 'big' behaviours by subsuming lesser behaviours en route (chapter 1) might easily come to grief for the same reasons.

It is worth adding that the standard device of asking judges to say what they think an item is measuring is not without blemish. When judges were asked to use the higher Bloom *Taxonomy* categories agreement was the exception rather than the rule (see refs. in Wood 1977, p. 205). Wood observed that the exercise was rather like asking people to sort fruit into apples, oranges, bananas and so on without giving them much idea of what an apple or a banana looks like. There is, in any case, a problem with the Bloom *Taxonomy*, the work which was responsible for the drive to test higher order skills via MCQ. The hierarchical structure of the *Taxonomy* has never been satisfactorily verified, even by sophisticated statistical methods.

The problem at the root of all this, and one which is frustrating an answer to the question of whether MCQ can test higher order skills, is that too often items have been so loosely worded as to permit a variety of problem-solving strategies and therefore a variety of opinions as to what the item might have been measuring. Thus the old chestnut that one student's recall is another student's comprehension.

What is missing is control of the kind Gagné (1970) was proposing when he called for measurement to be distinctive – 'distinctiveness in measurement has the aim of ruling out the observation of one category of capability as opposed to some other capability' (p. 111). To use one of Gagné's examples, the principle that 'a parallelepiped is a prism whose bases are parallelograms' may not have been learned because the learner has not acquired one or more of its component concepts, whether 'prism' or 'base' or 'parallelogram'. Thus the first stage of measurement would be to determine whether these concepts have been acquired.

When two types of measure correlate highly and it is inferred that they seem not to be measuring anything very different, the stock response is to argue that one or the other can be dispensed with, preferably the more expensive or troublesome one. This conclusion does not follow at all, as Choppin (1974) demonstrated. Suppose, he says, that two measures, X and Y, correlate 0·98 and that X is found to correlate 0·50 with some other variable Z. Examination of the variance shared between the variables shows that the correlations between Y and Z may lie anywhere between

0·33 and 0·67. Consider other arguments. If the high correlation comes about because the open-ended questions are doing the same job as the multiple choice items (eliciting factual content and so on), then the essay paper is obviously not being used to advantage. It is not performing its special function. In science subjects there may be some truth in this. But if there are grounds for supposing that the processes called for by the two tests are different in kind, and separate functions are being satisfied, all that high correlation means is that, relative to each other, persons produce the same kind of performance on both tests.

That various tests administered to the same children should produce high correlations need come as no surprise; as Levy (1973, pp. 6–7) remarked, children developing in a particular culture are likely to accrue knowledge, processes or whatever at different rates but in a similar order, a view shared by Anastasi (1970). What no one should do is to conclude from this that it is a waste of time to teach some aspect of a subject just because tests based on the subject matter correlate highly with tests based on other aspects of the subject. As Cronbach (1970, pp. 48–9) pointed out, a subject in which one competence was developed at the expense of the other could go unnoticed since one or more schools could on average be high on one competence and low on the other without this showing up in the correlation between scores. It is the **across-schools** correlation, which is formed by correlating average scores for schools, that will expose uneven development of the two competences. Here is a useful check, but how often is it performed?

Areas have been pinpointed where research has been thin when it might have been substantial. As usual, the reason is that it is tricky research to do. Finding out whether MCQ punishes 'first-rate' minds or tests so-called higher order skills is not easy, but there should have been more activity. The soft research has to do with the 'nuts and bolts' of the MCQ and there has been no lack of that (thus the length of this chapter). Would that the same time and effort had been put into studying essay tests. But that illustrates another plus point about MCQ. The time and effort spent has resulted in a good understanding about how the simple multiple choice item is best constructed and presented and answered. It is now possible to be quite prescriptive on a number of issues. These are:

number of alternatives;
use of 'none of these';
scoring systems and instructions (to deal with guessing);
answer until correct;
changing answers;
confidence weighting;
differential weighting.

Wood (1977) treats all of these issues and earlier references can be found there. What follows is an update.

Number of alternatives

> Despite their extensive use of multiple-choice tests, the examination boards in the UK appear not to have published any research support for the very widespread adoption of the five-option format in public examinations in science subjects.

So claims Hodson (1986, p. 85). He quotes the London Board as stating that such items **have** five options, rather than that the board **uses** five-choice items; the Cambridge Test Development and Research Unit (TDRU) as stating that five-choice items are used because they 'discriminate between candidates slightly more effectively' and because 'the role of the guessing factor may be reduced' (TDRU 1975); and the JMB as having decided that each subject area may employ four- or five-choice items according to the stated preference of the subject panel.

Remarking, quite reasonably, that conclusions regarding the optimum number of alternatives are uncertain, Hodson set out to investigate the effects on test statistics of reducing the number of alternative responses in multiple choice Chemistry tests (at O level and A level) from five to four. In so doing, he may have knocked on a door that was already open.

Ramos & Stern (1973) tested about 2400 college students in French and Spanish Language reading with four- and five-choice items, the four-choice items being formed by removing the least popular distractor. They found no differences between the two test forms in average test score, item difficulty or item biserial correlation. There was a slight fall in internal consistency from 0·91 to 0·87, but owing to the large sample size this result lacks strong practical implication. Ramos & Stern concluded that elimination of the fifth option will not seriously harm multiple choice items. This was also Hodson's conclusion, having conducted a similar kind of experiment.

The argument for five options over four is the one advanced by the TDRU – that the proportion of candidates who **guess** the correct answer will be reduced. Before dealing with the subject of guessing, it is reasonable to ask why set the limit at five; why not six, seven or more? Well, in fact, there are examples of six, such as Alice Heim's AH2/AH3 tests. There is actually an instance of **sixteen**! The Graduate and Managerial Assessment (GMA) tests (Blinkhorn 1985) present items in triples, each triple dealing with the same material, rather like the old **multi-facet** items (Schools Council 1965). Sixteen options were generated for each triple so that while probably only five to seven apply realistically to any one item, the candidate who wants to proceed by elimination is going to take longer than if the item had its own four or five options. A generalised version of this idea, whereby options for all items are sited at the beginning of the test, was put up by Gulliksen (see Wainer 1983), and, under the name of multiple matching tests, has been tried in practice by Budescu (1988). The format worked well with vocabulary tests which, being almost pure power tests with large numbers of short items and short answers, tend to encourage guessing. Whether the format works as well with fewer and longer items and options, remains to be seen. Budescu noted that the length of time required to scan and evaluate all the options may be too heavy a price to pay in order to eliminate the guessing factor.

Whatever view of response behaviour we take, the item writer must strive to produce distractors which are plausible alternatives to the correct response and sufficiently close to it to attract attention. If relatively strong distractors cannot be generated, there seems little point in using a weak distractor simply to 'make up the number'. To the extent that item writers have difficulty squeezing out a fourth distractor, it is in order to stop at three and settle for four-choice items. In any case, distractor-richness is a direct function of the item situation, so that mixtures of four- and five-choice items should be expected. Warnings that mixtures would fox candidates, or else interfere drastically with production and scoring of machine-readable answer sheets, are almost certainly overdone.

Any analysis of response behaviour is bound up with a consideration of how items can be solved. Bruce Choppin (1974) distinguished between 'forwards' items, which must be solved first before consulting the alternatives, and 'backwards' items, which can be solved by substitution or elimination. It has been generally supposed that 'forwards' items are superior because a question ought to be self-standing and not rely on what is in the alternatives in order to make it sensible. Choppin's point was that 'forwards' items are certainly the ones to have but that the lack of opportunity (or reduced opportunity) to eliminate alternatives makes them more vulnerable to random guessing, and therefore to reliability seepage. His conclusion, based on an international research study, was that items with at least five alternatives should be used, whether of the 'forwards' or 'backwards' kind.

In the light of Choppin's analysis, and other prophylactic measures which have been taken against guessing, it might seem perverse to introduce the **three**-choice item, but every now and then someone comes forward to champion this particular format. This has been continuing since 1925 at least. The latest piece of work (Owen & Froman 1987) reported that differences in measurement characteristics between three-choice and five-choice items were negligible (the three-choice items were formed by discarding the two distractors with poorest discrimination).

Where differences were found, they were to do with time spent per item which naturally favoured the shorter item. Using these authors' figures as a rough guide, it would seem that 60 three-choice items could be answered in one hour, compared to 50 five-choice items, which would offer the prospect of validity and reliability gains.

The use of three-choice items is also commended by Straton & Catts (1980), who experimented with different item/option combinations, given that the total number of options remains constant. As usual, it is unclear how well any of these studies would generalise to a British situation. Being realistic, it is hard to imagine three-choice ever being tried here, given the residual animus against multiple choice and the fond belief that guessing is rampant. That said, examples can be found in the corpus of psychological tests; the Mechanical Comprehension test in the Technical Test Battery (Saville & Holdsworth 1979) for one.

Use of 'none of these'

The 'none of these' or 'none of the above' option arouses strong feelings among item writers. Some refuse to use it under any circumstances, believing that it weakens their items. Others use it too much, as an easy way to make up the number when short of distractors. The TDRU item writer's manual (1975) asserted that 'none of these' is best avoided altogether and, if it must be used, it should only be in cases where the other options are unequivocally right or wrong. Bishop, Knapp & MacIntyre (1969) reported that the biggest difference between the distributions of responses to questions framed in multiple choice and in open-ended form was between the 'none of these' category in the former and the 'minor errors' category in the latter. This means that when placed alongside unequivocal alternatives the 'none of these' option was not sufficiently attractive to be effective.

The literature is saying that when 'none of these' is used as the correct answer, the item becomes more difficult than it would be in the one correct answer format (Tollefson 1987). Presumably the reason is that you have to be very confident that you know the right answer in order to reject three or four plausible answers. Otherwise there will be a premium on elimination, but the absence of the correct answer makes elimination a more difficult task than when it is there.

There is a case for using 'none of these' with multiple completion items where it can deny candidates the opportunity to glean information from the coding structure, which is inevitably not exhaustive. Again, the effect will be to make the item more difficult. Choppin took the view that 'none of these' sets a more complicated task to the candidate without increasing reliability and validity, and later studies bear out the last part of this statement.

Scoring systems and instructions to deal with guessing

If on encountering an item candidates were always to divide into those who knew the right answer for certain and those who were so ignorant that they were obliged to guess blindly in order to provide an answer, scoring would be a simple matter. A correct answer could be awarded one point, anything else zero, and a correction could be applied to cancel out the number of correct answers achieved by blind guessing. Alas, life is not as simple as this. A candidate who does not know the right answer immediately may act in any one of the following ways:

1 Eliminate one or more of the alternatives and then, by virtue of misinformation or incompetence, go for a particular wrong answer.
2 Eliminate one or more of the alternatives and then choose randomly among the remainder.
3 Fail to eliminate any of the alternatives but choose a particular wrong answer for the same reasons as in 1.
4 Make a random choice among all the alternatives, in other words do what is popularly known as guessing.

Actually, these possibilities are just bench marks on a continuum of response behaviour, anchored at one end with certain knowledge and at the other with complete ignorance. An individual's placement on this continuum with respect to a particular item depends on the relevant knowledge s/he can muster and the confidence s/he has in it. It follows that the distinction between an informed answer and a shrewd intuitive guess or between a wild hunch and a random selection is necessarily blurred; also that with enough misapprehension in his/her head an individual can actually score less than s/he would have got by random guessing on every item. In other words, one expects poor candidates to be poor 'guessers', and by the same token, good candidates to be good 'guessers'.

That undeserved reward can be obtained through blind guessing is a permanent blemish on multiple choice, one that is not removed by so-called guessing corrections. Any guessing correction is properly called a correction for individual differences in confidence, as Gritten & Johnson (1941) pointed out a long time ago. Correcting directly for such differences is beyond our capacity. The best we can do is to contain the damage by reducing omitting (the real culprit in all this) to a point where confidence differences have no real distorting effect on the estimation of achievement or ability.

Blind guessing is most likely to occur when items are difficult and when people are short of time. Choppin's study produced incontrovertible evidence of blind guessing (as well as some interesting differences between countries) but the items were difficult, and it was queried whether all had had the opportunity to learn the subject matter. Making sure testing conditions are appropriate is therefore an immediate antidote. The other area where control can be imposed is in the rubric. The wording of instructions to create the right psychological impact is decisive. In this respect, the problem is less psychometric than one of design. It is a fact that if the instructions for answering a test warn candidates that they will be penalised for guessing (where what is meant by guessing may or may not be specified), those who choose to ignore the instructions and have a shot at every item will be better off, even after exaction of the penalty, than those who comply with the instructions and leave alone items they are not certain about, even though an informed 'guess' would probably lead them to the correct answer. The advice that 'hunches are more right than wrong' still seems good, despite assertions that partial information, like a little learning, is a dangerous or, at least, an untrustworthy thing (Angoff 1987).

Exactly the same considerations apply to instructions which attempt to persuade candidates to omit items they do not know the answer to, by offering as automatic credit the chance score, that is 1/5 in the case of a five-choice item. On the face of it this seems a good way of controlling guessing, but the snag is that the more able candidates tend to heed the instructions more diligently than the rest and so fail to do themselves justice. Because their probabilities of success are in truth greater than chance, they are under-rewarded by the automatic credit, whereas the weakest candidates actually benefit from omitting because their probabilities of success are below the chance level. Wood's (1976) study indicated that instructions which encourage candidates to attempt all questions are best.

Not everyone is happy with a policy that seems to condone random guessing, whatever the collective equity gains. Some medical examiners have worried that the practice of random guessing on test items by medical students might lead to random guessing with respect to patient management in the clinical years (Friedman *et al.* 1987; Fleming 1988). Physicians, they say, need to apply intelligent guessing based on partial information; how though to distinguish between random and intelligent guessing? Friedman *et al.*'s answer, the so-called Discouraging Random Guessing approach to test administration, turns out to be simply the punitive formula score criticised earlier, where formula score is denoted $X = R - (\text{number wrong})/(A-1)$, R being the number of right answers and A the number of options per item.

Let us be clear what the correction formula does. All incorrect responses go down as failed random guesses and are penalised to compensate for the successful random guesses. If Akeroyd (1982) is right that up to 20% of responses can be classified as confidently wrong (as it were), there is immediately an injustice which results in an overall deflation of students' marks from what they should be. Then there is the intimidation factor already mentioned. Better $+1$ from a successful informed guess and $-\frac{1}{4}$ from an unsuccessful informed guess, than nothing from two omitted responses. Again the effect of complying is to shrink the marks. Interestingly enough, the medical examiners' study found that non-compliance was most marked among the more able students, but also that compliance, when it occurred in this group, was characterised by an ability to spot the hard items and to omit those. Low ability students could not spot the difference.

These findings do not necessarily conflict with those of Wood. Content comes into it; also the extent to which students are motivated to do well. Nevertheless, the objections to formula scoring remain.

It is a proper question to ask whether there is a best scoring system (not a correction) which both deters unwanted response behaviour and rewards partial information. Akeroyd (1982) has studied this problem. He finds no merit in **elimination scoring**, where the candidate indicates the responses s/he confidently believes to be wrong. An item is scored by awarding one point for each incorrect choice that is identified, but deducting K points (where K is equal to the number of options minus one) if the correct answer is identified as incorrect. Consequently, with five-choice items, scores may range from -4 to $+4$. Akeroyd remarks that this 'savage penalty' leads to even greater injustices than the formula scoring penalty for guessing method. He notes, however, and he is right in this, that elimination scoring is a useful way of learning about candidates' response behaviour. What this method does is to give credit for partial knowledge, that is -1, 2 or 3. If a candidate is guessing blindly throughout, the expected item score is zero, whereas on a test conventionally scored it is equal to one divided by the number of options.

Perhaps, in laying emphasis on what is wrong rather than what is right, elimination scoring induces a negative cast of mind. Certainly, there can be no such thing as a 'forwards' item; all must be 'backwards'. The meagre literature on the topic suggests that it does discourage guessing (as it should do given the penalties) without producing gains in reliability. Bradbard & Green (1986) argue that the technique is best suited to testing bodies of knowledge where partial knowledge can be elicited.

Akeroyd offers, as the most promising system to date, what he calls the **dual response** system. For four-choice items there will be:

1 mark for indicating the correct answer;
$\frac{1}{2}$ mark for indicating TWO answers, one of which is correct;
$\frac{1}{4}$ mark for an omission;
0 mark for an incorrect answer OR combination of answers.

Akeroyd comments that the merit of this system is that it allows the student a full range of guessing possibilities. If s/he can eliminate two distractors the student has 100% chance of $\frac{1}{2}$ mark, not 50/50 chance of 1 mark. If s/he can eliminate only one distractor the student should still make the dual response: s/he has a 67% chance of $\frac{1}{2}$ mark rather than 33% chance of a full mark, although over the whole test the expectations are the same. The award of $\frac{1}{4}$ mark for omissions eliminates fluctuations of scores due to random guessing.

Akeroyd claims that adoption of this scoring method gives the student a more reliable score (that is fluctuations due to blind guessing are smoothed out to a great extent) and there is no overall shrinkage of scores. It also reveals to the examiners and item writers something about the incidence of informed and blind guessing.

Nothing is known about how the dual response system will work in practice. Akeroyd remarks that when systematic research has indicated the 'best' system for correcting for guesses which have a probability of success in the 20–50% range, we can then start investigation of systems which allow for a 'best guess' and a 'fall back' second choice. 'In my opinion', he adds, 'such systems are currently too complicated for the present generation of multiple choice examiners.' Some might think that this remark is true also of the dual response system, and perhaps of all rubrics. There is empirical evidence (Cross & Frary 1977) that even highly motivated examinees do not always understand, remember or follow the instructions of the simplest scoring rule, which is taken to be the penalty for guessing rule. There is, of course, an even simpler rule, number of items correct, and it may be prudent to stick with this.

Answer until correct

The answer-until-correct procedure is just that – examinees continue to make attempts until they get the right answer. Evidently this is best accomplished through computer-driven administration, but it can work in a pencil-and-paper mode, as when examinees are asked to scratch off some sort of coating to reveal an answer. An example is the Computer Rules test (Blinkhorn 1987).

The obvious virtue of the method is that it gives immediate feedback to the examinee and may therefore stimulate learning. In this respect, the nature of the exercise is qualitatively different from that posed by conventional methods.

The effect of the response mechanism is to produce, for every item, a full or partial ranking of options. Scoring is then a direct function of this ranking, depending on the number of alternatives. If there are 3, then a correct answer first off attracts a mark of 2 and a correct answer at the second attempt scores 1.

Data from answer-until-correct lends itself to testing hypotheses about partial knowledge. Dalrymple-Alford (1970) was an early contributor to this literature. Later work is associated with the name of Wilcox (for example 1982) and there is the paper by Garcia-Perez (1990).

Changing answers

If individuals differ in their willingness to supply an answer at all, it is easy to imagine them differing in their readiness to change their answers having already committed themselves. The conclusions Wood drew from the literature in 1977 still stand. Candidates should review their answers; directions to stick with the first response to an item are misleading, or as McMorris & Weideman (1986) put it, 'counsellors should not discourage students from changing answers'.

Confidence weighting

The decision to change an answer may be read as a sign of unwillingness to invest one answer with complete confidence. The idea that individuals might be asked to signify their degree of confidence in the answers they make, or in the alternatives open to them, has seemed to some a move which would not only constitute a more realistic form of answering **psychologically** but would also yield more **statistical** information.

Known variously as confidence weighting, confidence testing, probabilistic weighting, probabilistic testing or even subject-weighted test-taking procedure, the basic notion is that individuals should express, through some code or other, their degree of confidence in the answer they believe to be correct, or else, by way of refinement, in the correctness of the options presented to them. Credit for laying the intellectual foundations of probabilistic weighting and for providing a psychometric application belongs to de Finetti (1965), although less sophisticated methods have been discussed in the educational measurement literature for some 40 years. Much energy has been expended on devising methods of presentation, instructions and scoring rules which will be comprehensible to the ordinary candidate. In one method candidates are invited to distribute five stars (each representing a subjective probability of 0·20) across the options presented to them. It is assumed that the individual's degree of belief or personal probability concerning the correctness of each alternative answer corresponds exactly with his personal probability distribution, restricted to sum to unity. The snag is that candidates may not care about some of the alternatives offered to them, in which case talk of belief is fatuous. Empirical evidence from other fields suggests that often individuals have a hard time distributing their personal probabilities; some fail to constrain their probabilities to add to unity, although the stars scheme gets over this, while others tend to lump the probability density on what they consider is the correct answer, which is not necessarily the best strategy.

Apart from worries about whether candidates can handle the technique, concern has been expressed that confidence test scores are influenced, to a measurable degree, by personality variables. The worry is that confidence response methods will produce variability in scores that cannot be attributed to knowledge of subject matter.

Having compared the validities of conventional testing and various confidence testing procedures, Koehler (1971) concluded that conventional testing is preferable because it is easier to administer, takes less testing time and does not require the training of candidates. A similar conclusion was reached by Hanna & Owens (1973) who observed that greater validity could have been attained by using the available time to lengthen the multiple choice test rather than to confidence-mark items.

The most recent study (Bokhorst 1986) asked examinees to make confidence judgements in addition to choosing the correct alternative. The test was first scored conventionally with a penalty for guessing and then again using confidence weightings. (Examinees were instructed that there would be two confidence levels, 'certain' and 'uncertain', and a third option would be to omit. Correct and incorrect responses given with confidence level 'certain' would be scored +4 and −4 respectively and 'uncertain' responses would be scored +1 and −1 in the same way. Omits would receive zero credit.) There is no evidence yet that confidence weighting leads to improved validity and this paper was no different. Reliability estimates were slightly improved, a result other investigators had shown. Otherwise, high test anxiety (which was estimated) was associated with low confidence and poor achievement. With practice in making judgements students may become less anxious and the validity coefficients might then change. As things stand, it is hard to push confidence weighting forward as a preferred response method.

Differential weighting of responses

Once item responses have been made in the normal manner, they can be subjected to all kinds of statistical manipulations in an effort to produce more informative scores than those obtained by simply summing the number of correct items. Individual items can be differentially weighted, groups of items can be weighted, even options within items can be weighted. Sadly, all these efforts have amounted to very little. If the intercorrelations among items or sections of tests are positive (as they invariably are) then differential weighting of items or sections produces a rank order of scores which differs little from the order produced by number right (Aiken 1966). At the time, Aiken claimed that his analysis reinforced the results of previous empirical and theoretical work and the position has changed little since. Most studies have been of empirical weighting (empirical because weights are allocated after the event) using an iterative computer solution so as to maximise the reliability or validity of the scores. Thus candidates have no idea when they take the test of the relevant score values of items. Not that this is anything new; in the normal course of events items weight themselves according to their discrimination values.

The empirical weighting method is, of course, open to the objection that it is the candidates rather than the examiners who are, in effect, deciding which options are most credit-worthy, even to the extent of downgrading the correct answer if the brightest group of candidates should, for some reason, happen to be drawn to another option (although it is very unlikely that such an item would survive as far as an operational test). There is also an element of self-fulfilment present since candidates' scores are being used to adjust candidates' scores; students who do well on the test as a whole have their scores boosted on each item, which only compounds their superiority. Echternacht (1976) was not exaggerating when he observed that one would have problems giving candidates a satisfying explanation of an empirical scoring scheme.

If empirical weighting leaves something to be desired, what about a priori weighting of the options? Here one asks informed persons, presumably examiners, to put values on the options, perhaps with a simple 4–3–2–1–0 scheme. Alternatively and preferably, although difficult, examiners could be asked to construct items in such a way that the distractors were graded according to plausibility. One might argue they should be doing this anyway. What happens when a priori or subjective weighting is tried out? Echternacht, using specially constructed items, found that the results it gave were not even as reliable as conventional number-right scoring and certainly inferior to the results obtained from empirical weighting. With empirical weighting he registered an increase in reliability equivalent to a 30% increase in length of a conventionally scored test and also reported an increase in validity. Note however that his items, which were quantitative aptitude items, cost 60% more to produce than items written in the usual way.

A study by Quinn & Wood (see Wood 1977 for details) compared subjective and empirical weighting with conventional scoring in connection with an O level English Language comprehension test. Difficulty was experienced ranking options in terms of plausibility (an indirect comment on the skill of the item writers). In the event neither subjective nor empirical weighting made much difference to the original rank ordering of candidates produced by conventional scoring. Any extra discrimination which graded scoring gives will naturally tend to be at the bottom end of the score range, since these are the people who get a lot of items 'wrong' and who stand to benefit from partial scoring. Note that the strength of the case for graded scoring is likely to vary according to the subject matter. In mathematics and the sciences, also the social sciences, graded scoring may work; in French and English perhaps the problems of interpretation are too great.

Discussion

Multiple choice items can demand more than recognition. Whenever candidates are obliged to work out an answer and then search among the alternatives for it (what are called 'forwards' items) processes other than recognition, which we generally call higher order skills, are liable to be activated.

Attempts to describe and classify these higher order skills have amounted to very little. Bloom's *Taxonomy* has promised more than it has delivered. Generally speaking, denotation and measurement of higher order skills has proceeded in an ad hoc fashion according to the subject matter. However, the failure to substantiate taxonomies of skills may not matter providing a penetrating analysis of what students ought to be able to do is carried out. It is suggested that more attention should be given to measuring what we say we are measuring, and in this connection Gagné's ideas are still relevant.

To get more out of the simple multiple choice form usually means increasing the information load. Care should be taken not to overdo the reading comprehension element.

Various item types other than simple multiple choice are available. Often ideas can be handled quite well within the simple multiple choice form without resorting to fancy constructions. Except for true–false and multiple true–false, all the other item types have in common that the instructions are lengthy and apparently complicated. This leads to the criticism that ability to understand instructions is being tested before anything else.

The multiple completion or selection item type suffers from the drawback that candidates have to code their answers using a table before making a mark on the answer sheet. Another shortcoming is that information is usually given away by the coding table and candidates may use it to their advantage, either consciously or unconsciously. As might be expected, the cleverer candidates appear to derive most advantage from it.

The various technical aspects of multiple choice item writing (number of options, use of 'none of these', use of negatives and so forth) have been studied intensively, but it is rare to find a study where the results can be generalised with confidence. However, some findings have achieved a certain solidity. For example, it is fairly certain that items containing 'none of these' as an option will be more difficult than those with all-specific options. This follows from the fact that 'none of these' is so many options rolled into one. Generally speaking, opinion does not favour the use of 'none of these', although there are those who would permit it with multiple completion items.

The traditional view that item writers should use as many options as possible, certainly four or five, continues to hold sway. Those who have promoted the three-choice item, which has from time to time looked promising, have not yet managed to substantiate their case. As to whether one should aim for four or five options, the point is not to be dogmatic about always having the same number, even if it is convenient for data processing purposes. The multiple matching format, whereby options for clusters of items are pooled, is worth further investigation.

Good candidates are good 'guessers', and poor candidates are poor 'guessers'. All candidates should be encouraged to make use of all the knowledge at their disposal. Yes, some partial information is untrustworthy, but using it will pay off more often than not. When candidates choose to omit questions it is usually the more able ones who do not do themselves justice, being reticent when they actually know the right answers.

Blind guessing does occur but only when the conditions are ripe for it. Under appropriate testing conditions its effects can be reduced until it is no longer a problem. Hysterical outbursts that multiple choice tests are no more than gambling machines are quite unjustified. All the evidence is that if tests are properly constructed, presented and timed, candidates will take them seriously.

Despite all the ingenuity and effort which has gone into developing methods for rewarding partial information, there is little evidence that any one method provides measurable gains. Differential weighting of item scores occurs, in any case, because items weight themselves according to their discrimination values. Confidence weighting is probably too elaborate for the average candidate. It is reasonable to conclude that if the items in a test are well constructed, if candidates are advised to go over their answers (since changing answers seems to pay), and if the testing conditions are such as to inhibit blind guessing with candidates being encouraged to attempt all items, number right suffices most needs. Certainly the suggestion that even highly motivated candidates have trouble following anything but the simplest instructions needs to be taken seriously.

References

Aiken L. R. (1966) Another look at weighting test items. *Journal of Educational Measurement*, **3**, 183–5.

Akeroyd F. M. (1982) Progress in multiple choice scoring methods, 1977/81. *Journal of Further and Higher Education*, **6**, 87–90.

Alker H. A., Carlson J. A. & Hermann M. G. (1969) Multiple-choice questions and students' characteristics. *Journal of Educational Psychology*, **60**, 231–43.

Anastasi A. (1970) On the formation of psychological traits. *American Psychologist*, **25**, 899–910.

Angoff W. H. (1987) Does guessing really help? *ETS Research Report*, *RR 87-16*. Princeton, NJ: Educational Testing Service.

Bishop A. J., Knapp T. R. & MacIntyre D. I. (1969) A comparison of the results of open-ended and multiple-choice versions of a mathematics test. *International Journal of Educational Science*, **3**, 147–54.

Blinkhorn S. F. (1985) *Graduate and Managerial Assessment: Numerical, Verbal and Abstract*. Windsor: NFER-Nelson.

Blinkhorn S. F. (1987) *Computer Rules Test*. Windsor: NFER-Nelson.

Bokhorst F. D. (1986) Confidence-weighting and the validity of achievement tests. *Psychological Reports*, **59**, 383–6.

Bracht G. H. & Hopkins K. D. (1970) The communality of essay and objective tests of academic achievement. *Educational and Psychological Measurement*, **30**, 359–64.

Bradbard D. A. & Green S. B. (1986) Use of the Coombs elimination procedure in classroom tests. *Journal of Experimental Education*, **54**, 68–72.

Breland H. M. (1977) Can multiple-choice test writing skills? *The College Board Review*, **103**, 11–13 and 32–3.

Budescu D. V. (1988) On the feasibility of multiple matching tests – Variations on a theme by Gulliksen. *Applied Psychological Measurement*, **12**, 5–14.

Choppin B. H. (1974) *The Correction for Guessing on Objective Tests*. IEA Monograph Studies, No. 4. Stockholm: IEA.

Cooper P. L. (1984) The assessment of writing ability: A review of research. *ETS Research Report RR 84-12*. Princeton, NJ: Educational Testing Service.

Cronbach L. J. (1970) Validation of educational measures. In *Proceedings of the 1969 Invitational Conference on Testing Problems*. Princeton, NJ: Educational Testing Service.

Cross H. L. & Frary R. B. (1977) An empirical test of Lord's theoretical results regarding formula scoring of multiple-choice tests. *Journal of Educational Measurement*, **14**, 313–21.

Dalrymple-Alford E. C. (1970) A model for assessing multiple-choice test performance. *British Journal of Mathematical and Statistical Psychology*, **23**, 199–203.

Dudley H. A. F. (1973) Multiple-choice tests. *Lancet*, **2**, 195.

Echternacht G. J. (1976) Reliability and validity of item option weighting schemes. *Educational and Psychological Measurement*, **36**, 301–10.

de Finetti B. (1965) Methods for discriminating levels of partial knowledge concerning a test item. *British Journal of Mathematical and Statistical Psychology*, **18**, 87–123.

Fleming P. R. (1988) The profitability of 'guessing' in multiple choice question papers. *Medical Education*, **22**, 509–13.

Frederiksen N. (1984) The real test bias: Influences of testing on teaching and learning. *American Psychologist*, **39**, 193–202.

Friedman M. A., Hopwood L. E., Moulder J. E. & Cox J. D. (1987) The potential use of the discouraging random guessing (DRG) approach in multiple-choice exams in medical education. *Medical Teacher*, **9**, 333–41.

Fry E. (1971) The orangoutang score. *Reading Teacher*, **24**, 360–2.

Gagné R. M. (1970) Instructional variables and learning outcomes. In Wittrock M. C. & Wiley D. E. (eds.) *The Evaluation of Instruction. Issues and Problems*. New York: Holt, Rinehart & Winston.

Garcia-Perez M. A. (1990) A comparison of two models of performance in objective tests: Finite states versus continuous distributions. *British Journal of Mathematical and Statistical Psychology*, **43**, 73–92.

Gritten F. & Johnson D. M. (1941) Individual differences in judging multiple-choice questions. *Journal of Educational Psychology*, **30**, 423–30.

Hanna G. S. & Owens R. E. (1973) Incremental validity of confidence weighting of items. *California Journal of Educational Research*, **24**, 165–8.

Hodson D. (1986) Multiple choice tests – are four options as good as five? *Education in Chemistry*, **23**, 84–6.

Hoffman B. (1967) Multiple-choice tests. *Physics Education*, **2**, 247–51.

Huxham G. J. & Lipton A. (1974) Do multiple-choice and essay tests measure different factors? *British Journal of Medical Education*, **8**, 204–8.

Koehler R. A. (1971) A comparison of validities of conventioned choice testing and various confidence marking procedures. *Journal of Educational Measurement*, **8**, 297–303.

Kuhn T. S. (1962) *The Structure of Scientific Revolutions*. Chicago: University of Chicago Press.

Levy P. (1973) On the relation between test theory and psychology. In Kline P. (ed.) *New Approaches in Psychological Measurement*. London: John Wiley.

McMorris R. F. & Weideman A. H. (1986) Answer changing after instruction on answer changing. *Measurement and Evaluation Counselling and Development*, **19**, 93–101.

Mathews J. C. (1967) The Nuffield Foundation Science Teaching Project V11: O-level chemistry examinations. *School Science Review*, **49**, 21–30.

Owen S. V. & Froman R. D. (1987) What's wrong with three option multiple-choice items? *Educational and Psychological Measurement*, **47**, 513–22.

Popham W. J. (1980) Domain specification strategies. In Berk R. A. (ed.) *Criterion Referenced Measurement: The State of the Art*. Baltimore, MD: John Hopkins University Press.

Ramos R. A. & Stern J. (1973) Item behaviour associated with changes in the number of alternatives in multiple-choice items. *Journal of Educational Measurement*, **10**, 305–10.

Ravetz J. R. (1971) *Scientific Knowledge and its Social Problems*. Oxford: Oxford University Press.

Saville P. & Holdsworth R. (1979) *Technical Test Battery*. Esher, Surrey: Saville & Holdsworth Ltd.

Schools Council (1965) *The Certificate of Secondary Education: Experimental Examinations – Mathematics 2*. Examinations Bulletin 7, London: Schools Council.

Straton R. G. & Catts R. M. (1980) A comparison of two, three and four choice item tests given a fixed total number of choices. *Educational and Psychological Measurement*, **40**, 357–65.

Test Research and Development Unit (1975) *Multiple Choice Item Writing*. Cambridge: TDRU.

Tollefson N. (1987) A comparison of the item difficulty and item discrimination of multiple-choice items using the 'none of the above' and one correct response options. *Educational and Psychological Measurement*, **47**, 377–83.

Vernon P. E. (1962) The determinants of reading comprehension. *Educational and Psychological Measurement*, **22**, 269–86.

Vernon P. E. (1964) *The Certificate of Secondary Education: An Introduction to Objective-Type Examinations*. Examinations Bulletin No. 4, London: Secondary Schools Examination Council.

Wainer H. (1983) Are we correcting for guessing in the wrong direction? In Weiss D. J. (ed.) *New Horizons in Testing*. New York: Academic Press.

Wilcox R. W. (1982) Some empirical and theoretical results on an answer-until-correct scoring procedure. *British Journal of Mathematical and Statistical Psychology*, **35**, 57–70.

Wood R. (1976) Inhibiting blind guessing: The effect of instructions. *Journal of Educational Measurement*, **13**, 297–307.

Wood R. (1977) Multiple choice: A state of the art report. *Evaluation in Education: International Progress*, **1**, 193–280.

5 Essay questions

Any treatment of essay questions must deal with the nature of extended writing, the construction of questions and the assessing of answers.

Psychometric enquiries into essay questions generally concentrate on the marking aspect (Coffman 1971; Cooper 1984) but there is much to be said about the other two areas. It might as well be recognised at once that the scoring of essays is a complex process, with many variables in multiple combination influencing the reader differentially (Chase 1986). Only one of these is the content of the essay, and it could be that this is of only modest importance in determining a score for an essay (Rafoth & Rubin 1984).

Nature of extended writing

There is no generally consistent theory of what constitutes language ability, including writing ability. Typically, views on which aspects of writing skills should be measured, and the best ways of measuring them, tend to differ from one study to another (IEA 1988, p. 15). Lack of a definition of 'good writing' makes the evaluation of effective writing difficult (Marsh & Ireland 1987, p. 353).

These are the messages from the literature. Yet no one doubts that there are recognisably different kinds of writing. The US National Council of Teachers of English in its *Standards for Basic Writing Programs* lists five kinds of writing or models of discourse – narrating, explaining, describing, reporting and persuading (NCTE 1979). These provide the organising principle for the Iowa Tests of Basic Skills (ITBS) *Writing* Supplement.

A classification of writing competences in terms of cognitive demand is increasingly favoured as it is acknowledged that good writing and good thinking are indivisible. Good writing is seen as the ability to generate ideas of substance, as well as the ability to express those ideas effectively (ITBS 1987*a*, p. 5). The IEA *Study of Written Composition* posited that the cognitive demands of writing divide into three classes:

1 the receptive, recognising and recalling modes of processing of information in

which the writer reproduces units, events and facts (for example copies, cites, makes notes);

2 the analysing and structuring modes of processing information in which the writer organises or reorganises reality (for example narrates, describes, explains, summarises);

3 the evaluating and general modes of information processing in which the writer expands reality, invents/generates reality (for example analyses, expounds, argues, creates a new possible world).

(IEA 1988, p. 23)

Except for 'persuading', which falls under **3**, the NCTE/ITBS scheme falls wholly into class **2**. This is likely to be true for most school and examination writing; certainly for examinations other than English Language where class **3** can be expected to figure more prominently.

A review of current examination practices in the IEA countries showed that school-leaving examinations, both in the language of instruction and in other school subjects, require mastery of explicit meaning, in particular the comprehension of texts and the production of autonomous text (IEA, pp. 27–8). In the five-year study of school-based writing in British schools carried out by Britton *et al.* (1975) referential (or informative) tasks constituted 62% of the empirical data. A later study in Scotland (Spencer 1983) found 75% of all school writing tasks across the curriculum to be informative.

In publishing a syllabus and setting an examination an examining board must decide what kinds of writing are to be stressed and therefore encouraged, and how they are to be weighted when it comes to task specification. The IEA study went through this process and on the basis of a general model of writing as conceptualised above (communication plus cognitive processing) arrived at 14 writing tasks. It would be interesting to know if any examining board has gone, or routinely goes, to this kind of trouble, either for English Language or any other subject.

Constructs of writing

Given data on tasks requiring different kinds of writing, methodologists are apt to enquire whether a more parsimonious representation of the data is possible. Are there non-task-specific aspects of the writing (call them constructs) which account for most of the observed score variation? Examples of constructs would be content, organisation, style, mechanics, handwriting. Various studies (such as Lehmann 1988) have strongly suggested that, for a **single given text**, the aspects of content, organisation and style be distinguished from each other as being analytically, and to some extent empirically, independent. What happens when there are several tasks is another matter. Lehmann, using West German data, found that only 'mechanics' (that is mastery of grammatical and orthographic conventions) and 'handwriting neatness' showed up as stable traits. Of the other constructs, 'organisation' was the least stable, an outcome supported by de Glopper's (1987) multitrait–multimethod analysis of Dutch data from the IEA *Writing Study*. Otherwise, specific task-related qualities seem to prevail. Lehmann concluded that his data did not support a concept of school writing which models achievement, independent of the nature of tasks, as a composite of a small number of stable individual traits. However, he did add that stylistic qualities seem to come closest to a general command of language and writing.

'Mechanics', as might be expected, is a key variable. Harris (1977) found that content and organisation, as opposed to mechanics, were more important in determining overall evaluations of writing samples, but that written formative feedback to students emphasised mechanics. We can assume that mechanics was more influential in the evaluation than these raters admitted.

Marsh & Ireland (1987), also using multitrait–multimethod analyses which are well suited to this kind of work, reported teachers' total inability to discriminate among multiple competencies, except perhaps for 'mechanics'. This is consistent with other research. It begins to look as if clearly differentiable components of writing effectiveness may not exist, or cannot be brought out, or are so highly correlated as to be of little practical value. This issue comes up again when we deal with analytical vs. holistic scoring.

Constructing questions

If the task specification requires students to describe, explain, illustrate, analyse and so forth, then the questions must be worded in such a way as to make this happen. The 'Discuss' type of question does not obviously stimulate the student to do anything in particular and is immediately suspect. Here is a field where we might have expected psycholinguists and discourse analysts to take a hand, but it has not happened (Swales 1982).

There is a set of instructional verbs which all examination compilers call upon, and without which they would be lost. They are sometimes called key commands – identify, describe, discuss, list, state, explain, compare and contrast, calculate, and so on. Much then depends on candidates having a good understanding of what examiners mean them to do through these key commands. That this understanding quite often turns out to be non-existent is a feature of many examiners' reports. Candidates are berated for insensitivity to key commands, and for tearing off quite irrelevant screeds. What is not so often asked is whether candidates are entitled to believe that compilers of examinations pay such close attention to the instructional verbs they use that when they, the compilers, choose

discuss rather than **describe**, this choice is well-motivated and capable of being defended. Swales (p. 20) claims to have found instances of the stylistic constraints against exact repetition that operate most conspicuously in continuous text. Thus, if the writer of the paper has a number of questions requiring terms to be **defined**, s/he will tend to alter (indeed sometimes to alternate) the form of words as the sequence of definition questions progresses. Horowitz (1986, p. 108) produces three examples of questions where some stylistic alteration would actually have been welcome, although a proper choice of instructional verb to signal what exactly was wanted would have been even better.

Example 1: Describe the causes of the War of 1812.
Example 2: Describe the technologies associated with horticulture and also those associated with agriculture.
Example 3: Describe the relationship between population growth, urbanisation, and the demographic transition.

Example 1, says Horowitz, requires a discussion of historical causes; example 2, a listing and perhaps a physical description; and example 3, a discussion of the interrelationships among three abstract concepts.

The meaning of **describe**, says Horowitz, varies so greatly among these prompts that there is little pedagogical value in placing them under one heading.

The instructional verb contains the primary instructions, but there are secondary instructions which can be incorporated into questions, or, if they are of a general nature, into rubrics at the beginning. These tell the writer what persona or point of view to assume, which sources to draw from, what to be sure to include or exclude and so on. The injunction on GCSE examining boards to induce positive achievement has brought signs of increasing use of secondary instructions. For the Midland Examining Group (MEG) the decision to include more cues was deliberate and, according to anecdotal report, the results were gratifying. The directions for the 1988 English papers place a limit of 150 words for one question, stipulate **one** paragraph only for another question, and for another, which is a conventional letter-writing task, add the helpful rider 'You will have to decide for yourself what kind of family they are and relate that information to the advice that you give'. Incidentally, the titles of the papers give the impression that there has been conceptualisation of the kinds of writing sought, even if, in the two syllabuses, quite different models are in play.

Syllabus B Paper 1 Argumentative and informative writing
Paper 2 Personal and expressive writing
Syllabus A Paper 2 Directed writing and continuous writing

Desirable though they appear on the surface, it remains an open research question whether explicit directions and extra cueing will produce more acceptable answers. Bell, Brook & Driver (1985, p. 210), writing about science papers, thought that cueing was not a significant issue. O'Donnell (1968), whose useful pioneering paper ought to have been followed up, found that pupils tended to avoid scientifically and rhetorically straightforward questions if they were prolix, and tended to opt for and do badly on brief but problematic questions of the 'Discuss' type. Obviously, much depends on how the cueing is set up, and we know next to nothing about this.

On all the impediments to understanding (unfamiliar vocabulary, complex sentence structures, overly dense presentation, specialist use of non-technical terms) Mobley (1987) has much of value to say, not necessarily drawn from research. She suggests (p. 22) that examiners are often reluctant to relinquish their 'formula' style of writing perhaps because they feel that to make a question paper more accessible would diminish its status. The belief, shared by many teachers and examiners, that the wording of the question helps to 'sort out' the candidates is, of course, true, but it is sorting them out linguistically rather than according to the stated objectives of the assessment. The importance of finding an appropriate level of presentation and laying out of the task or problem was highlighted by Eggleston (1983) – 'all too often children do not fully understand what they are being asked to do' (p. 14). That was said in the context of mathematics; in the context of science Johnstone & Cassels (1978) claimed that many students score low exam marks entirely through a failure to understand the language in which questions are couched. They reckoned that changing no more than a single word often brings about a marked improvement.

Marking answers

Lack of agreement between markers (raters) is endemic to the marking enterprise and the practical question is how to eradicate the worst disparities and understand the reasons for the rest. In that respect, nothing has changed since Hartog & Rhodes (1936). In recent times research has concentrated on pinpointing the sources of error, and on how to arrange the presentation of questions and the deployment of markers to best effect.

Using only one marker is clearly risky, but how many markers do you need? Coffman (1966) reported that the correlation between responses by two raters (that is the single-rater reliability) to the same short essay was about 0·38, though the reliability of the sum of five raters' responses was

0·76. Huddleston (1954) reported that highly trained examiners for English compositions on the College Board examination were able to achieve a single-rater reliability of about 0·55 for a long paper on a single topic. Wood & Quinn (1976) reported average correlations between examiners (10) of 0·54 and 0·48 for the same O level English Language essay and summary respectively. Diederich (1974) reported that 'even after working with an English staff for some time, I have rarely been able to boost the average correlation between pairs of readers above 0·50, and other examiners tell me that this is about what they get' (p. 33). French (1966) suggested that with extensive training and monitoring, the single-rater reliabilities could be as high as 0·70, but that when untrained raters from various academic disciplines were asked to evaluate essays, according to their own judgements of what constitutes writing ability, the single-rater reliability was only 0·31.

Hall (1972), in a review of research conducted in the US, England and Australia prior to 1972, concluded that single-rater reliability of about 0·60 appears to represent 'the limit of the extent of agreement one can generally expect between single judges marking one essay'. Marsh & Ireland (1987), summarising work to date, concluded that single-rater reliabilities generally vary between 0·3 and 0·8 depending upon the length and topic of the essay, the amount of freedom students have in selecting and responding to the essay, the experience of the raters, the extent of training given the raters and the control exercised in the marking environment. In nominating the upper figure of 0·8 and detailing all those conditions, they had in mind an exemplary Australian marking procedure where great efforts were made to standardise marking. The single-rater reliability for short in-class essays marked by classroom teachers tends to be substantially lower than estimates obtained in large, corporate marking studies.

As Godshalk, Swineford & Coffman (1966) noted (pp. 39–40), the reliability of essay scores is primarily a function of the number of different topics to be tackled and the number of readings the essays get. 'The increases which can be achieved by adding topics or readers are dramatically greater than those which can be achieved by lengthening the time per topic or developing special procedures for reading.'

Sources of error

Rater error is but one source of unreliability even if it is the one which catches the eye, as was the case with Hartog & Rhodes. Four variables influence the reliability of the estimate of writing ability when actual writing samples are used – the writer variable, the assignment or the topic variable, the rater variable and the colleague variable (Braddock, Lloyd-Jones & Schoer 1963). One expects writers to vary (there are better and poorer ones) so we have between-writer variation. Writers are known to vary according to assignment or topic, so we have within-writer variation. This source of variation indicates the need to call for multiple samples from an individual writer but **in the same mode of discourse**. (Correlation between sources on different modes of discourse is validity evidence, for example separating mechanics from organisation.) The rater variable refers to the tendency of raters to disagree within themselves, thus there is within-rater variation; and the colleague variable refers to the earlier discussion – the tendency of any two raters to disagree. So, we have:

between-writer variation;
within-writer variation;
within-rater variation;
between-rater variation.

In brief, the problems are that different raters tend to assign different grades to the same paper, that a single rater tends to assign different grades to the same paper on different occasions, and that these differences tend to increase as the essay question permits greater freedom of response. The preferred method for teasing out and quantifying these sources of variation, including those associated with the writers themselves, is a **generalisability** study (chapter 11) and there have been a few of these, such as Godshalk *et al.* (1966), although not enough. In general we know very little about within-rater variation. It has been demonstrated that the agreement between the same examiner's marks on two different occasions is scarcely any better than that between two different markers (Macnamara & Madaus 1969, pp. 11–12).

Between-writer variation will dominate any generalisability analysis, as it must otherwise raters would have nothing to get hold of. Concerning within-writer variation, the generalisability question to be answered is, 'What is the relationship between the obtained score and the score the student would have received had s/he been assigned a different essay topic on a different occasion?' The ITBS manual (1987*a*, p. 25) notes that published estimates of what it calls 'score reliability' are rare. In presenting estimates of between-rater reliability and score reliability, the manual notes how they differ substantially in magnitude (score reliabilities are much lower) and warns that between-rater reliability alone should not be used as an estimate of test reliability. It is instructive to view the score reliabilities by mode of discourse (p. 27):

narrative 0·69
explanation 0·50

description 0·38
informative report 0·40
persuasive essay 0·37

Evidently, essay tests that emphasise content, organisation and style (complex features whose quality may vary considerably from topic to topic) are less reliable than those that emphasise language mechanics (skills which are more or less uniformly deployed from topic to topic). This, of course, squares with the earlier finding that mechanics is the one feature raters can fasten on to; and, in general, illustrates how without reliability there is no prospect of discriminant validity.

Ever since Hartog & Rhodes, the prevailing view seems to have been that disagreement between examiners is reprehensible and that every effort should be directed towards stamping out individual differences and idiosyncracies. However there have been those, notably Wiseman (1949) and Britton, Martin & Rosen (1966), who have recognised the value of acknowledging **differences** between markers.

> we may more tentatively propose that examiners, where they differ, differ in the areas of their most sensitive discrimination and that this is the very element in their judgement that we should wish to incorporate into our assessment. (Britton, Martin & Rosen, pp. 10–11)

Now it is one thing to assert that rater disagreement does not constitute error; quite another to go as far as this. What is clear is that a candidate should not be the victim of an examiner's quirks which have nothing to do with the exercise. Wood & Quinn (1976, p. 236) tell of the examiner who was incited to fury by any essay on the subject of 'Going to a football match' which failed to condemn hooliganism outright. 'Lout' he would gouge on the scripts.

To accommodate markers' different perceptions, Wiseman proposed **multiple marking**, now 40 years ago. He established that one could treat a rater's score like a test item and combine the marks into a more reliable score, just as the Spearman-Brown formula is used to predict the effect of increasing test length. And this is precisely what happens; we saw that Coffman (1966) managed to boost a single-rater reliability of 0·38 to 0·76 when the scores of five raters were summed.

Wiseman's original conception of multiple marking did not go uncriticised. Cox (1968) argued that increasing the number of markers did nothing to improve discrimination between essays in terms of their real merits. Pilliner (1969) replied that Cox's criticism was only valid when markers agreed poorly, or not at all, in which case any increase in reliability would say more about the obstinacy with which each marker clung to his own judgements than about the quality of the essays they were marking. Where a 'fair' measure of agreement or single-rater reliability exists (say 0·50–0·60), then Pilliner demonstrated that an increase in the number of markers attenuates the effect of markers' idiosyncracies and enhances the precision with which differences in the real merits of the essays are assayed. These findings have been confirmed in many countries, and the practice of multiple marking has become fairly well established in large-scale assessments, and even class-wide or school-wide testing (IEA 1988, p. 54).

It is sometimes asked whether the benefits of moving from single marking to double marking are outweighed by the benefits of moving to triple marking, bearing in mind that the Britton *et al.* recommendations were for three markers. Wood & Quinn looked at this issue and found that moving from one to two markers produced the biggest improvement in overall rater reliability; specifically that the reduction in marker error more than compensated for the narrower mark spreads associated with double marking. Lucas (1971) came to the same conclusion after analysing the marking of a Biology examination. Wood & Quinn also demonstrated that there is nothing to be gained from attempting to pair examiners according to known or suspected marking characteristics rather than in some random or quasi-random way.

Analytic vs. holistic or impression marking

Analytic marking, whereby markers are asked to target judgements to nominated skills or features of writing, is sometimes linked with multiple marking as if one were a prerequisite for the other (e.g. IEA 1988), but this is not necessarily so. Impression or holistic marking, whereby examiners make swift overall judgements, will work quite as well with multiple marking; indeed Britton *et al.* advocated it.

Analytic scoring obviously presupposes that markers will be able to discriminate effectively between skills or attributes or features. The work reported earlier (Marsh & Ireland) was pessimistic on that score. The ITBS manual asserts (p. 8) that current thinking among many researchers is that:

> (1) analytic scoring is too time-consuming (and hence too expensive) to be practical in large-scale testing programmes; and (2) analytic scoring may distort and misrepresent the writing process.

The manual is quick to point out that those who adopt this last view do not necessarily insist that the whole is more than the sum of its parts; they do believe that the features that determine the quality of a piece of writing are too numerous and too complexly related for categorisation to be fruitful (Lloyd-Jones 1977). The IEA study, which opted for analytic marking, was obliged to allow impression marking in addition, so as to satisfy some countries who argued that their raters were used to giving such a rating and that the analytic score prevented them from giving a rating that was more than the sum of the parts (IEA, p. 50).

While noting that it was not possible to say whether impression marking was more or less valid than analytic marking, Wood & Quinn were of the view that the practical consequences of any differences which would occur would not be great. By switching from analytic to impression marking (even without introducing multiple marking at the same time) a candidate's result would probably be no more affected than if s/he were to be marked by one examiner rather than another. Incidentally, they also found that examiners' marking behaviour on the essay question was barely predictable from that on the summary question; whether the marking method was analytic or impression did not matter.

ITBS itself adopted what amounts to a hybrid of analytic and impression marking – **focused holistic scoring**. A single score is assigned to each essay. That score is determined in part by the extent to which the essay manifests features common to all good writing (although, as noted at the beginning, there is no agreement on this) and in part by the degree to which it fulfils the aims of a particular mode of discourse. The criteria for each score point are defined by scoring protocols and illustrated by actual student papers. Each new group of scorers is trained to conform to these established criteria through a process that includes both discussion and practice in scoring a set of preselected training papers.

Essays are scored on a four-point scale, and each essay is scored by two independent raters. If the two scores assigned an essay are identical or are within one point of one another, the essay's final score is the sum of these two ratings. If the two scores differ by more than one point, the essay received a third rating by the chief examiner. The final score in these cases is the sum of the two nearest ratings. If the chief examiner's rating falls midway between the scores assigned by the first two markers, the essay's final score is twice the chief examiner's rating. In an aside, the manual notes (p. 9) that while the procedures for resolving score discrepancies appear complicated, well-trained scorers will probably find that they are rarely necessary. A third rating was required for only one of the 5652 standardisation essays. The manual states that schools that find it necessary to resolve large numbers of score discrepancies may wish to interrupt their scoring and repeat their training sessions (shades of GCSE!).

The ITBS *Writing* supplement is indeed intended to be marked in the schools. Extensive training and scoring materials are supplied by ITBS.

All the background and data teachers need are to be found in the *Handbook for Focused Holistic Scoring* (ITBS 1987*b*), including pupil norms based on a national standardisation exercise involving the collection of some 20000 essays. Given the developmental evidence that students' progress in writing occurs unevenly across modes of discourse (the ability to take another person's point of view generally develops later than the ability to tell a coherent story), norms differ substantially from mode to mode as well as from grade to grade.

In comparing analytic and holistic methods of scoring there are reliability–time trade-offs to be taken into account. Given that a number of holistic readings can be given to a paper in the time it takes to arrive at an analytical total, it would seem preferable to opt for scores based on the sum of readings of several readers rather than compound error by having a single reader assign three (or more) different scores (Cooper 1984, pp. 37–8). Cooper maintains that, for psychometric as well as practical reasons, the holistic method is usually favoured for large-scale assessments; but evidently not in the IEA, except as a gesture.

Handwriting

It is deeply ingrained conventional wisdom that handwriting affects the evaluation of a piece of writing. Conventional wisdom is right in this case – markers with neat handwriting significantly mark down untidy essays (Hughes, Keeling & Tuck 1983). *Ceteris paribus*, neat essays get higher marks than untidy ones (Chase 1968; Briggs 1970; Markham 1976). Just what the size of the effect is likely to be when so many other effects are present remains to be ascertained. What, though, would we expect from markers with untidy writing? Some American work (Huck & Bounds 1972) found that they did not differentiate significantly between neat and untidy essays; so there was a marker-neatness/essay-neatness interaction. The New Zealand workers (Hughes *et al.*) did not find this. In distinguishing between handwriting which is merely lacking in aesthetic appeal and handwriting which is so bad as to be difficult to read in parts, they suggest that the Huck–Bounds interaction is possible in the former case but not in the latter; in other words, if it is indecipherable everyone reacts to it adversely.

With British handwriting much more variable than, say, American writing, it follows that the range of writing which can be labelled 'untidy' is that much greater and that the likelihood of more people being marked down because of it is increased, unless, of course, increased tolerance on the part of examiners has a cancelling effect. The examining boards seem not to have sponsored a handwriting study. Perhaps they sense it would result in adverse publicity. After all, how do you get examiners to ignore messy writing, and how do you get candidates to improve their scrawl?

Operational marking procedures and real time experiments

When the mathematical statistician D. V. Lindley reported to the Royal Statistical Society on his innovative marking experiment (Lindley 1961), Brereton, the old Secretary of UCLES, was quick to applaud its peculiar interest for him, which was that, unlike the Hartog experiments, it was based on an actual examination marked by the examiners concerned (Lindley, p. 308). So taken was Brereton that he chided Lindley gently for not going far enough. How do we find out about an examiner's performance at the top and bottom of the range? As an examiner goes through the marking of some hundreds of scripts, does he, owing to fatigue, change his characteristics? Brereton then proceeded to dilate on the need to maintain a balance between absolute reliability and an examination which is best educationally (but that is another story). Even so, one might ponder whether a sanguine attitude to correctable marking behaviour is consistent with an examination which is best educationally.

Lindley, who was delighted to find that he had been doing operational research without knowing it, was well aware of the limitations of his experiment. He could estimate bias and inconsistency for each examiner but he was unable to study behaviour across the whole range (this can always be rectified). More seriously, and this was a point Douglas Pidgeon made in the discussion, he had not been able to estimate candidates' variability, or within-writer variation as it was termed earlier. Lindley conceded that the lack of such estimates (a sign again of how they are neglected) is a severe restriction on the value of the results. As for marking variability over time, Lindley said he intended to carry out an investigation in English Language to investigate the point: 'one of the pair of photostats will be marked early in the marking period, and one towards the end'. There is no published record of that investigation, assuming it was carried out.

Another contributor to the discussion (Sandon in fact) suggested that there was some small evidence (Farrell & Gilbert 1960) that the marker's powers of discrimination increase with time; also that this effect will be more pronounced with impression-marked questions than marked-for-details questions (to use his term), the reasoning presumably being that there will always be more interpretative latitude with impression marking than analytic, and that exposure to new scripts serves, in a cumulative way, to shape and refine what will attract reward. If true, it would follow that questions which are poorly subscribed will be less reliably marked than well-subscribed and compulsory questions. Whether one can go on to argue that winter examinations will be less reliably marked than summer examinations is doubtful without further knowledge of how many scripts it takes before examiners are marking as reliably as they can. What it does suggest is that scripts marked early in a sequence might benefit from being looked at again, something which can be easily taken care of under double-marking conditions.

The operational significance of Lindley's work was seen immediately by Penfold (during the discussion). The information supplied by experiments embedded within the marking process would make it possible for examiner bias to be corrected statistically **as marking progressed** by the expedient of adjusting scores to remove the noise contributed by systematic sources of variation. Correcting for inconsistency (erratic marking) would be more difficult, thought Penfold, because there is no statistical adjustment which will do it. Perhaps the best course would be to eliminate high inconsistency markers from the marking team.

There is no evidence that the British examining boards ever took up the idea of ongoing calibration. Wood & Wilson (1974) attempted to revive interest in routine monitoring of marking behaviour in real time using another approach which did away with the need for an experiment. With all candidates for the London Board's O level English Language paper having to do a multiple choice paper in addition to the essay and summary, Wood & Wilson were able to exploit this concomitant information to judge examiners' marking behaviour, in particular their use of the mark scale. They concluded that examiners were discriminating between candidates in a non-uniform way.

Lindley used a balanced incomplete block design to estimate marker effects. Incomplete designs have the virtue of being cheaper than complete designs, since not every marker has to mark every paper. Ebel (1951) was one of the first to consider the problem of estimating reliability from incomplete designs. The latest application (Braun 1988) utilises **partially balanced incomplete block designs** which are superior to the balanced variety in that they cut down on the number of readings required of each marker at the cost (the tolerable cost) of an increase in variance in the estimates of the difference between some pairs of markers.

Braun's experiment is certainly ingenious, although it is a pity he overlooked Lindley's work. Not only does the designed experiment produce the information for the adjustments, the data can also be plugged into a variance components (generalisability) analysis which permits estimates of the relative contributions of the different sources of variability to the loss in reliability. Moreover, these same data can be used to estimate an upper bound for the reliability that can be attained through these types of adjustment. This, incidentally, confirms the superiority of ANOVA and regression methods over correlational methods, remarked upon by Maxwell in commenting on Lindley's study. Lindley, himself, observed that while they (the regression methods) are more work, you get so much more out of them.

Braun's claim to have carried out the first systematic study of the effects of different kinds of calibration-on-mark reliability appears justified. He sees operational calibration based on single marking as a preferred alternative to double or triple marking. Not only is it virtually cost-free but, as he demonstrates, it can outperform double marking in reliability estimate terms. The snag (and this is an old methodological issue) concerns the behaviour of examiners when marking photocopies. In Lindley's study it was said to make no difference, but in Braun's study some markers said that they treated the essays marked experimentally somewhat differently than they normally would. There is a validity threat here and it is not clear how it can be dealt with. To the extent that examining boards, in their efforts to calibrate examiners, require them to mark photocopies of a sample of scripts before marking proper commences, the same problem is present.

In the light of the research so far, it might be asked what examining boards should be doing to introduce quality control routinely into large-volume marking procedures. They could bring examiners to one place to train them and generally keep them under tabs. This is what ETS does. Coffman, who worked this system for many years, intimated that the problem with bringing markers together is brainwashing; too much training and regulation and you lose, if not the most sensitive areas of discrimination (cf. Britton *et al.*), then those authentic judgemental differences of opinion which enhance validity (Coffman, personal communication). Coffman may have been worried about over-regulation but the boards would be wrong to assume that there is nothing to be gained from holing up examiners. Hartog & Rhodes found they could improve consistency a good deal if they gave a few tips to examiners as they went along.

Coffman would entertain solo marking at home, but only on the proviso that script allocations were randomised prior to shipping out. This the boards do not typically do, though for English as a Foreign Language UCLES does operate such a procedure. The result is that examiners may receive a disproportionate number of scripts from a particular type of centre, or perhaps only ever see scripts from one type of centre. Overall calibre of scripts seen is bound to have an effect on marking behaviour. Were scripts to be randomised, Coffman would insist on examiners marking to a forced distribution, say on a scale 1–9, with examiners constrained to supply fixed percentages at each mark. Sets of scripts at each mark ought then to be comparable. According to Coffman, this idea goes back to Diederich at ETS in 1950. The objection that standards might drift from year to year, making the forced distribution chosen inappropriate, is countered by the reply that if this is happening the boards have no particular machinery for dealing with it anyway, and even if they did, the sources of error they have introduced by virtue of loose practices elsewhere are likely to cancel out whatever it is they are doing.

This does not exhaust the good ideas for training readers in circulation. These are mostly to be found in the USA; what they have in common is seriousness and thoroughness. The procedures worked by the Iowa Basic Skills testing programme have been described; elsewhere Patience & Auchter (1988) describe a system for training chief readers to be responsible for decentralised marking sites and Christopher (1988) discusses how readers may slowly evolve into an interpretative community.

Discussion

Three aspects of essay marking were considered – the existence of different types of writing, constructing questions and marking answers. While there may be no strong agreement on what constitutes good writing, it is possible to recognise different kinds of writing – narrative, argumentative and so on. Those responsible for setting tests and examinations should have an elaborated model of which kinds of writing they are looking to assess. The specifications for the questions should follow from this model. There is evidence that some kinds of writing can be assessed more reliably than others. This ties in with the clear research finding that markers are quite unable to distinguish between different features of writing – mechanics, organisation and so on – except perhaps for mechanics. It follows that the prospects for analytic marking are not good, but also that impression marking must be overly influenced by mechanics to be acceptably reliable.

When it comes to the wording of questions and rubrics, very little is known about what candidates make of what they are instructed to do. It is fair to speculate that there may be little shared understanding between examiners and candidates concerning what instructional verbs like 'Describe' signify. That, at any rate, is what examiners' reports are always saying. Both sides must be at fault; the dreaded 'Discuss' and 'Compare and contrast' have a lot to answer for. Much more needs to be found out about cueing (the best ways to do it) and its effects.

Any analysis of marking reliability needs to distinguish between four kinds of variation: between-writer, within-writer, between-marker and within-marker. Published estimates of reliability are invariably restricted to between-marker (single-rater reliability), but the within-writer factor, manifested in uneven performance across tasks requiring the same kind of writing, is just as important. Within-marker variability also needs attention and there are some pointers in the literature suggesting increased variability over time. The preferred way to study all these sources of variation, and that extends to handwriting effects also, is to carry out variance component or generalisability analyses.

The reliability of essay scores is primarily a function of the number of different topics to be tackled and the number of readings the essays get. Providing single-rater reliabilities are in the region 0·5 to 0·6 and upwards, the use of multiple marking is effective in producing a more reliable marking procedure. Moving to double, rather than triple, marking is quite adequate. An alternative to multiple marking is to calibrate markers according to information derived from a designed statistical experiment embedded in the operational marking arrangements. An examining board which disdains both of these prophylactics, and also allocates scripts non-randomly, is vulnerable to the charge that it has no effective control over reliability loss.

References

Bell B., Brook A. & Driver R. (1985) An approach to the documentation of alternative conceptions in school students' written responses. *British Education Research Journal*, **11**, 201–13.

Braddock R., Lloyd-Jones R. & Schoer L. (1963) *Research in Written Composition*. Urbana, Ill.: National Council of Teachers of English.

Braun H. I. (1988) Understanding scoring reliability: Experiments in calibrating essay readers. *Journal of Educational Statistics*, **13**, 1–18.

Briggs D. (1970) The influence of handwriting on assessment. *Educational Research*, **13**, 50–5.

Britton J. N., Martin N. C. & Rosen H. (1966) *Multiple Marking of Compositions: An Account of an Experiment*. London: HMSO.

Britton J. N., Burgess N., Martin N. C., McLeod A., & Rosen H. (1975) *The Development of Writing Abilities*. London: Macmillan.

Chase C. I. (1968) The impact of some obvious variables on essay test scores. *Journal of Educational Measurement*, **5**, 315–18.

Chase C. I. (1986) Essay test scoring: Interaction of relevant variables. *Journal of Educational Measurement*, **23**, 33–42.

Christopher R. (1988) Training of essay readers: A process for faculty and curriculum development. In *Notes from the National Testing Network in Writing, Vol. VIII*, 15–16, City University of New York.

Coffman W. E. (1966) On the validity of essay tests of achievement. *Journal of Educational Measurement*, **3**, 151–6.

Coffman W. E. (1971) Essay examinations. In Thorndike R. L. (ed.) *Educational Measurement* (2nd edition). Washington DC: American Council on Education.

Cooper P. L. (1984) The assessment of writing ability: A review of research. *ETS Research Report*, RR 84–12. Princeton, NJ: Educational Testing Service.

Cox R. (1968) *Examinations and Higher Education: Survey of the Literature*. London: Society for Research into Higher Education.

Diederich P. B. (1974) *Measuring Growth in English*. Urbana, Ill.: National Council of Teachers of English.

Ebel R. L. (1951) Estimation of the reliability of ratings. *Psychometrika*, **16**, 407–24.

Eggleston S. J. (1983) Learning mathematics. *APU Occasional Paper No. 1*. London: DES.

Farrell M. J. & Gilbert N. (1960) A type of bias in marking examination scripts. *British Journal of Educational Psychology*, **30**, 47–52.

French J. W. (1966) Schools of thought in judging excellence of English themes. In Anastasi A. (ed.) *Testing Problems in Perspective*. Washington, DC: American Council on Education.

de Glopper K. (1987) Convergent and divergent validity of analytical ratings of writing skill. In Degenhart R. E. (ed.) *Assessment of Student Writing in an International Context* (Publication Series B. Theory into Practice 9), 153–68 Jyvaskyla: Institute for Educational Research.

Godshalk F., Swineford F. & Coffman W. E. (1966) The measurement of writing ability. *College Board Research Monographs*, No. 6.

Hall P. B. (1972) Multiple impression marking of essays at a large-scale public examination. Unpublished M.Ed. thesis, Department of Education, University of Sydney.

Harris W. (1977) Teacher response to student writing: A study of the response patterns of high school English teachers to determine the basis for teacher judgements of student writing. *Research in Teaching English*, **11**, 175–85.

Hartog P. & Rhodes E. C. (1936) *The Marks of Examiners*. London: Macmillan.

Horowitz D. (1986) Essay examination prompts and the teaching of academic writing. *English for Specific Purposes*, **5**, 107–20.

Huck S. W. & Bounds W. G. (1972) Essay grades: An interaction between graders' handwriting clarity and the neatness of examination papers. *American Educational Research Journal*, **9**, 279–83.

Huddleston E. M. (1954) Measurement of writing ability at the college-entrance level: Objective vs. subjective testing techniques. *Journal of Experimental Education*, **22**, 165–205.

Hughes D. C., Keeling B. & Tuck B. F. (1983) Are untidy essays marked down by graders with neat handwriting? *New Zealand Journal of Educational Studies*, **18**, 184–6.

International Studies in Educational Achievement (1988) *The IEA Study of Written Composition I: The International Writing Tasks and Scoring Scales*. Gorman T. P., Purves A. C. & Degenhart R. E. (eds.) Oxford: Pergamon Press.

Iowa Tests of Basic Skills (1987*a*) *Writing: Teacher's Guide*. Chicago, Ill.: Riverside Press.

Iowa Tests of Basic Skills (1987*b*) *Writing: Handbook for Focused Holistic Scoring*. Chicago, IL: Riverside Press.

Johnstone A. & Cassells J. (1978) What's in a word? *New Scientist*, 18 May.

Lehmann, R. H. (1988) Research on national and international writing assessments: Towards a validation of the IEA rating system as applied to German student compositions. Unpublished paper, School of Education, University of Hamburg.

Lindley D. V. (1961) An experiment in the marking of an examination. *Royal Statistical Society Journal, Series A*, **124**, 285–312.

Lloyd-Jones R. (1977) Primary-trait scoring. In Cooper C. R. & Odell L. (eds.) *Evaluating Writing: Describing, Measuring, Judging*. Urbana, IL: National Council of Teachers of English.

Lucas A. M. (1971) Multiple marking of a matriculation Biology essay question. *British Journal of Educational Psychology*, **41**, 78–84.

Macnamara J. & Madaus G. F. (1969) Marker reliability in the Irish leaving certificate. *Irish Journal of Education*, **3**, 15–21.

Markham L. R. (1976) Influences of handwriting quality on teacher evaluation of written work. *American Educational Research Journal*, **13**, 277–83.

Marsh H. W. & Ireland R. (1987) The assessment of writing effectiveness: A multidimensional perspective. *Australian Journal of Psychology*, **39**, 353–67.

Mobley M. (1987) Making ourselves clearer: Readability in the GCSE. *Working Paper 5*, London: Secondary Examinations Council.

NCTE (1979) *SLATE: Support for Learning and Teaching of English*, **4**, No. 2.

O'Donnell W. R. (1968) An investigation into the rôle of language in a Physics examination. Monograph, Moray House.

Patience W. & Auchter J. (1988) Establishing and maintaining score scale stability and reading reliability. In *Notes from the National Testing Network in Writing, Vol. VIII*, 14–15, City University of New York.

Pilliner A. E. G. (1969) Multiple marking: Wiseman or Cox? *British Journal of Educational Psychology*, **39**, 313–15.

Rafoth B. A. & Rubin D. L. (1984) The impact of content and mechanics on judgements of writing quality. *Written Communication*, **1**, 446–58.

Spencer E. (1983) *Writing Matters Across the Curriculum* (SCRE Publication 79). Edinburgh: Hodder & Stoughton.

Swales J. (1982) Examining examination papers. *English Language Research Journal*, **3**, 9–25.

Wiseman S. (1949) The marking of English compositions in grammar school selection. *British Journal of Educational Psychology*, **19**, 205.

Wood R. & Quinn B. (1976) Double impression marking of English Language essay and summary questions. *Educational Review*, **28**, 229–46.

Wood R. & Wilson D. T. (1974) Evidence for differential marking and discrimination among examiners of English. *Irish Journal of Education*, **8**, 36–48.

6 School-based assessment including Records of Achievement

A categorical justification for including school-based assessment in GCSE has been made by the Secondary Examinations Council (SEC). School-based assessment is there to test 'aspects of attainment which may not easily or adequately be tested by (final) papers' (SEC 1985, p. 2). In affirming that school-based examining can do what one-off external examining cannot, SEC was merely codifying received opinion. A 1984 Australian report (McGaw *et al.* 1984) saw the strengths of school-based assessments to be that they:

> can be used on a substantial sample of student performance, over time and over the full range of the syllabus requirements;
> can assess aspects of a course not accessible to external examination.

The report went on:

> We recognize, however, that school assessments can have serious deficiencies too. We see these to be that the assessments:
> can be biased for or against a student by the relationship between teacher and student;
> can, in some cases, take undue account of early performance in a course and, relatively, too little of the level a student finally reaches;
> can change the relationship between teacher and student by casting the teacher in the role of judge instead of that of supporter in the preparation for external assessment;
> can be undertaken with variable criteria from school to school.

Of these deficiencies, the second can ostensibly be taken care of by specifying precisely when assessments shall be undertaken, while the fourth is being tackled in GCSE by the Southern Examining Group, at least, who claim to be providing teachers with detailed mark schemes and asking them to mark work as if they were marking examination scripts (Owen 1988). The third deficiency, what Torrance (1986) calls the 'uneasy dual role', seems endemic to the school-based assessment enterprise, although no easier to take for that.

The first deficiency is perhaps the one which worries most observers and always will. What research there is suggests that in certain circumstances teachers will be unduly swayed, although, again, the steps that are being taken in GCSE to make school-based assessment more analytic and less impressionistic will tend to ameliorate unwanted influences. What we do not have is a British study which has sought to quantify the effects of this particular kind of bias.

That teachers will be influenced by all sorts of considerations (tastes, preferences, prejudices and so on) was brought out in a study by Wood & Napthali (1975). The starting point for the research was an apprehension that attempts to standardise assessments through the use of apparently specific schemes purporting to describe achievement constitute both a recognition and a concealment of the possibility that teachers vary both in what they regard as achievement and in their capacity to pick out defined attributes or behaviours, that is to use such schemes. A rather thorough Irish–American study (Pedulla, Airasian & Madaus 1980; Kellaghan, Madaus & Airasian 1982) found that teachers' judgements of students' IQ, English and Mathematics performance were confounded with their judgements of other academically related behaviours, such as attention span and persistence. The possibility that ratings of social behaviours such as manners/politeness and behaviour in school might also intertwine seriously with academic judgements was rejected. By contrast, standardised test results were not confounded with these academically related behaviours to any great degree. What did emerge was that teachers' ratings of pupils were more often raised than lowered when they were given access to test results (Kellaghan *et al.* p. 260), an example of teachers being swayed by factors other than the evidence of achievement they gather themselves.

Validity considerations

In justifying the inclusion of teacher-assessed elements in GCSE by reference to the principle of 'fitness for purpose', the Department of Education and Science (DES) has, as Torrance (1986, p. 2) noted, effectively made teacher involvement in assessment an issue of validity – the validity of the examination. This is important because it means that school-based assessment is not something which can in future be marginalised or bargained away. In other words, if the *General Criteria* (DES 1985) are to be observed, it is not something it would be nice to have but something which is imperative. Moreover, the need to produce evidence for the teacher–examiner to assess means that the range of attainments will be expanded, into research skills, interactive skills, motor skills, skills of adaptation and improvisation in the widest sense (SEC 1985, pp. 2–4). In effect, school-based assessment becomes an engine for enriching the curriculum as it is delivered. Not only is there better correspondence between what is done in schools and what is examined, which itself enhances validity, but the result is fuller and richer. That, at any rate, is the hope.

At bottom, the issue is whether a real integration of curriculum and assessment can be achieved within schools or whether, because of the identity of GCSE as an examination designed and organised by the SEC and examining bodies, the teachers will be unable to function as both encouragers and examiners of attainment.

Reliability considerations

The *General Criteria* also stipulate that 'any scheme of assessment and moderation must... not be allowed to dominate the educational aims or inhibit good teaching and learning practice' (DES p. 6).

This is indeed a most pregnant statement of intent. Those familiar with such statements will recognise the juxtaposition of two outcomes known to be antithetical, with the pious injunction that one should not be allowed to overwhelm the other when the strong suspicion already exists that this is precisely what will happen. The whole history of external examining is a tale of curbing and reining in heterodox educational practices, in the interests of fairness to all. Whatever is done, however partial, should be done to all in the same way. Nothing should be done to jeopardise reliability.

We are talking, again, about the trade-off between reliability and validity. It is a most poignant predicament, because the trade-off can only go so far – reliability places a limit on validity.

Torrance (p. 37) says that if the examining groups continue to treat teacher involvement in assessment solely in terms of the technical issues of marker reliability and moderation, then curricular flexibility will be the least visible feature of the new system and to that extent validity will suffer. The trouble with that statement is that the examining groups are running an examination and therefore **have** to care about reliability. Tedious it may be to have to observe this dictum, but it is simply no use having the most wonderful examination in the world if it cannot be marked and graded reliably. The experiences may have been good but what is the point if the rewards are distributed quite haphazardly?

So, while it is possible to be critical of the boards' collective efforts in maintaining acceptable levels of reliability for written examinations (chapter 11), they cannot be expected to be neglectful of reliability considerations where school-based assessment is concerned just because it is seen as an agent of educational reform. The easiest way to bring coursework assessment into disrepute would be to take a stand-off, laissez-faire attitude to it, so that people will think that anything goes. A similar argument applies to the introduction of 'authentic' tests of language use where the suspicion is that supporters want to go soft on reliability (chapter 19).

It is, however, a good question to ask what the appropriate level of effort is for ascertaining reliability of school-based assessments, commensurate with the effort which is put into the externally examined side, especially if the respective weightings are 50:50. Ideally, a system as light and as unobtrusive as possible would be best, so that the schools are not hampered in what they are trying to do (if indeed they are trying to do something); but is that going to be enough? It may be that any system is perceived as too heavy, just as the present system may be already quite light judged by any reasonable criterion.

On one aspect of reliability, the availability of repeated observations, the teacher is better placed than the external examiner, as the McGaw report noted. The opportunity is certainly there to firm up a sound estimate of a student's achievements. What, though, if **bias** gets in the way? Bias here is defined as the discrepancy between what a potentially biased assessor will award and what a consensus of uninfluenced assessors will award. It is sometimes supposed that teachers confuse industry or effort with achievement, but a recent American study (Wright & Wiese 1988) says they can keep the two separate. The Irish–American study (Pedulla *et al.*) was not so sure. On the face of it, attention span and persistence do not seem very far removed from industry and effort, perhaps just different orders of magnitude.

What of the influence of students' extra-academic characteristics? The literature contains reports of different behaviour towards high and low achievers (Pidgeon 1970), students perceived to come from different social classes (Nash 1973), boys and girls (Carter 1952; Kellaghan *et al.* p. 200) and good-looking and plain children (Dion 1974). Dweck (1976) observed teachers directing more criticism towards boys and also evaluating them less positively on academic tasks. Dipboye, Artey & Terpstra (1977) found assessors to be strongly biased by physical attractiveness, a preference which prompted Cook (1988, p. 62) to talk of 'face-ism akin to racism'.

Gender-related teacher–student interactions have also been reported. Dion maintained that women teachers are likely to be much more lenient towards an attractive boy than they are to an unattractive girl (see also Archer & McCarthy 1988 and references there). Spear (1984) sought to discover whether teachers' expectations can either reinforce or counteract girls' under-achievement in science. She found that work attributed to a boy was rated higher than identical work attributed to a girl; also that teachers (male and female) tended to express higher expectations for boys than for girls. More recent work (Worrall & Tsarna 1987) reported that science teachers expected lower achievement from girls, although this appeared not to influence their teaching disposition adversely. There was also the suggestion that the effect works in reverse for boys in languages.

The most pervasive and potentially most serious consequence of teachers' suggestibility (or even biddability) would be if they were to substitute estimates of ability or IQ for estimates of achievement. Speculation to this effect was published by Murphy (1974) who argued that teachers, having suitably motivated the children and provided them with the relevant stimulating environment, see good or bad performance as the natural consequence of the child's innate ability or IQ. Success or failure in academic matters is in the natural order of things, as such ubiquitous classroom explanations as...'not quite having it...', 'being a bit dull...', 'rather stupid...' constantly testify (Murphy, p. 334). The ability of young children to rank themselves for academic ability has been brought out by Crocker & Cheeseman (1988), among others.

So school-based assessment could be about ability, whereas external examinations are indubitably about achievement. That is one travesty of school-based assessment as the SEC and DES intend it to be. Another is when teachers treat the task as prediction of what students will do in an examination. The fact that teachers are able to predict examination performance quite closely, is, from the point of view of the proper function of teacher assessment, neither here nor there. In the context of entry for differentiated papers, Good & Cresswell (1988) reported that teachers are able to predict examination grades correct to ± 1 grade for approximately 85% of the candidates, with only between 2% and 3% of the predictions being out by more than two grades. Earlier Murphy (1979) had mounted a typical prediction exercise and found reasonably strong agreement. When Murphy asked teachers to use their own criteria, considerable disparities were revealed between the two sets of rank orders. Murphy was inclined to think that the more teachers' assessments are taken out of the control of external examinations, the more they will differ from the results of external examinations. Of course, that may only mean a regression to estimating IQ.

Given what can go wrong with teachers' assessments, it is curious that examining bodies over the years, and now the DES in the *GCSE General Criteria*, have been so ready to agree that the teacher's rank ordering of students is perfect. It is doubtful if they would place such trust in any one examiner marking over a run of 30 scripts or so. Remember, too, that this declaration of faith was made in the days before teachers were trained in assessment. Although it is not customary to discuss reliability in terms of ordinal measurements, and there is no well worked out theory for it, a common sense interpretation of the statement 'The teacher's rank order is sacrosanct' would be that the teacher's judgement is perfectly reliable. Certainly, this would follow if Lord & Novick's essentially 'bootstrapping' proposal that each observed rank be treated as an observed score were to be adopted (Lord & Novick 1968, p. 215).

What the teacher finds hard is to ascertain **level**; to attach an accurate score or mark or grade to each rank. That is why there is moderation. It is not quite conventional wisdom, but there is a common belief that teachers overestimate their students' achievement. (The finding in Kellaghan *et al.* that teachers only revise upwards when given test data is consistent with this belief.) As with all these issues, there is too little to go on but a recent experiment (Spear 1989) suggests that teachers habitually mark generously as a way of encouraging students. Spear notes how such a habit might backfire in raising false expectations. Be that as it may, whatever kind of calibration the teacher actually uses, an invitation to re-mark students would presumably result in marks which fell in the same rank order. A lower bound on reliability, conventionally calculated, can then be theoretically estimated as the lowest product–moment correlation possible compatible with a perfect rank-order correlation, and given a certain sample size. Whatever answers come out of this exercise, the result is unlikely to be worse than the reliability levels of 0·80–0·90 we would expect to get from, say, essay papers (chapters 5 and 11). Little has been published on the reliability of school-based assessments since the early JMB study (Hewitt 1967). Interestingly, that study reported an average correlation of 0·83 between the school's assessment and the assessment of an independent moderator (for 20 candidates in each of 10 schools). Not one of the correlations fell below 0·60. It may be that school-based assessment can be trusted after all.

It follows anyway on the premiss that the teacher's rank order is true, that school-based assessment will pass muster on reliability grounds. Given the validity enrichment it promises, it should then enjoy parity of esteem with other components, once moderation has been applied. Where this bright scenario could go seriously adrift is if teachers subvert the proper function of teacher assessment, as seen by SEC, and end up impoverishing validity.

Moderation

The moderation problem can be seen as one of distinguishing between the making of what are very proper corrections to counter grade inflation and the making of unjustified overcorrections downwards when in truth there are good and sufficient reasons why a teacher should offer assessments which, according to examination results, are too generous. Suppose a teacher sets out to bring most of her students to a high level of achievement, by, for example, using a mastery learning strategy or just by taking very seriously the injunction to encourage and reward positive achievement. Suppose also that she succeeded, but that her efforts do not show through in the external examination to the same degree (perhaps because of the very factors inherent in examinations which pull down some students' performances). The act of statistical moderation would be to deprive some of these students of grades they may well have earned. Visiting or postal moderation might do the same. Stockwell (1988) reports on a CSE board moderation procedure (East Midlands) which involves lowering the marks awarded to the complete school-based coursework rather than rearranging the order or marks of individual candidates. Methods for scaling marks or grades are dealt with in chapter 10.

Weighting

The objections to statistical moderation are, in any case, well known. If instrument Y exists to measure things other than instrument X manages, how can it be right to use X to scale Y? The *GCSE General Criteria* specify the conditions under which statistical moderation may be applied in the GCSE. These include an overlap of assessment objectives between internally and externally assessed components, and a high correlation between components. Here the DES is hedging; the term 'overlap' is too vague, as is 'high' correlation, and there is no indication that the latter requirement would ever be routinely checked, or indeed the other requirements for linear scaling identified by Good (1988).

If it is correct to say that less is known about the properties of school-based assessment than about other components to be mixed in, then there must be legitimate concern about the effects of mixing in school-based assessment, and in particular about the possibility that school-based assessment will exert more weight in actuality than was planned. This last outcome can certainly happen if care is not taken. Component marks need to be standardised separately before being entered into the mix and steps have to be taken to accommodate the presence of correlations between components. Methods exist for doing this (Adams & Wilmut 1981; Cresswell 1987; Govindarajulu 1988). These methods do presuppose a more or less uniformly high reliability level across components, an assumption which could be sustained for school-based assessment on the basis of the reasoning above, even if empirical confirmation is hard to come by.

Records of Achievement

All the findings reported earlier, concerning the suggestibility of teachers in the face of biasing influences, are refocused in an interesting way when it comes to a consideration of Records of Achievement (RoA). At first glance it might seem that RoA would be even more suspect than school-based assessment in its examination form, yet reflection suggests that the greater openness and transparency, which are a feature of RoA, ought to conduce to fairer assessments, and to the validity enrichment SEC hoped school-based assessment would deliver.

Considered here are the national evaluation of pilot schemes by the PRAISE team (Broadfoot *et al.* 1988), the HMI report on developments in RoA (DES 1988), the RANSC report on RoA (DES 1989), together with what can be gleaned from CPRA documents (UCLES 1988) concerning experience with the pilot scheme involving UCLES and Cambridgeshire. Appropriately, greatest attention is given to assessment issues. Self-assessment is the most obvious 'new' issue to emerge. The CPRA introduction talks of 'enhancing active learning'.

RoA has obvious diagnostic possibilities. The HMI report notes, however, (p. 12) that often documents rich in diagnostic information were issued and copies unhelpfully filed, rather than followed up with pupils. Perhaps the reason is the reason noted in chapter 8 *Diagnostic assessment* – teachers are unable or unwilling to follow through. With what the CPRA, for one, provides in the way of materials, there is less excuse for doing nothing than is the case with diagnostic testing programmes which go off at half-cock.

A problem facing RoA compilers is that of converting a mass of information about the individual into a summative record. The same problem faces the school which has to produce school-based assessments, but there it seems to be more recessed, or perhaps less acknowledged. The PRAISE team (p. 54) saw that issues of validity were raised, as indeed they are. Did the summative records represent a selection from statements in formative and interim records, or were they different in kind in that they were in some way synoptic? The PRAISE team commented that free prose formats seem better able to portray the achievement of the pupil in a holistic way but noted (p. 56) that summarising is a skill and many teachers will need in-service support before they feel confident in statement writing. Comment banks were thought to be of limited value but that, if they were to be utilised, there should be separate comment banks for formative and final summative records, the latter containing comments which are more synoptic but fewer in number.

Among the weaknesses it identified the HMI report cited 'unduly limited opportunity for self-assessment by pupils' and 'a lack of clearly defined assessment criteria, capable of being understood by pupils' (p. 45). Given that self-assessment is difficult for most pupils anyway, the need for clear, intelligible assessment criteria is paramount. This is as true for teachers as for students.

Commenting on the same issue, the PRAISE team raised the question of whether pupils are able to assess themselves accurately and in a way which is free from understandable anxiety. They say that even when presented with specific categories of criteria for assessment, pupils are apt to judge their achievement in relation to their perception of the range of achievement in their teaching groups. They call this the 'persistence of norm-referencing' (p. 25). The RANSC report makes the same point (para. 4.10), adding that their perceptions of teacher expectations, their views on what is socially acceptable and their anxiety not to lose face also come into play. That students should behave like this at first is quite understandable. The tendency to make relative statements is culturally very strong. However, what is likely to make them continue to do it is the same difficulty with the wording of assessment criteria. One example in the PRAISE report (p. 25) is 'can hypothesise'. The teacher felt that when making self-assessments some pupils placed themselves along a continuum from poor to good rather than studying the statements closely to see which most accurately described them. They are unable to do this because the language defeats them. HMI says (p. 18) that target-setting needs to be encouraged and that the targets need to be specific, to be in the forefront of pupils' minds, and to be met by pupils through the completion of specific pieces of work.

Evidence is slowly beginning to emerge of substantial differences between pupils of different sex, race and prior attainments in their approach and attitudes towards RoA. Thus the PRAISE report (p. 125). One LEA suggested that boys have more time spent on them, an observation which tallies with the literature, for example Kelly (1988) who, on the basis of a meta-analysis, estimated that teachers, on average, spend 44% of their time with girls and 56% with boys. Furthermore, said this particular LEA, boys were challenging more and actually modifying statements as a result of dialogue even though they find it more difficult to express themselves freely. By contrast the RANSC report says that there is some evidence that girls take to RoA and understand the purpose of the formative processes better than do boys (para. 3.17). They tend to be more forthcoming and skilled in discussion and value the opportunity for one-to-one contact with their teachers (providing they are of the same sex). On the other hand, boys tend to have a keener sense of the external audience for the records, and concentrate on concrete achievements rather than relationships.

Differences with respect to race are showing up presently as an issue with language. The PRAISE team reports concern that pupils who admit their first language is not a European language will be disadvantaged rather than have their mastery of two or more languages recognised as an achievement (p. 126). The RANSC report makes the point rather differently, arguing (para. 3.18) that where teachers are not closely familiar with particular cultural models they may not fully recognise the achievements of certain pupils.

The HMI report, but not the RANSC report, has nothing to say about differences whether with respect to sex, race or class, perhaps mirroring what the PRAISE team report saw (p. 126) as a worrying reluctance to address the issue of pupil differences, despite the invitation to do so.

The HMI report (pp. 28–9) draws the distinction between **authentication**, which involves checking the evidence of pupils' achievements on which the content of the RoA is based, and **validation**, **accreditation** and **verification**, which are to do with the efficacy of the assessing, recording and reporting processes; in other words, whether procedures are being operated properly. Authentication is therefore a kind of moderation, and a particularly difficult kind at that. As the PRAISE report notes (p. 172), traditional product-based approaches to moderation are clearly not appropriate for RoA where the products are so highly individualised. Rather, it is the processes supporting the production of the final record, as much as the statement itself, which need to be monitored. Quality assurance procedures have tended to draw on practices developed in further and higher education in relation to the validation of courses of study and the accreditation of institutions to issue particular awards. These do not speak to authentication, which remains highly problematic.

Discussion

Even if school-based assessment was, in the main, less reliable than it apparently is, it would still be possible to say of it what Thouless said of essays, '...that this unreliability can be reduced by improved methods of marking and that there is no reason for regarding it as so great that essays cannot be included as elements in an examination if it is felt that their inclusion has desirable educational effects' (Thouless 1969, p. 210). That the inclusion of coursework in principle has a greater educational effect than the inclusion of essays, which are involved anyway in coursework, is surely beyond doubt, providing, that is, that the validity enrichment claims made for it are delivered and that it does not degenerate into a series of mini-examinations or, even worse, a mimicking of the examination itself. It is necessary to add that school-based assessment will always be vulnerable to accusations of contamination through teacher bias, Records of Achievement less so, and if the SEC and examining bodies are to have answers, appropriate enquiries need to be undertaken;

or else a respectable defence of the proposition that such bias is endemic in the system.

References

Adams R. M. & Wilmut J. (1981) A measure of the weights of examination components and scaling to adjust them. *The Statistician*, **30**, 263–9.

Archer J. & McCarthy B. (1988) Personal biases in student assessment. *Educational Research*, **30**, 142–5.

Broadfoot P., James M., McMeeking S., Nuttall D. L. & Stierer B. (1988) *Records of Achievement: Report of the National Evaluation of Pilot Schemes (PRAISE)*. London: HMSO.

Carter R. S. (1952) How invalid are marks assigned by teachers? *Journal of Educational Psychology*, **43**, 218–28.

Cook M. (1988) *Personnel Selection and Productivity*. London: Wiley.

Cresswell M. J. (1987) A more generally useful measure of the weight of examination components. *British Journal of Mathematical and Statistical Psychology*, **40**, 61–79.

Crocker A. C. & Cheeseman R. G. (1988) The ability of young children to rank themselves for academic ability. *Educational Studies*, **14**, 105–10.

DES (1985) *GCSE General Criteria*. London: HMSO.

DES (1988) *Report by HM Inspectors on Developments in Records of Achievement 1986–1988*. London: DES.

DES (1989) *Records of Achievement: Report of the Records of Achievement National Steering Committee (RANSC)*. London: HMSO.

Dion K. K. (1974) Children's physical attractiveness and sex as determiners of adult punitiveness. *Developmental Psychology*, **10**, 772–8.

Dipboye R. L., Arvey R. D. & Terpstra D. E. (1977) Sex and physical attractiveness of raters and applicants as determinants of resumé evaluation. *Journal of Applied Psychology*, **62**, 288–94.

Dweck C. S. (1976) Children's interpretation of evaluative feedback: The effect of social cues on learned helplessness. *Merrill-Palmer Quarterly*, **22**, 105–9.

Good F. J. (1988) A method of moderation of school-based assessments: Some statistical considerations. *The Statistician*, **37**, 33–49.

Good F. J. & Cresswell M. J. (1988) Can teachers enter candidates appropriately for examinations involving differentiated papers? *Educational Studies*, **14**, 289–97.

Govindarajulu Z. (1988) Alternative methods for combining several test scores. *Educational and Psychological Measurement*, **48**, 53–60.

Hewitt E. A. (1967) The reliability of GCE O-level examinations in English language. *JMB OP 27*, Manchester: Joint Matriculation Board.

Kellaghan T., Madaus G. & Airasian P. (1982) *The Effects of Standardized Testing*. Boston: Kluwer-Nijhoff Publishing.

Kelly A. (1988) Gender differences in teacher–pupil interactions. *Research in Evaluation*, **39**, 1–24.

Lord F. M. & Novick M. R. (1968) *Statistical Theories of Mental Test Scores*. Reading, Mass.: Addison-Wesley.

McGaw B. *et al.* (1984) *Assessment in the Upper Secondary School in Western Australia*. Perth: Ministry of Education.

Murphy J. (1974) Teacher expectations and working-class under achievement. *British Journal of Sociology*, **25**, 326–44.

Murphy R. J. L. (1979) Teachers' assessments and GCE results compared. *Educational Research*, **22**, 54–9.

Nash R. (1973) Keeping in with teacher. *New Society*, 24 December.

Owen S. (1988) Marksmanship for the GCSE. *Education*, 6 May.

Pedulla J. J., Airasian P. & Madaus G. F. (1980) Do teacher ratings and standardized tests of students yield the same information? *American Educational Research Journal*, **17**, 303–7.

Pidgeon D. A. (1970) *Expectation and Pupil Performance*. Windsor: NFER Publishing Company.

Secondary Examinations Council (1985) *Course Work Assessment in GCSE*, Working Paper 2. London: SEC.

Spear M. G. (1984) The biasing influence of pupil sex in a science marking exercise. *Research in Science and Technological Education*, **2**, 55–60.

Spear M. G. (1989) The relationship between standard of work and mark awarded. *Educational Research*, **31**, 69–70.

Stockwell P. (1988) GCSE coursework assessment. *Mathematics in Schools*, January, 12–13.

Thouless R. H. (1969) *Map of Educational Research*. Windsor: NFER Publishing Company.

Torrance H. (1986) School-based assessment in GCSE: aspirations, problems, and possibilities. In Gipps C. V. (ed.) *The GCSE: An Uncommon Examination*, London: Institute of Education, 30–42.

University of Cambridge Local Examinations Syndicate (1988) *Cambridge Partnership for Records of Achievement*. Cambridge: UCLES.

Wood R. & Napthali W. A. (1975) Assessment in the classroom: What do teachers look for? *Educational Studies*, **1**, 151–61.

Worrall N. & Tsarna H. (1987) Teachers' reported practices towards girls and boys in science and languages. *British Journal of Educational Psychology*, **57**, 300–12.

Wright D. & Wiese M. J. (1988) Teacher judgement in student evaluation: A comparison of grading methods. *Journal of Educational Research*, **82**, 10–14.

7 Criterion-referenced testing including graded assessment

In 1963 there appeared three seminal papers in educational measurement. Carroll (1963) introduced the notion of time to mastery which Bloom later turned into the mastery learning paradigm; Cronbach (1963) showed how matrix sampling could be used in evaluation work; and Glaser (1963) introduced the notions of criterion-referencing and criterion-referenced testing (CRT), differentiating them sharply from norm-referencing and norm-referenced testing. This last paper was to mark a watershed. Educational measurement should no longer be seen as a branch of psychological testing; moreover, the preoccupation of psychological test theory with aptitude and with selection and prediction problems, all of which involve norm-referencing, ought to be shrugged off. It is true, as Glaser acknowledged, that others had made this distinction previously (Hamilton (1929) for one) but it was his paper which caught the imagination. It can be said to mark the point at which educational measurement began to detach itself from psychometrics.

Since then there has been much embellishment, but little invention. Notions like minimum competency testing and graded assessment are only developed versions of the original paradigm, given particular twists. The contrast with norm-referenced testing has most certainly been overdone. To give but one example, it was argued, quite seriously, by two educational philosophers that norm-referencing constituted a violation of students' civil rights inasmuch as students were ranked publicly and might therefore feel humiliated (Guy & Chambers 1973, 1974). Under criterion-referencing this could not happen. The timing of this attack was particularly unfortunate because before long, in the USA and especially Florida, the courts were hearing a succession of cases in which litigants claimed that their civil rights had been denied as a result of taking minimum competency tests built on the most impeccable criterion-referenced principles (*Debra P.* vs. *Turlington* 1981, being merely the best known). These students had been refused leaving certificates, compelled to stay on at school and so on. This was one of the silliest examples of praising criterion-referencing by damning norm-referencing.

It has been said that if you scratch a criterion-referenced interpretation, you will very likely find a norm-referenced set of assumptions underneath (Angoff 1974). That is to say, a norm-referenced interpretation can nearly always be placed upon a criterion-referenced interpretation, simply by admitting comparisons. People vary in the time taken to reach the criterion (mastery), the number of criteria met and so on. A driving test is certainly criterion-referenced, but note that the results can also be interpreted in a norm-referenced way as in, 'He needed four tries, his sister two, but I passed first time.' Or, as Skehan (1984, p. 217) has noticed, there is often a reliance on covert (or not-so-covert) norm-referenced terms, such as 'Generally can get by without serious breakdowns' or '...better than an absolute beginner'.

Glaser's purpose, in inventing CRT, was to dramatise the need, as he saw it, to provide answers to the question 'Can X and Y do Z?' rather than 'Did X score higher than Y on Z?' which norm-referenced testing addresses. Emphasis should be on calibrating individual growth rather than on inducing between-individual variation, and testing should be firmly coupled with the instruction which has preceded it. This is what distinguishes educational measurement from psychological measurement. One deals in achievement, which can be described in detail (in principle), and the other in ability, which people are presumed to have more or less of (the so-called 'strength' model). To the extent that examining boards trade in achievement, and teachers trade in ability, any mixture of the two is liable to be degraded. The irony is that teachers are better placed to practise authentic criterion-referencing, given that they can make sure that instruction and assessment are tightly coupled, something the boards can never do. But teachers are also in a much better position to norm-reference, notably by ranking according to ability what to them are manageable numbers of students.

Operationally, the distinguishing characteristic of a CRT is not, as was once thought, the existence of a standard or passing score, but rather the detailed specification of the content or behaviour domain to be assessed. Only by spelling out what people were supposed to know and be able to do would it be possible first to test and then to report in those terms. That is what the development of grade-related criteria for the GCSE is supposed to have been all about. The interesting thing there is how daylight has appeared between criterion-referenced grading and the so-called grade descriptions (Forrest & Shoesmith 1985, pp. 8–9). Whereas, in principle, grade-related criteria are predetermined standards of performance which examiners are required to apply exhaustively, as if they are operating a **conjunctive** scoring model (chapter 10), grade descriptions are merely meant to convey what Orr & Nuttall (1983, p. 9) call 'post-hoc generalisations about the skills and knowledge mastered by the majority of candidates that have obtained a certain grade'. Such descriptions are irredeemably actuarial (in addition to being an act of faith); as Forrest & Shoesmith note (p. 9), success in a task cannot be seen as a criterion for the award of grade C to an individual candidate, for it is only a statistical expectation and not a certainty as required of a criterion. Perhaps French *et al.* (1987, p. 19) are right in saying that grade-related criteria were never intended to be criteria in the sense of criterion-referencing, but that only means that the GCSE cannot be treated as an example of CRT, or anything like.

As to post-hoc generalisations, the nature of achievement at school is characteristically so bitty and unrelated that the sort of hierarchical structure of performance required to support really trustworthy generalisation (a perfect Guttman scale) is inconceivable. Those well-meaning revisionists who tried to wring meaning out of grades retrospectively came to grief precisely for this reason (Kempa & Odinga 1984). That was before criterion-referenced grading and grade descriptions were tried, but there is no reason to suppose that the outcome will be any different now unless anyone believes that teaching, which is the most likely agent for removing bittiness, has changed significantly as a result of GCSE and grade criteria. In these circumstances the application of a conjunctive scoring model, instead of perhaps a compensatory or **disjunctive** model (chapter 10), is not unduly restrictive but is doomed to fail; for minimum competency and mastery tests, the passing level has always been set at 80% or so, never 100%. Forrest & Shoesmith put it this way (p. 12):

> The more simplistic proponents of such a scheme describe it as certificating success rather than failure as at present but there is an ironic sense in which the boot is on the other foot: your grade is determined by the simplest task in which you fail, no matter how complex those in which you succeed.

Technical characteristics of criterion-referenced testing

Although the various treatments of CRT reliability have spawned any number of competing estimators, the topic is basically straightforward. As with norm-referenced tests, validity is much less well conceptualised and explicated. The belief that CRT is all about passing scores is reinforced by a look at the CRT reliability literature. Seizing on what was obviously most different from norm-referenced testing, investigators have devised statistics which use, as raw material, the numbers judged to pass or fail (master or non-master) on both test and retest, and those who are judged pass/fail or fail/pass. Loss functions can be imposed, with differential weights assigned to false positives and negatives. It is then possible, by routine methods, to calculate the reliability of the classification, and in this respect the problem is no different from any other classification problem where the judges or instruments are fallible. Examples of competing estimators can be found in Traub & Rowley (1980) and Feldt & Brennan (1989). Companion solutions for CRT item analysis, which is just a parallel problem with items replacing tests, are presented in chapter 9.

In the different situations where there is no such thing as a passing score but the tests are built on CRT principles, like GCSE, these new statistics do not apply, except in the sense that we could imagine judges using grade descriptions disagreeing about whether a candidate was grade C or otherwise. The old statistics would still appear to be appropriate and the question arises as to whether improved reliability performance might be expected, by virtue of the tightening up of specifications and targeting of marking which ought to ensue from a properly implemented CRT regime.

At first glance it would appear that validity in the CRT context must be solely a matter of content validity. It is indisputable that one of the important contributions of the CRT movement has been an increased emphasis on content. The absolute interpretations of the measures are dependent upon clear specifications of the content domain and on the degree to which the measure is representative of the domain. Rather as people confuse an intention with the deed, there has been a tendency to suppose that the content validity of CRTs is unproblematical, if not assured.

Content validity is dealt with elsewhere (chapter 12), as has been the related topic of specifications (chapter 1). The question here is whether it is enough. Reference to the *Standards for Educational and Psychological Testing* (APA 1985) suggests not – 'Questions of validity are questions of what may properly be inferred from a test score; validity refers to the appropriateness of inferences from test scores.' Now content validity is a test characteristic; it will not vary across different groups of examinees. However, the validity of test score interpretations will vary from one situation to another. To use an example provided by Hambleton *et al.* (1978, pp. 38–9), if a CRT is administered by mistake under highly speeded test conditions, the validity of interpretations based on test scores obtained from the test administration will be weaker than if the test had been administered with more suitable time limits.

The undesirability of thinking of different kinds of validity as alternatives, or as Guion (1980) put it 'roads to psychometric salvation' one of which must be taken, is pointed out in chapter 12. That said, it is still appropriate to ask whether construct validity has any relevance to CRT validation. A clue that there are constructs involved in CRT comes from the term **minimum competency** testing. Some competence or other is implied, but what is it? Could it be 'literacy' or 'numeracy'? Messick (1981) has pointed out how little effort has been made to unpack these terms. Is a basic skill one that enables performance in a wide variety of situations at some functional level of environmental complexity? Is it a skill that facilitates later learning in the same area or across areas? Evidently there are constructs in play, even if they are grossly under-conceptualised. As Messick remarks, 'what sort of construct is it if we do not know anything about it above the mastery or minimum competency threshold?' Or, to use Skehan's example (p. 216), how shall we know whether someone who succeeds with an easy lecture could cope with a more difficult one? Logically, says Skehan, to obtain criterion-referencing one would need as many tests as there are types of lectures, given that these cannot be ordered along one dimension of difficulty.

These examples show how over-extended inference can become. This is not supposed to happen with CRT. It is meant to deal in low-level inferences, those that are tied closely to the definition of an item domain and rely upon well-established principles of sampling theory. The drawbacks of such test construction procedures were mentioned in chapter 1. Typical low-level inferences are:

> Given any 4, 5 or 6 digit numeral the pupil can round off the numbers to the nearest hundred;
>
> and
>
> Given two unlike fractions with denominators of 2, 3, 4, 5, 6, 7, 8, 9, 10 or 12 the pupil can find their sum or their difference.

As Linn notes (1980, p. 557) this high degree of specificity is very desirable for some purposes. These objectives are coupled much more tightly to particular instructional activities than is possible with a global score for arithmetic computation. For other purposes, however, the narrowness of the skills tested and the proliferation of scores limits their utility. It will be recalled (chapter 1) how Popham, the high priest of CRT, burdened down by amplified objectives, tried to escape the confines of low-level inference by going for 'important' behaviours. Would Popham consider 'numeracy' and 'literacy' to be important behaviours? It would be interesting to know.

A good, modern, successful example of criterion-referenced testing: the Degrees of Reading Power (DRP) test

Dissatisfaction with the narrowly specific scores led Koslin, Koslin & Zeno (1979) to argue that an alternative type of measure is needed for purposes of measuring long-term educational outcomes. The outcome they had in mind was 'reading with comprehension' and to measure it they devised the Degrees of Reading Power (DRP) test. It has proved very popular in the USA. Cronbach (personal communication) thought it quite the best example of a criterion-referenced test that he had seen; its great virtue is that it has a ready and valuable application, with strong remedial possibilities.

The DRP is similar to a cloze test in that words are deleted from a prose passage and the examinee has to select the deleted word. It differs from the typical cloze passage, however, in the choice of words for deletion and in the number of words deleted. Fewer words are deleted on the DRP (for example seven deletions for a passage of several paragraphs) than is found on the typical cloze test. Also, only familiar words (ones that occur with high frequency in prose) are deleted or used for distractors. The purpose of limiting deletions to highly familiar words is to minimise the dependence of the DRP scores on the particular vocabulary of the response options. A third, and probably the most important feature of the words selected for deletion, is that 'processing surrounding prose is both necessary and sufficient to choosing the right answer' (Koslin *et al.* p. 316).

The scaling of the DRP is accomplished by scaling the difficulty of the passages. That is, passages are initially indexed by a readability formula, and difficulty ordering of the passages is then verified after the test is administered. Scaling is done using latent trait model methods, specifically Rasch. Perhaps here is an application where Rasch really does work. Certainly, one of the most attractive features of the model (and item response theory generally) can be exploited; that is to say, the reading ability of students can be assessed on the same DRP unit scale. It then becomes possible to match students with texts and (because of Rasch scaling) to make predictions as to how well they will cope with text of a certain DRP difficulty. According to a DRP pamphlet 'normative information for the DRP indicates that fewer than 50% of high school seniors can read material of 67 DRP units of difficulty with 90% comprehension' (College Board, 1983). The overall average for American magazines has been calculated as 65 DRP units.

By now the DRP people will have calculated the readability of many texts. Since reading difficulty will vary within a text, the readability reports go to the trouble of reporting difficulties for various sections, as in this example (taken from College Board 1986, p. 6):

Composition: Models and Exercises. Glatthorn & Fleming. Harcourt, Brace and World, Inc., 1965. 274 pp. (S)

65 63 61 68 58** 63

** Variability is very high (more than 11 DRP units) among the samples in this section of the book.

It may be asked whether DRP qualifies as a criterion-referenced test. An ability such as 'reading comprehension' is certainly much broader than the specific skills that most CRTs are intended to measure. Linn has no doubt that the DRP satisfies the primary requirements of a criterion-referenced test. Indeed, he says (1980, p. 557) 'it is in many ways an outstanding example of a test that is designed to measure a broad and important ability over a wide range but that has a well-defined domain and produces scores that are directly interpretable in terms of the difficulty of the prose that an individual can read with comprehension'.

Several kinds of evidence were obtained to validate the proposition that texts can be arranged in difficulty and examinees arranged in ability to comprehend prose on a common scale. Surface linguistic variables such as average word length and average sentence length were used to predict mean and median Rasch difficulties for passages. The study demonstrated that 'giving students the intact text to read just before they took a comprehension (hard cloze) test lead to "mastery" level performance *if and only if* the readability of the text was in a range relative to the student's ability as predicted by the DRP (that is if the probability of success equalled $p = 0{\cdot}75$)' (Koslin *et al.*, p. 327).

The DRP is certainly an ambitious undertaking and we have seen nothing like it in this country. There are tests built apparently on criterion-referenced principles, like the graded tests to be discussed next, but nothing which is as powerful as DRP. It is a pity, therefore, that the College Board has decided not to market the instrument any more, although it will still be available from the developer (Haney & Madaus 1989). It appears that the lack of norms drew complaints, surely premature, but norms have now been developed just as the College Board withdraws support.

Graded assessment

Considering what claims are held out for it, there has been very little systematic research into graded assessment. It has attracted nothing like the resources pumped into records of achievement. We might have expected at least a DES evaluation by now, but nothing has appeared.

Having noted that graded tests are often labelled 'criterion-referenced', Pennycuick & Murphy (1986*a*, p. 275) preferred to follow Harrison (1982) in avoiding the term which they said, rightly, has a wide range of meanings. Harrison seems to have been bothered by what he saw as the restriction of CRT to what the candidate 'knows' rather than 'can do', pointing out (p. 37) that the performance of language acts is realised through communicative tasks rather than with knowledge of the language.

More puzzling is his belief that in order to specify objectives, which he acknowledges is characteristic of CRT, subject specialists have to become expert at psychometrics, or else testing experts have to specialise in every subject for which they set up test systems. This is a misconception. Elsewhere (p. 38) Harrison realises that the syllabus for Graded Objectives in Modern Languages (GOML) actually 'sets out the aspects of language which are needed to communicate successfully – the criteria for a criterion-referenced assessment'.

There is no question that graded assessments, if properly constructed, are authentic examples of CRT. Of the three key features of graded tests listed by Pennycuick & Murphy, the third is quite characteristic of CRT:

1 emphasis on student success;
2 a progressive sequence of levels;
3 tasks to be mastered by candidates being clearly specified.

But not everyone makes the connection. That it is perfectly possible to talk about graded assessments without ever mentioning CRT, is evidenced by the SSCC study *Graduated Assessment in Mathematics* (Close & Brown 1987). This could be because, as one suspects, the tests were not constructed from stated objectives and careful specifications; also that the results were not reported in terms of what students know and can do in detail.

If, as the ideology implies, CRT should throw up the wherewithal for diagnosis and remediation, the SSCC study was somewhat disappointing, more so as it was meant for low achievers: 'The marking and record keeping system did not assist teachers in making diagnoses or planning remedial programmes of work' (Close & Brown, p. 4).

In terms of research on graded tests, there is little besides the SSCC study to go on. The LEAG work will be interesting when it appears (25000 students, 19 authorities); hopefully, the evaluation will be more hard-headed and less Panglossian than the newspaper piece about it promised (*Independent*, 21.4.88). The SSCC investigators would, one imagines, have been just as enthusiastic and well-disposed to graded assessment; the difference was that they found many shortcomings which will need to be put right. Nor were they able convincingly to support the (amazingly) good outcomes reported (Close & Brown, pp. 4–5) namely:

> increased pupils' confidence and self-esteem;
> increased pupils' enjoyment of their mathematics lessons;
> encouraged almost all pupils to work harder throughout their 4th and 5th years.

Perhaps it does not take much to improve on the 'one shot'

examinations, and GASP (Swain, 1988) and GAIM and GAMLL and GACDT and the rest will easily establish their superiority once the results are in. Against that, the SSCC team, although it was not necessarily comparing GAIM and 'one-shot', was adamant that **all** its recommendations for improvement would need to be implemented for any graded assessment scheme to be successful. The obvious drawback to chunked-up, lockstep systems is that they will sink beneath their own weight. What will be especially interesting to see is whether the genuine CRT idea of individual growth mentioned in the *Independent* piece – 'The children have to realise that the only competition is against themselves' – ever sinks in.

There are technical issues connected with graded testing which Pennycuick & Murphy (1986*a*,*b*), despite their distaste for 'detailed technical research of the type that has been done for 50 years on existing systems' (1986*b*, p. 310), spend some time dealing with. There is the question of which instructional strategy is best suited for graded assessment (they list five) and there is the crucial issue of what is meant by mastery. Noting that teachers may wish to distinguish between a 'pass' level and 'mastery', Pennycuick & Murphy observe that there is a tension in many graded test schemes between setting cut-off scores which demonstrate a sufficient level of mastery and at the same time ensuring a high pass rate, given that it is expected that candidates will not be entered for a test unless it is clear they have a good chance of passing it. Mastery levels must be predetermined, but they ought not to be too high or too low. The lower the cut-off, the less precisely is known about successful candidates. Finally, there is always the question of whether scoring should be based on a **conjunctive** or perhaps a **disjunctive** model (chapter 10).

Summing up

There has been reluctance in some quarters to concede that graded tests may be an example of criterion-referenced tests, but it looks as if at the moment they are actually the best and most prominent example in this country of the genre. Glaser, in launching CRT, hoped to shift attention away from between-individual variation to within-individual variation – from psychometrics to what Carver (1974) called 'edumetrics'. Graded assessment does just that, at least in principle and maybe in practice.

To implement criterion-referencing in large-scale examinations is problematical, as the efforts to date show. No doubt there has been a cargo cult mentality in evidence, believing that notions like grade-related criteria and grade descriptions would overnight eradicate the bad practice and inequities associated, sometimes unfairly and erroneously, with norm-referenced examinations. The emphasis on criterion-referencing in GCSE will be beneficial insofar as it promotes clearer thinking about what students are expected to be able to do and reduces the effects of capricious question selection, but the gains are bound to be modest.

References

American Psychological Association (1985) *Standards for Educational and Psychological Testing*. Washington: APA/NCME/AERA.

Angoff W. H. (1974) Criterion-referencing, norm-referencing and the SAT. *College Board Review*, **92**, 2–5.

Carroll J. B. (1963) A model of school learning. *Teachers College Record*, **64**, 723–33.

Carver R. C. (1974) Two dimensions of tests: Psychometric and edumetric. *American Psychologist*, **29**, 512–18.

Close G. & Brown M. (1987) *Graduated Assessment in Mathematics*. London: Department of Education and Science.

College Entrance Examinations Board (1983) Is there a 'real world' reading standard for high school graduates? *Degrees of Reading Power* pamphlet. New York: CEEB.

College Entrance Examinations Board (1986) Readability report sample. *Degrees of Reading Power*. New York: CEEB.

Cronbach L. J. (1963) Course improvement through evaluation. *Teachers College Record*, **644**, 672–83.

Debra P. vs. Turlington (1981) 644f. 2nd 397 (5th Cir.)

Feldt L. S. & Brennan R. L. (1989) Reliability. In Linn R. L. (ed.) *Educational Measurement* (3rd edition). Washington, DC: American Council on Education/Macmillan Series on Higher Education.

Forrest G. M. & Shoesmith D. J. (1985) *Monitoring Standards in the General Certificate of Secondary Education*. Manchester: Joint Matriculation Board on behalf of the GCE examining boards.

French S., Slater J. B., Vassiloglou M. & Willmott A. S. (1987) *Descriptive and Normative Techniques in Examination Assessment*. Oxford: University of Oxford Delegacy of Local Examinations.

Glaser R. (1963) Instructional technology and the measurement of learning outcomes: Some questions. *American Psychologist*, **18**, 519–21.

Guion R. M. (1980) Content validity – the source of my discontent. *Applied Psychology*, **11**, 385–98.

Guy W. & Chambers P. (1973) Public examinations and pupils' rights. *Cambridge Journal of Education*, **3**, 83–9.

Guy W. & Chambers P. (1974) Public examinations and pupils' rights revisited. *Cambridge Journal of Education*, **4**, 47–50.

Hambleton R. K., Swaminathan H., Algina J. & Coulson D. B. (1978) Criterion-referenced testing and measurement: A review of technical issues and developments. *Review of Educational Research*, **48**, 1–47.

Hamilton E.R. (1929) *The Art of Interrogation*. London: Kegan Paul.

Haney W. & Madaus G. F. (1989) Searching for alternatives to standardized tests: Whys, whats, and whithers. *Phi Delta Kappan*, **70**, 683–7.

Harrison A. W. (1982) Review of graded tests. *Schools Council Examinations Bulletin 41*. London: Methuen Educational.

Kempa R. F. & Odinga J. L. (1984) Criterion-referenced interpretation of examination grades. *Educational Research*, **26**, 54–6.

Koslin B. L., Koslin S. & Zeno S. (1979) Towards an effectiveness measure in reading. In Tyler R. W. & White S. H. (eds.) *Testing, Teaching and Learning: Report of a Conference on Research on Testing*. Washington, DC: National Institute of Education.

Linn, R. L. (1980) Issues of validity for criterion-referenced measures. *Applied Psychological Measurement*, **4**, 547–62.

Messick S. (1981) Constructs and their vicissitudes in educational and psychological measurement. *Psychological Bulletin*, **59**, 575–88.

Orr L. & Nuttall D. L. (1983) Determining standards in the proposed single system of examining at 16+. *Comparability in Examinations Occasional Paper 2*. London: Schools Council.

Pennycuick D. B. & Murphy R. J. L. (1986*a*) The impact of the graded test movement on classroom teaching and learning. *Studies in Educational Evaluation*, **12**, 275–80.

Pennycuick D. B. & Murphy R. J. L. (1986*b*) Mastery, validity and comparability issues in relation to graded assessment schemes. *Studies in Educational Evaluation*, **12**, 305–12.

Skehan P. (1984) Issues in the testing of English for specific purposes. *Language Testing*, **1**, 202–20.

Swain J. R. L. (1988) GASP: The graded assessments in science project. *School Science Review*, **70**, 152–8.

Traub R. E. & Rowley G. L. (1980) Reliability of test scores and decisions. *Applied Psychological Measurement*, **4**, 517–46.

8 Diagnostic assessment

It seems likely that the term 'diagnostic' assessment was first used in connection with learning disabilities, which is perhaps the closest education comes to medicine. The effect of borrowing from the rather powerful medical model is apparently to legitimise the educational usage but, in reality, **diagnosis** and **remedial** have become weasel words, debased by wishful thinking and a mimicking of what is fondly supposed to be best medical practice. Diagnosis is such a self-evidently **good** thing to be doing that diagnostic assessment must be a virtuous activity and any pre-existing reservations about assessment ought to be abandoned. The same applies, incidentally, to Feuerstein's (1980) 'dynamic assessment', which is teaching through testing. In both cases we are dealing with marketing concepts like product labelling and consumer reaction.

Facile analogies with health care are merely part of the hype. Just before her demise from the Inner London Education Authority, Frances Morrell proposed that testing at 7, 11 and 14 be seen as corresponding to health checks at those ages (*Independent*, 20.3.87). Although well meant, not the least objection to this analogy is that children, other than the severely handicapped, do not even receive health checks routinely, at least not any probing enough to expose specific weaknesses. A rather robust view is taken, and the 'normal' child is left to soldier on as best it can. The same is true, but more so, in education, and that is a far worse state of affairs since there is so much more to do. If we were talking about the educational equivalent of the graze, that would be all right, but we are not; it is more like bone breaks and the walking wounded. To believe you can treat the mind as if it were the body is a very peculiar and deceptive form of dualism.

Goodness knows what range of lay perceptions diagnostic assessment invokes. It sometimes seems as if it is enough to set a number of questions – more or less any questions – and diagnostic material will be available for groups **and** individuals simultaneously. By appending a miscellany of questions disarticulated from any kind of rationale, the TGAT report (DES 1987, Appendix E) manages to foster exactly this impression. It is regrettable that the only substantive thing it has to say about diagnostic assessment is wrapped up in a rather convoluted attempt to reconcile diagnostic and formative purposes:

> We do not see the boundary between the formative and diagnostic purposes as being sharp or clear. If an assessment designed in formative terms is well matched to the pupil, it is likely to provide some information which will help in the diagnosis of strengths and weaknesses. Some assessments of this kind will be of value as indicators of learning problems which require further investigation. Further diagnostic investigations would, however, often involve the use of highly specialized tests of relevance to only a limited set of circumstances and pupils. (para. 27)

Note how the medical model pokes through. A broad screening throws up signs, following which detailed personalised investigation is undertaken, or so it is fantasised.

For the educational world, the problem with this methodology is that the broad screening device is not necessarily sharp enough to throw up trustworthy signs. The supposition is that it can, but when the question is asked, 'Can this test of reading comprehension reliably differentiate between one subskill and another, say, basic word meaning and literal comprehension?', the answer is liable to be in the negative if the data are interpreted at all rigorously.

The unreliability of profile interpretation is, indeed, notorious. Thorndike (1972, p. 67) concluded that with existing instruments (of all kinds) the development of accurate diagnostic interpretations of score differences is unlikely. Coles (1978) delivered the same judgement on learning-disability batteries. Thorndike did add, however, that if salvation exists, it lies in the fact that most of the actions following from diagnostic judgement are reversible; if they are unfounded, they are likely to result in wasted time or effort rather than any critical loss. For those on the receiving end, there is some comfort in this, but it offers scant encouragement to teachers who are loath to commit the time to diagnostic and remedial work, or feel they do not have it to give.

The profile interpretation problem is just a version of the construct validity problem highlighted in other chapters (chapters 5, 7, 12 and 15). For an explicit treatment in diagnostic terms, Lyons' (1984) investigation of reading comprehension subskills is as illustrative as any. At the heart of his critique (p. 293) is a warning against expecting too much in the way of diagnostic power from criterion-referenced tests:

> Matching items to skills does not automatically produce a valid measure of a domain. As a validity study (reported here) of one criterion-referenced reading competency test shows, these tests like any other need careful validation. In particular, one cannot assume that their subscales provide valid diagnoses of reading comprehension subskills.

Having carried out a construct validity analysis of five reading comprehension subskills, Lyons concluded that there is no convincing evidence of discriminant validity (see the 'burnout' example in chapter 12). Farr had said the same earlier – 'The most serious deficiency in using standardized reading tests to diagnose reading achievement is a lack of discriminant validity' (Farr 1969, p. 81). The data Lyons analysed came from multiple choice tests, but the same problems occur with informal reading inventories (Schell & Hanna 1981). Lyons' conclusion, that the good sense approach in testing for reading comprehension is extreme caution in interpreting and using subskills scores, can be extended to any kind of test or examination where the intention is to profile and to make inferences about differential achievement.

The push towards proliferating subskills and subtests can be seen as attending to validity, but without necessarily (in fact almost certainly not) attending to reliability. That results in a conflict. As Fulcher (1987) says, in the context of language testing, high validity and low reliability are a contradiction in terms. Fulcher cites the English Language Testing Service (ELTS) (chapter 19) where profiles are drawn up on the basis of subtest scores. It is necessary to be certain that the reliability of each subtest is high, and calculate the reliability of score differences in order to be fairly sure that any differences reflect a true difference of actual ability in the examinee. Only ELTS will know whether this has been done.

Profiles are an example of what has been called **deficit measurement** (Bejar 1984). The focus is on discrepancies in performance between actual and expected achievement. Although the better than expected performances in a profile are acknowledged, the concern in diagnostic work is with weaknesses, otherwise there is no remedial enterprise. Deficit measurement incorporates the estimation of so-called underachievement and of learning disabilities. Unfortunately, as noted by Wood (1984) and by Bejar (1984), there is more than a little circularity in defining diagnosis as deviation from some model. If there turn out to be too many individuals in the population with unusual response patterns, then by definition the model does not fit.

Nitko (1989, p. 455) lists five categories of diagnostic assessment. One, in which a deficit is defined as failure to acquire necessary pre-instructional knowledge and skill, need not concern us, but the other four, which include deficit measurement or trait profile differences, just dealt with, are worth considering. What follows draws heavily on Nitko's presentation.

Mastery of behavioural objectives

In the mastery of behavioural objectives approach, a deficit is defined as failure to master one or more end-of-instruction objectives.

The meaning of mastery/non-mastery, and any subsequent remedial action, depends crucially on the congruence between the intent of instruction, the statements of the objectives and the items created for the tests. Unfortunately, written statements of behaviour are usually too ambiguous to guarantee or even approximate to this three-way congruence. In particular, the more or less mechanical methods of item construction are not sound enough to deliver tight coupling between items and objectives (chapter 1).

Objectives-based diagnostic tests are generally plagued with measurement error, principally because the tests tend to have too few items per objective. This comes about through operational expediency; with objectives generally defined at an atomistic level, the proper test length would require students to tackle far too many items. The resulting error is reflected in decision consistency indices (chapters 7 and 9) which describe the extent to which students are likely to be classified the same, that is thrown into the same broad diagnostic category, when either the same test form is readministered or an alternative form of the test is administered.

While the behavioural objectives approach to diagnostic testing has the virtues of focusing on specific and limited things to teach and on what the student is producing, it is too flawed to stand by itself. The information obtained from such tests is limited to only one aspect of diagnosis and testing – the overt behavioural manifestation of what is to be learned. This information provides insufficient help to teachers concerning appropriate remedial instruction. To know that a student has not mastered an objective does not provide enough guidance. Like the trait profile approach, the behavioural objectives approach is far from being fully diagnostic.

It is sometimes claimed that teachers are making diagnoses all the time in the interchanges between themselves and students. It is something which happens instinctively; in fact, without diagnosis there is no teaching, another way of saying that without mistakes there is no learning. No doubt this is a rosy view of what goes on in the classroom, and can hardly be true of larger classes, but it does raise the question, 'If the teacher knows so much, why would diagnostic tests provide more, and why, in particular, would the teacher not devote the time given over to taking the tests and interpreting the results to working with students who need it?'

Error analysis

In error analysis the task is to arrive at a diagnosis from the errors the student makes. Error detection can be on an individual basis, as in one-to-one interviews, or on a group basis, as in the use of classroom tests.

Superficially, error analysis is at a lower level of abstraction than deficit measurement; the emphasis is on delving into the nitty-gritty of single item or question responses. The sophistication comes in trying to arrive at some conceptualisation of what is causing the student to make mistakes. This, in turn, means trying to determine the rules by which the student works. They do not have to be correct, but they are systematic. Finding such 'systematicities' is the essence of diagnosis (Glaser 1981). Without them, diagnostic enquiries are liable to turn into mere error hunts without any shape or pattern, in the same way that a catalogue of the apparent flaws in a human being's physique is not meaningful, in and of itself.

Error analysis in mathematics

The Denvir & Brown (1986) work is a testimony to the fact that you cannot waltz into classrooms and start to chalk up errors. Their work is based on a carefully formulated scheme built on others' research. For example, they note that there are thought to be three main types of strategy for solving simple additional problems – 'Count All', 'Count On' and 'Recall'. The first two of these are widely regarded as characteristic of distinct stages of development of number understanding. Consequently, they say, it should be possible to make inferences about a child's understanding of number from observing that child's repertoire of strategies.

Building on state-of-the-art insights and speculation Denvir & Brown developed a diagnostic instrument for assessing children's understanding of number. Their experience in using that instrument – a classroom test for group administration – is described in chapter 16 where comparison is made with the information which can be gained from one-to-one interviews. The point is made there that ultimately diagnosis is a function of how much time can be spent on an individual.

When doing error analysis in mathematics, the favoured methodology has been to use multiple choice (MCQ) tests produced by using, as distractors, actual wrong answers given to the same questions in open ended (OE) form. An early example was Frederiksen & Satter (1953). The motivation was as much to combine the advantages of the open ended form (more information) and the multiple choice form (more reliable and quicker to mark) as to produce a diagnostic instrument.

A British–American investigation (Bishop, Knapp & McIntyre 1969) was carried out in a way which stands up well today. The two versions were randomly distributed between 300 boys and girls in their first year at secondary school and the results compared, in terms of both total scores and students' distribution over the answer choices for each question. The total scores on the MCQ version were significantly higher than those on the OE version, 14 of the 20 questions showed a significantly different distribution pattern and five questions showed a significant difference between the proportion getting the correct answer. These differences were accounted for by the unavoidable non-parallelism of the distractors in some of the questions, by the relative unpopularity of the 'none of these' choice, and by the different mathematical abilities tested in the questions. However, only three questions showed a significant difference between distributions over the 'major errors' alone, suggesting clear possibilities for using MCQ tests to diagnose errors among large numbers of pupils provided that, as in this experiment, the distractors are empirically derived.

This last point is important. The researchers invited item writers to submit distractors from their own heads, as it were, and found that while some of these artificial distractors might be superior for some purposes, they were, in this case at least, very different from the wrong answers most commonly given by pupils.

Error analysis has a long history in psychology. Piaget began by doing just this kind of work (Tuddenham 1966). Later, Sigel (1963) applied the technique to intelligence tests, and a little later Jacobs & Vandeventer (1970) and then Thissen (1976) used it on Raven's Coloured Progressive Matrices test. Sigel concluded that while children may be consistent in the errors they make, type of error and total score are unrelated, but Jacobs & Vandeventer inclined otherwise.

Error analysis in science

There is now a large body of research which examines students' misconceptions in a variety of science subject areas (Driver 1989). Students' conceptions which are different from those generally accepted by the scientific community, what Kuhn (1962) called 'normal science', have been labelled 'preconceptions' (Novak 1977), 'alternative frameworks' (Driver 1982), or 'children's science' (Gilbert, Osborne & Fensham 1982). These conceptions are really just Glaser's 'systematicities' (Glaser, personal communication).

The usual method for obtaining information about students' misconceptions has been through one-to-one interviews. Now the multiple choice test method has been picked up, although an exponent like Treagust (1988) is apparently oblivious of the early literature noted by Bishop *et al.* and of that paper. Thus the Israeli Tamir gets credit which might easily have gone to Bishop *et al.* or to earlier workers. Assessment types working in science education are particularly prone to ignoring other literatures and to reinventing the wheel, although their opposite numbers in medical education can be just as bad. Perhaps this somewhat tribal behaviour is harmless and only those who care about attributing precedence universally worry about such things.

The Treagust approach to constructing diagnostic tests is actually quite exemplary. The specifications for the tests are built on a series of propositional knowledge statements, such as oxygen is taken in during respiration, and on a concept map, both validated by science educators, secondary science teachers and science specialists. Thus it is supposed that errors can be traced directly to a particular breakdown in understanding. For example, Treagust argues that science teachers need to pay more attention to the essential meaning of intermolecular and intramolecular forces and to illustrate the different concepts clearly with good examples. Of course, the teacher still has to be able to do something about correcting misconceptions, and may not have the resources. Treagust recognises this (p. 168) – 'efforts to help teachers address observed misconceptions based on information from these two diagnostic tests are currently being investigated'.

Error analysis, while a necessary operation, is subject to several practical problems. Many different kinds of errors are made by pupils, and these are difficult to classify and to keep in mind while analysing a pupil's performance. Frequently pupils demonstrate the same erroneous overt behaviour for different reasons, so remedial instruction could be misdirected; and the amount of individual testing and interpretation required seems prohibitive (the point made earlier) given the amount of instructional time available. Some of these practical problems could be addressed by using 'intelligent' computer-assisted testing, in which the programs embodying expert systems present the tasks, identify and classify the errors, describe the probable causes of the errors and suggest remedial instructional procedures (Snow & Lohman 1989, p. 314). Perhaps statistical models could be incorporated into such a system, whereby the program would receive feedback on the success of its recommended remediation, match this with student and teacher characteristics and revise its future recommendations in light of past experience. (Such programs currently do not exist, however.)

More serious than practical problems of implementation is the problem that, if diagnosis only classifies errors, it still fails to identify the cognitive procedures and processes a learner has used to produce the errors observed, and to give teachers insight into the appropriate knowledge structures and cognitive processes a learner needs to acquire to reach the desired outcome. As Bejar (1984) points out, error enumeration and classification focus on the negative aspects of performance. As such they are insufficient for understanding why learners produce errors. The point is nicely made by two different dictionary entries for 'diagnosis'. One (Collins 1987) talks of diagnosis as 'finding out what's wrong' or 'not working properly'; the other (Webster 1968) talks of 'careful investigation to determine the nature of the thing'. That is where the knowledge structure approach comes in.

Knowledge structure

A shortcoming of the diagnostic testing approaches dealt with so far is their strong ties to the surface features of subject matter – those teachable 'bits' of disposable knowledge which do not necessarily add up to anything. The deeper competence, which is seen as a developmental construct, has been neglected. In designing curricula and teaching strategies we have to ask, 'What develops', and, having got an answer, 'What should we measure?' The operationalist is fixated on performance – whatever we can measure is what develops (Wood & Power 1987). Ideally, diagnosis should focus on how a learner perceives the structure or organisation of content and how s/he processes information and knowledge to solve problems. It follows that a test designer's understanding of typical student knowledge structures is important for building diagnostic tests.

From the long-term developmental perspective only the broad contours of competence in knowledge-filled domains are known. What is clear is that as students become more proficient, their knowledge becomes more interconnected, more deeply organised and more accessible. A most useful distinction is between 'experts' and 'novices'. In studies of differences between experts and novices in physics problem solving, Glaser and his colleagues (Chi, Glaser & Rees 1982) noticed that novices use painstaking means–ends analysis, working backwards from the unknown with equations that they hope are relevant to the problem. Experts, in contrast, apply correct equations in a forward direction, indicating that they have a solution plan in place before they begin. Nothing separates experts and novices so much as the experts' capacity for fast recognition and perception of underlying principles and patterns. It is as if the expert virtually sees a different problem from the novice (Glaser & Bassok 1989). This has been verified in a variety of domains, perhaps most interestingly by Lesgold *et al.* (1988).

When Denvir & Brown (1987) argue that in order to make diagnostic assessments, three aspects of learning need to be considered – what the child knows, how this relates to a framework of knowledge and how children learn – they are talking the same language as Glaser and his colleagues. In contrast, the TGAT report has nothing to say about how knowledge is structured and how children learn. The impression is left that diagnosis and remediation are vaguely benign activities which teachers will perform acting on information from tests. It is a bit like a doctor interpreting signs of distress knowing less about the body than William Harvey.

Discussion

Trying to do diagnostic work with tests as currently conceived is almost certainly a waste of time. 'At present, tests (with the exception of the important informal assessments of the good classroom teacher) are not designed to guide the specifics of instruction' (Glaser 1986, p. 45). Even so, people will persist with what are two distinct approaches.

Deficit measurement is the most common approach to diagnostic assessment. The second major approach, error analysis, is more clinical in nature. That is, by examining the pattern of errors a student makes, it may be possible for a trained observer or analyst to infer the nature of the student's difficulties, where 'trained' implies that the analyst has a worked-out scheme of how understanding of concepts, principles and so on typically develops. Bejar (p. 181) expresses the difference between deficit measurement and error analysis in this way – whereas deficit measurement tends to emphasise response consistency, error analysis focuses on the content of items. The duality in this formulation is limiting; it would be better if the two could be integrated. The linkage may be through the construct validation enterprise. Authenticating diagnostic legitimacy on the basis of some differences is a construct validation task. Errors are one class of diagnostic signs and accounting for their empirical characteristics is, therefore, engaging in construct validation. Glaser's systematic rules can be thought of as constructs, the more so as he calls them 'intelligences' (Glaser 1981). Given the record on discriminant validity, it is futile to carry on with deficit assessment without attention to error analysis.

Back at the sharp end, recognition that teachers need assistance in remediation, meaning time and materials, has often been conspicuously missing from the diagnostic assessment rhetoric. To suppose that they will know immediately what to do may be quite mistaken. The whole issue of how the results of diagnostic tests are to be assimilated into lessons and into the teacher's characteristic teaching style and disposition remains to be dealt with. British teachers are notoriously atheoretical; how many would be abreast of the sort of state-of-the-art thinking characteristic of researchers like Denvir & Brown? Placing in front of them the sort of instrument illustrated in Appendix E of the TGAT report, and then expecting them to do the rest, is not going to work.

References

Bejar I. I. (1984) Educational diagnostic assessment. *Journal of Educational Measurement*, **21**, 175–89.

Bishop A. J., Knapp T. R. & McIntyre D. I. (1969) A comparison of the results of open-ended and multiple-choice versions of a mathematics test. *International Journal of Educational Science*, **3**, 147–54.

Chi M. T. H., Glaser R. & Rees E. (1982) Expertise in problem-solving. In Sternberg R. J. (ed.) *Advances in the Psychology of Human Intelligence*, vol. 1. Hillsdale, NJ: Erlbaum.

Coles G. S. (1978) The learning-disabilities test battery: Empirical and social issues. *Harvard Educational Review*, **48**, 313–40.

Collins (1987) *English Language Dictionary* (*Cobuild*). London: Collins.

Denvir B. & Brown M. (1986) Understanding of number concepts in low attaining 7–9 year olds: Part I. Development of descriptive framework and diagnostic instrument. *Educational Studies in Mathematics*, **17**, 15–36.

Denvir B. & Brown M. (1987) The feasibility of class administered diagnostic assessment in primary mathematics. *Educational Research*, **29**, 95–107.

Department of Education and Science (1987) *Report of the Task Group on Assessment and Testing* (TGAT). London: DES.

Driver R. (1982) Children's learning in science. *Educational Analysis*, **4**, 69–79.

Driver R. (1989) Students' conceptions and the learning of science. *International Journal of Science Education*, **11**, 481–90.

Farr R. (1969) *Reading: What can be Measured?* Newark, Del.: International Reading Association.

Feuerstein R. (1980) *Instrumental Enrichment*. Baltimore, MD: University Park Press.

Frederiksen N. & Satter G. A. (1953) The construction and validation of an arithmetic computation test. *Educational and Psychological Measurement*, **13**, 209–27.

Fulcher G. (1987) Tests of oral performance: The need for data-based criteria. *English Language Testing Journal*, **41**, 287–91.

Gilbert J. K., Osborne R. J. & Fensham P. J. (1982) Children's science and its consequence for teaching. *Science Education*, **66**, 623–33.

Glaser R. (1981) The future of testing. *American Psychologist*, **36**, 923–36.

Glaser R. (1984) Education and thinking: The rôle of knowledge. *American Psychologist*, **39**, 93–104.

Glaser R. (1986) The integration of testing and instruction. In *The Redesign of Testing for the 21st Century: Proceedings of the 1985 ETS Invitational Conference*. Princeton, NJ: Educational Testing Service.

Glaser R. & Bassok M. (1989) Learning theory and the study of instruction. *Annual Review of Psychology*, **40**, 631–66.

Jacobs P. I. & Vandeventer M. (1970) Information in wrong responses. *Psychological Reports*, **26**, 311–15.

Kuhn T. S. (1962) *The Structure of Scientific Revolutions*. Chicago: University of Chicago Press.

Lesgold A. *et al.* (1988) Expertise in a complex skill: Diagnosing X-ray pictures. In Chi M. T. H., Glaser R. & Farr M. J. (eds.) *The Nature of Expertise*. Hillsdale, NJ: Erlbaum.

Lyons K. (1984) Criterion referenced reading comprehension tests: New forms with old ghosts. *Journal of Reading*, **27**, 293–8.

Nitko A. J. (1989) Designing tests that are integrated with instruction. In Linn R. L. (ed.) *Educational Measurement* (3rd edition). Washington, DC: American Council on Education/Macmillan Publishing Company.

Novak J. D. (1977) *A Theory of Education*. Ithaca, NY: Cornell University Press.

Schell L. M. & Hanna G. S. (1981) Can informal reading inventories reveal strengths and weaknesses in comprehension subskills? *The Reading Teacher*, **35**, 263–8.

Sigel I. E. (1963) How intelligence tests limit understanding of intelligence. *Merrill-Palmer Quarterly*, **9**, 39–56.

Snow R. E. & Lohman D. F. (1989) Implications of cognitive psychology for educational measurement. In Linn R. L. (ed.) *Educational Measurement* (3rd edition). Washington, DC: American Council on Education/Macmillan Publishing Company.

Thissen D. (1976) Information in wrong responses to the Raven Progressive Matrices. *Journal of Educational Measurement*, **13**, 201–14.

Thorndike R. L. (1972) Dilemmas in diagnosis. In MacGintie W. H. (ed.) *Assessment in Reading*. Newark, Del.: International Reading Association.

Treagust D. F. (1988) Development and use of diagnostic tests to evaluate students' misconceptions in science. *International Journal of Science Education*, **10**, 159–69.

Tuddenham R. D. (1966) Piaget and the world of the child. *American Psychologist*, **21**, 207–17.

Webster (1968) *New English Dictionary*. New York: Webster.

Wood R. (1984) Doubts about 'underachievement', particularly as operationalized by Yule, Lansdown and Urbanowicz. *British Journal of Clinical Psychology*, **23**, 231–2.

Wood R. & Power C. N. (1987) Aspects of the competence – performance distinction: Educational, psychological and measurement issues. *Journal of Curriculum Studies*, **19**, 409–24.

9 Item analysis

Conventional or classical item analysis procedures suitable for norm-referenced tests were worked out a long time ago and there is little new to say about them – the Wood (1985) review is still applicable. Because it lends itself to neat mathematising, there is a reluctance to abandon the field and so we find a certain amount of titivating at the edges, like the paper by Harris & Kolen (1988) which compares three methods of estimating the point-biserial correlation coefficient standard error.

Item analysis refers always to multiple choice tests. There could be a question analysis for essays and structured response tests but, since these are seldom, if ever, pre-tested, one has not emerged (the efforts of Morrison (1974) notwithstanding). Recent application of Rasch model analysis to the marking and calibration of essay tests (Pollitt & Hutchinson 1987) may presage the development of a proper question analysis. Research issues these days are aimed at whether modern methods of item analysis, that is those based on item response theory (IRT), are superior to classical methods and, if they are, whether it is economic to adopt them; also what item analysis procedures, if any, are most suitable for criterion-referenced tests.

Not everyone will agree that the classical side is exhausted; for some there is still a great unresolved issue – whether or not to use the biserial or the point-biserial correlation coefficient as an index of item discrimination. It is necessary, therefore, to say something on this subject.

Item discrimination for norm-referenced tests

A discrimination index is meant to communicate the power of an item in separating the more from the less capable on some latent attribute. The idea is that the higher the correlation between candidates' scores on an item and their scores on the test, the more effective the item is in separating them. Naturally, this relationship is a relative one; when included in one test an item could have a higher item–test correlation than when included in another, yet produce poorer discrimination.

The point-biserial correlation is a special case of the general Pearson product–moment correlation, where one of the variables (test score) is regarded as continuous and the other (item score) can take one or other of two discrete values, typically 1 for correct and 0 for incorrect. The biserial correlation is based on the assumption that both variables are continuous, but that one has been divided at some point into two groups. The passers are thought to differ from the failers only in having more of whatever the item measures, that is as having enough to get over the threshold and get the item right. The two variables are each assumed to follow a normal Gaussian distribution in the population of persons from whom the sample is drawn. That same assumption is made for the dichotomised scale (item continuum) when p is transformed to z and Δ.

The point-biserial is not like any well-behaved product–moment correlation which can take values between −1 and +1. With the point-biserial that will not work because it has a curtailed range. If the distribution of scores in the total group is normal, the point-biserial can never go beyond 0·8 (Thorndike 1982, but see Carroll 1987). Furthermore, because the point-biserial is a function of item difficulty, the range of possible values depends on the percentages of passers and failers, contracting as the split becomes more uneven. For an item difficulty of 0·10, that is a very hard item, the maximum point-biserial value is 0·58.

The biserial correlation is **not** a form of product–moment correlation; rather it should be thought of as a measure of association. In theory, it can take any value between −1 and +1. In practice, values greater than 0·75 are rare, although in exceptional circumstances it can exceed 1, usually due to some peculiarity in the test score or criterion distribution or else to correction for chance success by guessing (Carroll 1987).

The point-biserial is always lower than the biserial; specifically, pbis = 0·82 bis when $p = 0{\cdot}50$ and shrinks with respect to pbis the further p gets away from 0·50, although the effect is only dramatic when p is very high or low.

While it is always a simple matter to convert from one coefficient or index to the other, their respective strengths and weaknesses need to be understood. Where the point-biserial is used there are considered to be only two distinct positions on the item continuum, right or wrong. But passers would seem to differ from failers more in degree than in kind, which makes the assumption of continuity underlying the biserial correlation more plausible, although the requirement that it should take a particular distributional form (normal) is harder to believe.

That the point-biserial is confounded by item difficulty is not necessarily a bad thing; in fact it may be argued that the point-biserial value is rather more informative about the item's contribution to the functioning of the test, because very easy or very difficult items make relatively few differentiations between more- and less-capable examinees. Even so there is no hiding the fact that the point-biserial is effectively a combined index of difficulty and discrimination. Those who believe that the two concepts should not be muddled up in a single index will incline towards the biserial. Because it is less influenced by item difficulty, it has been thought that the biserial might prove to be invariant, or at least reasonably stable, from one examinee group to another. This is necessarily a matter for empirical investigation and there are still no results to show it.

For what it is worth, personal experience indicates that even with ostensibly parallel groups of candidates, biserial estimates for the same item can 'bounce' around beyond what would be expected from a 'guestimated' margin of error, guestimated because no really good estimate of precision is available for this statistic (a mark against it). Standard errors for the point-biserial are available and Harris & Kolen (1988) have shown that even when it is suspected that the normality assumption will not hold, it is better to use the standard error formula assuming normality.

The biserial plays a part in item characteristic curve theory (in the equation for estimating the steepness parameter of the curve); the point-biserial does not. Against that, and importantly, the point-biserial fits directly into the algebra of multivariate analysis. When it comes to estimating test parameters from item parameters, as when trying to engineer score distributions, it is the point-biserial which is needed. For bread-and-butter item analysis this is an important plus. Indeed, it may be stated quite generally that any item statistic which does not bear a definite (preferably a clear and simple) relationship to some interesting total test score parameter (Lord & Novick 1968) is of limited value for practical test construction purposes.

Evidently both biserial and point-biserial have shortcomings, serious enough to rule either out if the objections were to be pressed. The practical user will find that as long as a markedly non-normal distribution of ability is not anticipated, substantially the same items will be selected or rejected, whichever index is used to evaluate discrimination. It is when item selection is linked to the engineering of test score distributions with desirable properties, as it ought to be for conventional group testing situations grounded in more or less norm-referenced contexts, that the point-biserial is preferable. Otherwise the best advice is to fasten on to one or other statistic, learn about its behaviour and stick with it. Switching from one to the other, or trying to interpret both simultaneously, is likely to be counterproductive. A Monte Carlo study of ten possible discrimination indices (Beuckert & Mendoza 1979) concluded that selection of an index should be based solely on ease of computation or the need for statistical tests of significance. Such advice ignores the need for linkage with test parameters and should be viewed circumspectly, but it may be regarded as a judgement on the utility of 'fringe' indices.

It would be wrong to call index *D* a fringe index, for when item analysis was done routinely by hand it occupied a central position. If, for any item, P_h is the proportion of correct answers achieved by the 27% highest scorers, and P_l is the corresponding figure for the 27% lowest scorers, then $D = P_h - P_l$. It may seem odd that just as good results can be obtained by discarding middle scores of the score distribution as by using the whole distribution, but providing the ability being measured is normally distributed, and that is a big proviso, this is the case. Incidentally, it has been shown that the correct percentage is more like 21% but even so 27%, or more conveniently 25%, cannot be far from optimal.

For those who want or need to carry out an item analysis by hand (and it is still a good way of getting the 'feel' of item performance) the 1969 Nuttall–Skurnik tables have been reissued (Nuttall & Skurnik 1987). Operationally, *D* agrees quite closely with biserial correlation estimates, even when the underlying distribution is non-normal. Like the point-biserial, and even the biserial, the *D* index is dependent on item facility. In particular, it decreases sharply as the facility approaches 0 or 1, when it must be interpreted with caution, but the test constructor will probably not be interested in these items anyway.

Modern item analysis methods

Whatever item statistics are concocted, being of a summary nature they are bound to be less informative than we would like. Evidently an infinite number of items can have different response patterns, yet possess the same discrimination index or difficulty. Guilford (1954, p. 419) expressed the limitations of the difficulty index very cogently, 'All we know is that if the respondent passes it, the item is less difficult than his ability to cope with it, and if he fails it, is more difficult than his ability to cope with it.' The most instructive way of examining an item response pattern is to plot a graph showing how success rate varies with candidates' ability, for which total test score usually stands proxy. The result is called an **item characteristic curve**. It is the coping stone of modern item analysis methods, but the idea is as old as educational measurement itself, dating from 1905 when Binet & Simon plotted curves to show how children's success rates on items varied with age. The movement towards summarising item response patterns only came with the streamlining of item selection procedures. Goldstein & Wood (1989) provide a retro-

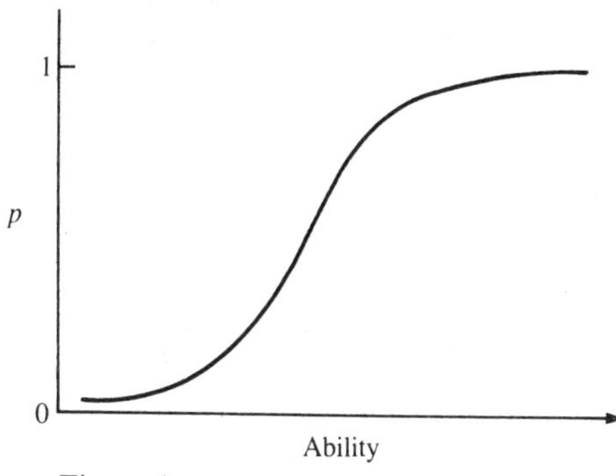

Figure 1.

spective of item response theory or, as they prefer to call it, item response modelling on the reasoning that the model **is** the theory.

To plot an item characteristic curve, the most obvious method would seem to be to plot success rates for as many groups as there are different test scores. In practice, however, this method is not only finicky but may also mislead, the reason being that success rates calculated from very small numbers of candidates obtaining certain test scores are unstable and thus may give a false impression of how an item performs. Since the relationship between the assumed underlying ability and test score is unknown, and the test scores are bound to be fallible, it is preferable to group candidates in terms of test score intervals, the supposition being that all candidates within a group possess roughly the same amount of the ability in question. When this is done, a curve like that in figure 1 results. A step-by-step method for producing an item characteristic curve is given in the appendix of Wilmut (1975). Since we cannot measure 'ability' directly, the unit of measurement for the ability dimension is test score expressed in standardised form.

The curve in figure 1 is the classic form – steep in the middle and shallow at the tails. Given anything like a normal distribution of ability, items with this characteristic are needed to produce discrimination among the mass of candidates in the middle of the score range. If, however, the focus of discrimination is elsewhere, say at the lower end of the ability range, then items with characteristic curves like that shown in figure 2 will be needed. Note that it is quite feasible to plot response curves for each distractor and to display them on the same graph as the item characteristic curve. It is then possible to inspect the behaviour of each distractor.

While item characteristic curves should be displayed for inspection whenever possible, they are not in a suitable form for theoretical exploratory and predictive work. It would, therefore, be useful if these

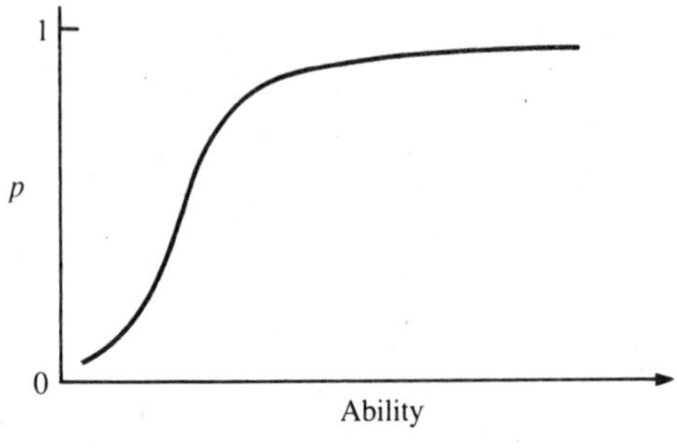

Figure 2.

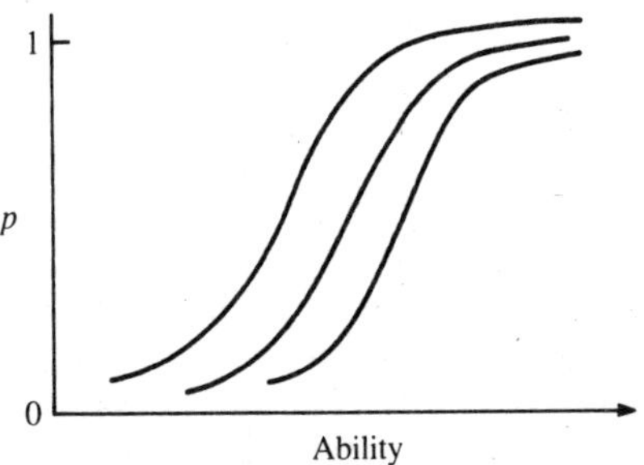

Figure 3.

curves could be represented by a mathematical function or functions. Repeated investigation has shown that if item characteristic curves are 'well behaved' they can be fitted by functions of the exponential type. Such functions then constitute a **model** of the item response process in which an individual's probability of success on an item is said to be governed jointly by his ability and by the difficulty and discrimination of the item.

Various models have been proposed to fit different families of curves. If items are extremely well-behaved and look like figure 3 (same discrimination but varying difficulties) they will fit what is called the Rasch model, that is the one-parameter logistic model, in which the one parameter is the item difficulty. If items are not so well-behaved and look like figure 4 (varying difficulties **and** discriminations) they will fit either the two-parameter logistic model or the two-parameter normal ogive model, which are very similar. Finally, if items look like what Levy (1973, p. 3) calls 'reality' (figure 5), then some will fit one model and some another, but not all will fit the same model however complicated it is made (within reason of course). The item analyst or constructor then has to decide whether or not to discard those items which fail to fit his favourite model.

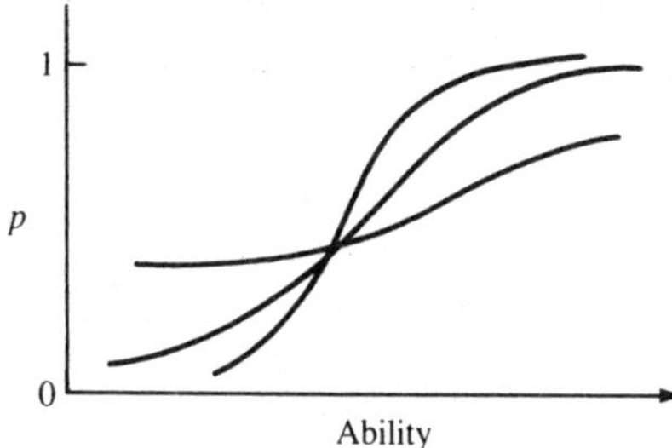

Figure 4.

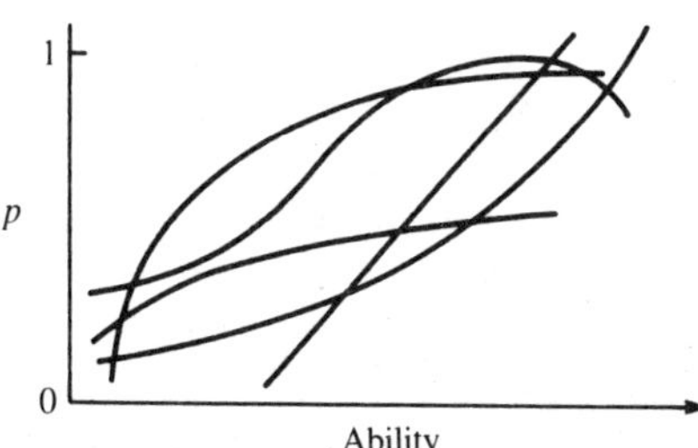

Figure 5.

With the most restrictive model, that of Rasch, quite a number of items may have to be discarded or, at least, put to one side; with the other models, which allow discrimination to vary, not so many items should be rejected. Anyone who believes that tangles of curves like figure 5 do not occur in practice should look at the plots in Raven (1986, pp. 69–70).

The utility of these item response models obviously depends on how many items are reasonably well-behaved and how many are like 'reality'. This is especially true where the Rasch model is concerned. Because it is the simplest model and can ostensibly be explained to lay people (notwithstanding Hoover's personal communication remark 'Try explaining Rasch to the principal of Betendorff High'), because less than fully numerate investigators are most comfortable with it, and because it requires less computing time than the competing two- and three- and even four-parameter models, there has been a general tendency to try to make Rasch work. This entails pushing robustness to the limit and hoping that departures from the model are without serious practical consequence. The worst consequences are likely to be in equating exercises where systematic errors are carried over from one level to the next and from an earlier equating to a later one (Divgi 1986). Henning (1989) has accused Divgi of exaggerating the objections to Rasch claiming that he (Divgi) had argued that the Rasch model is never a viable IRT model with multiple choice items. Divgi's (1989) reply challenges Henning to defend the propriety of deleting 'misfitting' items and 'misfitting' people, and asks whether the practical benefit of specific objectivity has ever been demonstrated.

The fact is that IRT models were never intended for use with multiple choice items. Guilford (1954, p. 363), reviewing Lord's original IRT work, pointed out that the assumption of unidimensionality and the exclusion of multiple choice tests place severe limits on the usefulness of the theory. But Henning is too partisan (see also chapter 19). He falls back on the old saw that, with Rasch, items must fit the model rather than the other way round. In so doing he fails to deal adequately with the objections that, in principle, all multiple choice items are poorly conditioned for Rasch due to guessing, and that item deletion following misfit will alter the construct(s) measured by the test. A proper balance is struck by de Gruitjer (1986) who argues that Rasch should never be used for optimal item selection when guessing plays an important part in item responses and that, in general, it might be too simple to be adequate.

In one important respect, there is nothing controversial about the Rasch model. Since each item response is weighted according to the discriminating power of the item, the Rasch model gives estimates which correlate perfectly with total test score (and, it follows, item difficulty estimates which correlate perfectly with classical item difficulties). Thus, it could be said that the Rasch model provides the necessary logical underpinning for classical analysis and the use of number correct score, which otherwise appear to be motivated by quite pragmatic considerations. It is because of these correspondences that investigators are apt to conclude, when comparing the results of classical and Rasch item analyses, that much the same outcome ensues, from which they go on to wonder whether the extra work and cost associated with modern item analysis methods is worth the candle. This is true whether the analysis is of a spelling test like Schonell (Newman *et al.* 1988) or of Civil Service Qualifying Tests (Johnson 1986). Fred Lord, the man who has done most to develop item characteristic curve theory, was candid enough to remark that 'applications of item response theory are generally more expensive than similar applications of classical test theory' (Lord & Stocking 1985).

Where these models do come into their own, and where classicai methods are inadequate (although Lord's (1971) 'flexilevel' testing was an exception) is in connection with individualised, or tailored, or adaptive testing; or, more generally, wherever different students are given different tests and it is necessary to place all students on the same measurement scale (equating). This topic is dealt with in chapter 13. The problem with that application lies in the assumption of unidimensionality, that is that a single latent trait underlies performance on an item. Lord may be right that this is a reasonable assumption where tests of verbal ability and spelling are concerned, but surely not in education itself, where diverse curricula and styles of teaching make it a priori reasonable that tests of attainment will be multidimensional (Goldstein & Wood 1989). The Rasch model requirement that all pairs of items should have relative difficulties which remain constant cannot be reconciled with focused instruction which deliberately seeks to shift, perhaps radically, those relative difficulties.

Classical item analysis was built for norm-referenced tests where discrimination is paramount. The Rasch model, by discarding high discrimination items, is automatically weakened as an instrument for norm-referencing. Johnson (1986) noticed significantly lower reliability coefficients (a direct result of reduced discrimination) and concluded that the Rasch model could not be recommended for developing Civil Service aptitude tests; those tests, note, for which Rasch was believed to be better suited (Thorndike 1982). There is a suggestion, however, that Rasch, by de-emphasising discrimination, could be more suitable for developing criterion-referenced tests although the objection concerning relative item difficulties would still apply.

Item analysis for criterion-referenced tests

Item analysis has always been a source of ambivalence among advocates of criterion-referenced testing. Unsullied doctrine requires belief in perfect congruence between objectives, item generators and items, so that items which function less than satisfactorily are not supposed to occur. Experience, however, indicates that there will always be subjective and uncertain elements in the formulation of objectives and therefore in the production of items, suggesting that there is room for some kind of analysis.

This empirical view is generally accepted nowadays, but in the beginning ambivalence led to some gratuitous inversions. It was argued that items with facilities as near as possible to 100% should be favoured above all others, when a moment's thought would have shown that such items can provide no evidence on the effectiveness of instruction or on progress towards mastery. What was wanted, it was said, were items with nonsignificant item–test correlations; items that discriminate positively usually indicate a need for revision. This, of course, was simply to misuse norm-referenced item statistics. If the idea is to find items which are sensitive to changes **within** individuals, then it is necessary to test items out on groups before and after they have received instruction. Items showing little or no difference, indicating insensitivity to learning, would then be discarded. The best items, in this view, are those which have *p* values approaching 0 prior to instruction, and *p* values approaching 1 subsequent to instruction.

Various refinements of the simple difference measure have been proposed. There seems good reason to view them all with suspicion (Van der Linden 1981). Noting that all the item analysis statistics (or validity coefficients, as he calls them) are based on the same idea of instructional sensitivity, require pre-test–post-test administration and entail gain scoring, Van der Linden acknowledged that such measures are welcomed in many papers as being typically criterion-referenced but argued that these coefficients have many disadvantages and serious interpretation problems. When the validity of instruction is not established, low pre-test–post-test differences may be due to poor instruction rather than to weak items. Two items with the same difference between pre-test and post-test *p* values may cover different intervals of the mastery continuum with different degrees of discrimination. The pre-test–post-test method mixes up two sources of information – the characteristics of the item and the differences between the pre-test and post-test mastery distributions – and blames the former for the peculiarities of the latter. By doing so, it is not surprising to find that it weeds out items of high quality.

Other work has exposed the shortcomings of the pre-test–post-test method (Harris & Subkoviak 1986). Item response theory has a solution to offer here, as Lord & Stocking explain:

> Suppose there is a pool of calibrated items, and subject matter experts have defined the mastery level. The test construction specialist then selects items from the pool that have the highest item information functions at that level. The test constructed in this way will measure most precisely at the mastery level, thus minimizing errors in classifying people. In addition, item response theory can aid in the determination of the optimal item difficulty, item weights, and cutting score, also the necessary test length. Various test designs may be compared in relative efficiency. (Lord & Stocking 1985, p. 2748).

A statistic which measures the power of an item to discriminate at a given cut-off point was proposed by Van der Linden (1981). Empirical work indicates that items selected by the Rasch statistic produce more reliable mastery tests than those composed of items selected by the pre-test–post-test method when the two selection methods are compared across multiple data sets. Once again, however, utility considerations intrude, not to mention doubts about the realism of Rasch model assumptions.

While latent trait statistics appear to be the best available indices for selecting criterion-referenced test items, in terms of compatibility with the purpose of mastery testing, their computational and conceptional complexity makes them problematic for routine use. If a simpler statistic could be devised, one which produced close agreement with the latent trait statistic, then it would be preferable to use. Harris & Subkoviak claim to have just such a statistic. Called the **agreement statistic**, it was found to overlap to a large extent with items selected by the latent trait statistic. An interesting analysis of the item characteristic curve suggests good reasons why there should be such strong agreement. It is recommended that the agreement statistic be used in practice.

A quite different approach to the problem was taken by Seddon (1987). Taking as his point of departure the purist view that item analysis is unsuitable for criterion-referenced tests – 'our position is that a random selection of items from the total domain rather than one based on item analysis should be used to construct an achievement test' (Harris, Pearlman & Wilcox 1977, p. 3) – Seddon devised a method of item analysis and item selection which apparently gives more accurate (domain) scores than those produced by random sampling. Tests constructed by this method were more effective than 93 out of 100 tests constructed by selecting items at random from a domain.

Of the other indices which have been proposed, Black (1987) produced a variant on the *D* statistic which takes into account disparity in size of above and below criterion groups, that is takes into account the score distribution shape. Evidently, there is a need to synthesise the various approaches to the problem and the mathematisers would do well to attend to it, rather than spawning yet more statistics.

References

Beuckert A. K. & Mendoza J. L. (1979) A Monte Carlo comparison of 10 item discrimination indices. *Journal of Educational Measurement*, **16**, 109–17.

Black T. R. (1987) A discrimination index for criterion-referenced tests. *British Journal of Educational Psychology*, **57**, 380–8.

Carroll J. B. (1987) Correcting point-biserial and biserial correlation coefficients for chance success. *Educational and Psychological Measurement*, **47**, 359–60.

de Gruitjer D. N. M. (1986) Small N does not always justify Rasch model. *Applied Psychological Measurement*, **10**, 187–94.

Divgi D. R. (1986) Does the Rasch model really work for multiple choice items? Not if you look closely. *Journal of Educational Measurement*, **23**, 283–98.

Divgi D. R. (1989) Reply to Andrich and Henning. *Journal of Educational Measurement*, **26**, 295–9.

Goldstein H. & Wood R. (1989) Five decades of item response modelling. *British Journal of Mathematical and Statistical Psychology*, **32**, 139–68.

Guilford J. P. (1954) *Psychometric Methods* (2nd edition). New York: McGraw-Hill.

Harris C. E., Pearlman A. P. & Wilcox R. R. (eds.) (1977) *Achievement Test Items – Methods of Study*. (*CSE Monograph Series in Evaluation, No. 6*). Los Angeles: University of California Center for the Study of Evaluation.

Harris D. J. & Kolen M. J. (1988) Bootstrap and traditional standard errors of the point-biserial. *Educational and Psychological Measurement*, **48**, 43–6.

Harris D. J. & Subkoviak M. J. (1986) Item analysis: A short-cut statistic for mastery tests. *Educational and Psychological Measurement*, **46**, 495–507.

Henning G. (1989) Does the Rasch model really work for multiple-choice items? Take another look: A response to Divgi. *Journal of Educational Measurement*, **26**, 91–7.

Johnson C. E. (1986) Qualifying tests for appointments-in-administration and executive office recruitment: A linkage feasibility study. *Recruitment Research Unit Report No. 28*. London: Civil Service Commission.

Levy P. (1973) On the relationship between test theory and psychology. In Kline P. (ed.) *New Approaches in Psychological Measurement*. London: Wiley.

Lord F. M. (1971) The self-scoring flexilevel test. *Journal of Educational Measurement*, **8**, 147–51.

Lord F. M. & Novick M. R. (1968) *Statistical Theories of Mental Test Scores*. Reading, MA: Addison-Wesley.

Lord F. M. & Stocking M. L. (1985) Item response theory. In Husén T. & Postlethwaite T. N. (eds.) *International Encyclopedia of Education: Research and Studies*. Oxford: Pergamon Press, 2745–8.

Morrison R. B. (1974) Item analysis and question validation. In Macintosh H. G. (ed.) *Techniques and Problems of Assessment*. London: Arnold.

Newman S. P. *et al.* (1988) An item analysis of the Schonell graded word reading test and Schonell spelling test. Unpublished paper. Department of Psychiatry, Middlesex Hospital.

Nuttall D. L. & Skurnik L. S. (1987) *Examination and Item Analysis Manual*. Nottingham: University of Nottingham School of Education.

Pollitt A. & Hutchinson C. (1987) Calibrating graded assessment: Rasch partial credit analysis of performance in writing. *Language Testing*, **4**, 72–92.

Raven J. (1986) *Manual for Raven's Progressive Matrices and Vocabulary Scales: Research Supplement No. 3*. London: H. K. Lewis & Co Ltd.

Seddon G. M. (1987) A method of item-analysis and item-selection for the construction of criteria-referenced tests. *British Journal of Educational Psychology*, **57**, 371–9.

Thorndike R. L. (1982) *Applied Psychometrics*. Boston, MA: Houghton Mifflin.

Van der Linden W. J. (1981) A latent trait look at pretest–posttest validation of criterion-referenced test items. *Review of Educational Research*, **51**, 379–402.

Wilmut J. (1975) Objective test analysis: Some criteria for item selection. *Research in Education*, **13**, 27–56.

Wood R. (1985) Item analysis. In Husén T. & Postlethwaite T. N. (eds.) *International Encyclopedia of Education: Research and Studies*. Oxford: Pergamon Press, 2734–42.

10 Scoring, weighting, combining and scaling

Scoring formulas are the outward expression of reward systems, which in turn delineate the value to be placed on achievements. A reward system indicates how individual items or questions are to be valued, and then how the corresponding scores are to be accumulated or combined, both within and across papers. **Weighting** is merely an extension of scoring in that scores are, in effect, multiplied (or divided) according to the weights allocated. A scoring procedure can always be adjusted beforehand so that questions are self-weighted. The purpose of weighting is not so much its convenience but what it signals to the world about the relative importance attached to papers. The business of **combining** scores on papers is less straightforward. There are statistical problems to be resolved, also decisions which can only be resolved by a principled consideration of what kind of achievement is to be rewarded. An obvious example in the examination context is the hurdle, where a certain paper has to be passed for overall success. The decision to put in a hurdle says, in effect, that a certain level of all-round performance is required.

Scaling, or **equating** as it is known in the USA, includes weighting as a special case but otherwise is not concerned with expressing value. The purpose of scaling is to place all scores ostensibly in the same metric, and it does this by deforming distributions of scores expressed in different metrics, either by stretching or by shrinking. If the linear scaling function is $y = \mathrm{a}x + \mathrm{b}$, then for weighting, the b disappears. Scaling does not have to be restricted to linear functions; equipercentile scaling is accomplished through a non-linear function.

A special case of scaling (or equating) is the very British problem of **comparability**, although it may not seem so at first glance. That is because the phenomenal task of placing all examination scores for all boards and all subjects on the same scale has never been attempted, nor ever will be. But it is still an equating problem. The various other ways in which comparability has been tackled constitute a literature of their own which has been more than adequately surveyed by Forrest & Shoesmith (1985) and I do not intend to deal with it here.

Scaling also has a meaning in relation to characterising the properties of items or questions; specifically it means calibration. The estimation of values for the parameters of the item characteristic curve (chapter 9) is a form of scaling. This usage, and the antecedents of the estimation of item difficulty and discrimination in latent trait theory (Goldstein & Wood 1989), originated with Thurstone (1925) who proposed that Binet test questions be located at a point on a chronological age scale such that 50% of children with an average age equal to that point passed the question. In psychological test parlance, a scale is a set of questions with known and desirable properties which act in concert in known and desirable ways.

Scoring

It is convenient to treat the scoring of multiple choice items before moving on to the more problematic issue of rewarding performance on extended answers to free response questions. The historical decision to award one point for a correct answer to a multiple choice item and zero for anything else has made scoring in this area seem unproblematical. Common sense bears this out. Even if it could be agreed that one item was worth more than another, the ratio of rewards is unlikely to be more than 1·5:1 and a rubric which nominated one item as worth 3 points and the next as 2 would only complicate matters. It is better to work on chunking up the question material so as to approximate parity of demand. Chapter 4 showed how attempts have been made, through varying the response mechanism, to offer rewards for partial information and for omitting items instead of guessing; also how distractors can be scored empirically when the purpose is prediction. The conclusion was that 0–1 scoring is satisfactory and defensible providing other conditions are met, notably clear instructions and adequate time to finish.

Items are, in any case, only of equal value on the surface. The point was made in chapter 4, and again in chapter 9, that items effectively weight themselves according to their discrimination. To get an item correct which everyone else gets correct is of no value to the individual in a norm-referenced set-up, or even in a criterion-referenced context if items have been selected using one of the discrimination statistics.

Turning now to the scoring of extended answers, it is evident that when examiners decree that such and such a question will be worth 25 marks and another 40, they are expressing directly their estimates of the relative importance and value of the respective tasks. Presumably, their judgements are time-related in that the 40-mark questions will be expected to take roughly half as long again as the 25-mark questions, although time spent and amount achieved are not necessarily correlated. Simon French (whose views we will come to when dealing with combining scores) does not believe that examiners can numerically answer questions of the form 'How much more important is paper 1 than paper 2?' In fact, he has grave doubts whether such questions are meaningful. 'We may say in everyday language that something is twice as important as another but that does not mean that we have in mind two unambiguously defined numbers, one twice the other' (French 1985, p. 276). French believes that examiners are not particularly sensitive to what the **achieved weight** of a paper should be, but that they do have a sufficiently keen idea of relative worth that when faced with profiles of candidates' scores they are able to apply certain principles and arrive at consistent and coherent judgements.

What French does not mention is the need to tell candidates what questions and papers are deemed to be worth so that they too can make decisions, notably in how to deploy their time. Quite how candidates deal with numerical question values is itself a fascinating study. We saw from the very limited evidence in chapter 2 that they do not necessarily choose well.

Were questions (and papers) to attract equal numerical values, French would have a stronger point. And indeed it is proper to ask why examiners should think it necessary to give 36 marks for this, 24 for that, and so on. Just as with multiple choice, why cannot they work on giving questions parity of demand? It might be a useful discipline.

This is not a topic susceptible to research (although see chapter 3 for some relevant data). The sort of empirical research one might think of doing, like calculating the effect on total scores, or some other variable, of swapping mark values around, so that the 40-mark question becomes a 20-mark question, cannot be done because the candidates have already used the information in the official mark values to make decisions to offer evidence of achievement in particular ways. This is especially the case when there is question choice combined with uneven mark values. The same objection might be levelled at post hoc research on multiple choice item values, but there the margins are so much smaller and of course there is no choice.

Weighting

Weighting is a topic which is subsumed under scoring and combining. Once it was realised that nominated weights and achieved weights were rarely the same after linear combination, due to the effects of covariance between papers, there ensued a lively debate on how best to ensure that the two were identical. But this is best dealt with under combining.

The use of differential empirical weighting to predict future performance using multiple regression methods is an interesting topic, although little pursued in this country. When the aborted Test of Academic Aptitude (TAA) was being developed in the early 1970s there was interest in trying to predict degree class in different subject areas using variable weights for the verbal and non-verbal elements. Were a general test of academic aptitude to be developed, then there might again be interest in this sort of calculation. An example of differential empirical weighting was the decision by ETS to score the SAT by the formula 2V+M (V = verbal, M = mathematical), done so as to minimise sex differences (Coffman, personal communication).

Combining

The practice of combining scores by addition, whether at the question or paper or test level, is so entrenched that it would come as a great surprise to many to be told that it does not necessarily have to be done this way and that, in fact, there are convincing reasons for abandoning the practice. The standard linear form for a combination can be written as $C = \Sigma\alpha_i$ for question or paper or test i, but there is no reason why it should not be written as $C = \Sigma\alpha_i^j$ where, instead of being set to 1, j can take values greater or less than 1. For instance, setting $j = \frac{1}{2}$ has the effect of compressing scores and reducing the effect extremes have on the combination score. A decision to use this formula (a convex function) would be to observe a principle of rewarding **steadiness**; a decision to set $j > 1$ (a concave function) would be to reward **erratic** performances (Plackett 1976). As it is, setting $j = 1$ merely observes some kind of roundabouts-and-swings principle, where individuals can make up for a poor performance with good performance elsewhere.

Green & Wigdor (1988, pp. 17–18) call roundabouts-and-swings a **compensatory** scoring model. They also propose **conjunctive**, **disjunctive** and **hybrid** scoring models. A conjunctive model requires that an individual successfully complete each of a series of composite steps, a disjunctive model requires success in only one of the components (hurdle) and a hybrid model is some mix of the other models. A compensatory–conjunctive model would permit the usual compensating scores, providing that one or two critical steps were done correctly (hurdle idea also). A sequence of steps could be scored in a compensatory manner, and then a cut-off point could be established to turn that sequence into a 0, 1 score depending on whether the performance was above or below the cut. The group scores could then be scored in a compensatory fashion. Green &

Example from French (1981)

Candidate	T	P
$C^{(1)}$	30	95
$C^{(2)}$	50	74
$C^{(3)}$	60	61
$C^{(4)}$	70	50

Wigdor note that if the steps in a task (items) are ordered with each step harder than those before it, so that success on a given item implies success on all previous items (technically, a perfect Guttman scale), then the conjunctive model is identical with the compensatory model.

There is room for invention in the linear combination or compensatory/hybrid methods, but French (1985) finds them wanting. He argues that they implicitly prohibit the examiners from making certain judgements which may be entirely reasonable. Suppose, he says, that there are two papers in a science subject, theory (T) and practical (P), and suppose further that four candidates gain the marks shown in the table. If the examiners hold theory to be more important than practical, but nonetheless demand that candidates, particularly good candidates, should show a roughly even performance in the two papers, then they might wish, quite reasonably, to award overall performance in the order:

1st – $C^{(3)}$, 2nd – $C^{(4)}$, 3rd – $C^{(2)}$, 4th – $C^{(1)}$

French maintains that it is a straightforward matter to show that no linear combination is consistent with this ranking. If we confine attention to weighted linear sums of marks, we are prohibiting certain overall rankings of the candidates and, moreover, the prohibited rankings may be perfectly reasonable expressions of the examiners' judgements.

French and the Decision Analytic Aids to Examining (DAATE) project (SEC 1987) are working on ways of allowing examiners to exercise judgement. By definition whatever emerges will fall into the class of hybrid models as defined by Green & Wigdor.

The problem of achieving desired weights in practice when using linear combination has exercised several minds. If nothing is done to take account of varying dispersions of marks across papers (after corrections to the mark ranges), then the paper with the largest standard deviation will exert more weight than it should, and conversely at the other extreme. Thus the desired weights need standardising by dividing by the standard deviation. This is not good enough, says French, and AEB workers think so too (Adams & Murphy 1982; Adams & Wilmut 1982). Weights should be additive, they say, that is the combined weight of two papers should be the sum of their individual weights. Thus we must question the validity of this definition of weight, or question the demand for additivity.

Be that as it may, correcting for dispersion only can never be enough. Covariances between papers must be taken into account. The variance of a simple linear combination is a series of covariance terms, only some of which are dispersions. The comprehensive solution to achieving desired weights is to take all the covariance terms into the reckoning. This approach, which requires an iterative solution, was investigated by the Test Development and Research Unit at Cambridge and later by the AEB workers. An improved solution has recently been proposed by Govindarajulu (1988). Still French is unhappy. Yes, we have additivity because the combined weight of two papers is now equal to the sum of their individual weights, but we have lost another intuitively desirable property. If one paper has twice the weight of another, then surely, he says, an improvement by a candidate on the first should be rewarded twice as much as an equal improvement on the second. Other definitions of weight allow this, albeit with differing scales of measuring improvement. With the introduction of covariances, an improved performance on one paper must be accompanied by corresponding improvements on the others. Besides, says French, covariances are too high-falutin for examiners and they will be at a loss to know what is going on.

Anyone who believes that examination systems ought to be as transparent as they can be, will understand French's remark. But what to do? At the very best, weights would have to be corrected for varying dispersions and that small step would leave many examiners behind. The fact is that examiners are accustomed to leaving the boards' officials to do the manipulation (let us not be unkind and call it the fudging) of numbers after scripts have been marked. This being so, French's own methods for making them aware of the consequences of the judgements they make, at the individual candidate level, are radical indeed.

If weights are announced, then they ought to apply to every candidate directly, with no manipulation afterwards. This somewhat literal interpretation was Cresswell's (1987) idea and it can be seen as harmonising with the French/DAATE programme, insofar as they preserve the intuitively desirable property lost by the covariance/aggregation solutions. Cresswell stresses the importance, in terms of equity protection, of Wood's (1978) stricture that candidates' results should not be affected by the company they keep. He rightly says this is particularly necessary where examinations are of the criterion-referenced kind. Incidentally, Cresswell points out that the covariance solution depends on linear relationships between marks, something Adams & Murphy (1982) had noted themselves. As Cresswell himself came to realise during the SEC project (see next section), structural realities implicit in differentiated paper systems may induce non-linear relationships between components.

Scaling

Discussion of scaling in the examination context has centred largely on the moderation of school-based assessments. GCSE has that problem too, but also a fresh set of problems created by the presence of differentiated systems of assessment. The SEC project represents a first crack at these new problems (which are actually old problems, old equating problems).

Scaling teacher assessments

When Vernon (1957) surveyed the scaling techniques adopted by local authorities in the post-war period in connection with 11+ selection, he noted nine distinct methods. These included a typically ingenious, if somewhat unworkable, proposal by the late Gilbert Peaker which involved scaling each primary school's estimates against results obtained later by that school's pupils in the secondary school.

Of those nine methods, only three have survived – linear scaling by equating means and standard deviations, nonlinear or equipercentile scaling and rank order conversion. The last technique may have fallen out of use altogether, although it was being used in 1978 by the State of New South Wales (NSW Dept of Education 1978). The suitability of linear and equipercentile scaling for coping with GCSE measurement problems is dealt with by Good & Cresswell (1988 *a*). Scaling methods based on item characteristic curve theory have been developed at the Educational Testing Service (ETS) for the purposes of equating, but these have not been taken up in this country.

In its pristine form the method of **rank order conversion**, or **rank allocation** (Wood 1978), requires no statistical manipulation, or understanding for that matter. The school prepares a rank ordering of students and then proceeds to assign the highest examination mark total (or grade) gained in that set of students to the top-ranked student, the second highest to the second rank, and so on. Evidently the precise distribution of scores, that is ability estimates, is reproduced, and this has some statistical appeal when it comes to combining the scaled school assessments with the examination results.

An obvious objection to the method is that with a small group an irregular distribution of examination marks may give an inaccurate picture of the distribution of achievement. To adapt Vernon's example (p. 194), the group might obtain marks of 82, 79 and then the rest in a bunch around 55 to 45. Yet the two students with the highest rankings might not be considered by the school as being actually much ahead of the 3rd and 4th on the list.

The more general objection is that students might be penalised by another student turning in a below-par examination performance or 'flop', to use McIntosh, Walker & Mackay's (1962) term. Quite which students will suffer from being assigned 'flop' scores is, of course, unknown unless efforts are made to identify students who have done particularly badly (something the NSW method does). The best guess is perhaps that the lowest examination mark is most likely to be a 'flop', and should not be assigned to anyone. This, in fact, is what the NSW method does. The lowest mark is ignored and the lowest rank is given a value by a formula which depends on the lowest and second lowest school estimates and the second lowest examination mark. Since this adjustment requires the school to produce estimated marks, it will not do where only ranks are available.

Vernon argued that the rank order conversion method was strictly unsuitable for small groups; the NSW Dept of Education argues that it is **necessary** for small groups ($n < 20$) on the grounds that the linear scaling method it prefers for larger groups becomes unstable. There is substance in this criticism, but otherwise Vernon must be right. Small groups present a problem in their own right, which probably has to be dealt with by other than statistical methods.

Whether or not it is the case that teachers, in the generality, prefer to draw up rank orders than to assign marks or grades, the requirements of GCSE now require them to arrive at marks. Thus, rank ordering which might once, in the absence of guidance, have been a natural method of reporting achievement, now seems careless of information and obsolete, whatever its technical shortcomings.

The method of **linear scaling** is easily the most heavily used, especially where psychological tests are concerned. T-scores, standard scores, stens, IQs and normal deviates are all examples of raw scores being subjected to linear transformation so as to produce desirable or just convenient scale properties, that is designated means and standard deviations such as 50 and 15 respectively.

The most obvious objection to linear scaling is that inaccuracies may occur if either distribution (exam marks, school marks) is skewed. This is more likely to happen with small numbers, which is no doubt why NSW reckoned the method unstable for $n < 20$. There are ways of normalising distributions by transformation, but as with all second-order manipulations, few connected with the examination will understand them and the valuable principle of transparency will be compromised. (Perhaps it is too late to worry about this when so much else in marking and awarding is opaque to examiners, never mind the public.)

Scaling school assessments in the GCSE is part of the general business of transferring marks to a common scale prior to grading. The same operations apply when there are differentiated papers. The existence of a common paper, which everyone does, is enough in principle to enable marks on easier and harder papers to be scaled to the common paper metric, or any other. The SEG researchers advise that linear scaling is probably the most satisfactory type of procedure 'if, as seems likely, the candidates' marks give a good indication of the difficulty of the various components' (Good & Cresswell, p. 79). This turns out to be a critical condition.

In making this recommendation, Good & Cresswell noted that many objections to scaling marks have been put forward since Backhouse (1976) applied linear scaling to the differentiated papers problem. Using Backhouse's own illustrative data for small groups ($n = 6$ and $n = 4$), and also data supplied by the WJEC, pioneers in the differentiated papers field (group sizes 10 and 10), I drew attention to what I believed to be a basic flaw in linear scaling (Wood 1978). It is that an individual's score as a result of scaling will depend to a large extent on the group s/he is in or, as one might say, the company s/he keeps. More importantly, the flaw appears whenever the bivariate structures between the common paper and the easier (harder) paper are quite different. The likelihood of this happening in practice is actually quite strong, precisely because of the way candidates are allocated. Common paper marks for those due to tackle the harder paper are likely to be on the high side and to be bunched; quite how their marks distribute on the harder paper depends on the skill of the paper constructors. For those tackling the easier paper, marks on the common paper may be quite well spread out, especially if there has been a good deal of conservative candidate allocation. The same sort of distribution may well occur on the easier paper for the same sort of reason. The outcome could be that the bivariate structure for the easier paper candidates will turn out to be approximately normal, while that for the others will be more or less doubly truncated and not well-behaved at all.

This is not to say that it is disadvantageous to be in the harder paper group. Of two mediocre candidates with the same common paper score, the one in the harder paper group will come off best since he will have his scaled mark improved through the efforts of his coevals on the common paper. Generally speaking, individuals will benefit more from having their raw marks **stretched** than **shrunk**.

In a rebuttal appended to my paper, Backhouse contended that he was interested only in the suitability of scaling techniques for large-scale examining and that large numbers will produce a smoothing of distributions; also that the end-product of the exercise is simply a guide for each candidate – 'For the great majority of candidates, agreements between the methods may be expected' (also scrutinised were the rank conversion method and a regression method). Good & Cresswell (1988*b*) came to the same conclusion (p. 185), namely that my objections, although theoretically valid, are unlikely to be of practical importance.

Seeking protection in the law of large numbers is respectable enough and Backhouse (and Good & Cresswell) may well turn out to be right. Not that drawing conclusions from small data sets is necessarily to be despised. As we have seen, French was prepared to draw conclusions from a data set of $n = 4$, defending himself on the grounds (fully shared by myself) that even-handedness requires that any 4 or 3 or 2 candidates be justly rewarded relative to each other. At the end of the day Good & Cresswell settle for the position that a decision not to scale, and the consequent need to grade levels separately, stores up so many more problems than scaling that it would be better to do linear scaling *faute de mieux*, although they do not put it quite like that. Provided the data are edited prior to fitting a linear relationship, then all will be well. In fact the standard work on equating notes, unsurprisingly, that linear methods are found to be poor when a true non-linear relationship exists (Petersen, Kolen & Hoover 1989).

This kind of recommendation puts a great deal of pressure on differentiated paper constructors. Having acknowledged (p. 47) that if able candidates take a common paper that is targeted at middle achievers then there may not be enough marks available for the best candidates to show their true levels of achievement (their terminology), Good & Cresswell (1988*a*) go straight on to advise that 'if the candidates for whom the papers are inadequate measuring instruments are removed', that is the very candidates they have just been talking about, then the marks of the remaining candidates, for whom the papers **are** appropriate, may be fitted by a straight line. Now deleting outliers and flops is one thing, but the outcome here, if the paper constructors were to fall down (and why would they not given that they are totally unaccustomed to engineering score distributions, never mind fine tuning), could be data editing on an unprecedented scale. The boards' software writers, never comfortable with statistically driven fixes at the best of times, would not be happy.

Linear scaling is but a regression method which ignores the correlation between the two sets of marks. I thought that treating the problem explicitly as a regression problem, which is also what Backhouse did (also Sandon much earlier, see Vernon p. 197), produces better solutions because stretching and shrinking is accommodated; that is what regression does. Backhouse was unhappy about the propriety of calculating 'imputed' scores, that is scores on the papers candidates did **not** do. I was unhappy too, thinking of consumer resistance or, as I would say now, loss of transparency, but I wonder if we were not being too tender-minded.

Note, however, that the regression method does not escape the 'company you keep' objection. Linear scaling in its simplest form also assumes that both sets of marks are equally reliable. Would we assume that school-based assessments and examination marks totals were equally reliable? Probably not, although then again we might persuade ourselves by some kind of roundabouts-and-swings reasoning that there is little in it. At any rate, the general solution with variables taken to be fallible involves, as Good & Cresswell acknowledged (p. 46), what is called a **structural regression** model, even if they prefer to coin the neologism structural linear scaling. Mention of this model recalls a famous debate involving the University College statistician the late N. W. Please and the HMI Inspector the late Gilbert Peaker. The debate (Please 1971; Peaker 1971) hinged on which was the appropriate regression line, y on x or x on y, but the argument was really about whether measurement error in one or both variables should be formally modelled.

Now Good (1988*a*, *b*) has taken the problem of moderating school-based assessment, and has formally modelled error in both variables, that is to say, the teacher's mark and the moderator's mark. Structural regression lines are fitted for each centre on the basis of assumptions made about the relative errors, for example mark errors are proportional to their variances. Choice of assumption turns out to be critical only for candidates at the extremes. If no error is assumed in the teacher's marks, the marks of the weakest candidates are inflated, and those for the strongest candidates depressed. If no error is assumed for the moderator's marks, assumption produces something in between. So it appears there are still grounds for concern, not least because of the problems induced by fitting equations for small centre sizes, and low correlation whether from small or larger centres.

Of all the scaling methods, Vernon preferred **equipercentile scaling** (p. 206). It was, he thought, as technically sound as any and easier to implement. Fairer too, in that scaled scores more nearly reflect the intervals between candidates, which was the objection to rank conversion. With equipercentile scaling it is not necessary to assume that a straight line

Anomalies arising with equipercentile scaling

	Common paper	Hard paper		Aggregate	
	Raw/scaled	Raw	Scaled	Raw	Scaled
Candidate A	40	20	35	60	75
Candidate B	29	31	44	60	73

describes the relationship between scores on the components. Good & Cresswell, in this earlier stage of their report before they opt for what are essentially brute force solutions, observe (p. 44) that a curvilinear function is likely to be required precisely because in differentiated paper arrangements one set of scores (or both) is going to be skewed because one paper is easier than the other. When the shapes of the score distributions are identical, or almost so, linear scaling can be thought of as a special case of equipercentile scaling.

With equipercentile scaling, two marks on different papers are defined as comparable if they are reached by the same proportion of a given group of candidates. In order to convert marks on one paper on to the scale of another, points representing pairs of marks reached by equal percentages of candidates are plotted and a smoothed curve is drawn through them (this procedure can be computerised). The main difficulty with equipercentile scaling, according to Good & Cresswell, is that it assumes that the achievement measured on one paper (the optional one) can be placed appropriately on the measurement scale of another (the common paper). To illustrate what can go wrong they use the data set shown in the table (well, barely a set as $n = 2$).

Both candidates scored a total of 60 raw marks, but candidate B achieved more of them on the hard paper. Nevertheless, after equipercentile scaling A was placed above B. Anomalies of this type are always likely to arise, say Good & Cresswell, if non-linear transformations are used. And, they might have added, with linear scaling too.

The standard work on scaling (Petersen, Kolen & Hoover 1989) points out (p. 252) that unlike equipercentile scaling, linear scaling or equating is entirely analytical and free from those errors of smoothing that can produce serious errors in the score ranges where data are scant or erratic, that is the extremes. Their judgement is that providing one is willing to assume that differences in the shapes of the raw score distributions are trivial, say due to sampling error, and may be disregarded, linear equating is to be preferred to equipercentile equating. With that assumption evidently not holding for structural reasons unconnected with error, it seems to be a case of the devil or the deep blue sea.

As a footnote to non-linear scaling methods, it is worth pointing out that the **equating methods** developed in recent years by ETS and the College Board are also of the non-linear kind, as they must be since the relationship between item performance and ability is conceived to be non-linear (the exponential normal ogive and logistic functions). In principle, using either separate random samples or common tests, the item parameters for all tests can be estimated, thus enabling the ability of an individual who responds to any of the tests to be estimated. Because they deal with items rather than the test scores, latent trait models require additional assumptions to be made. These, however, give issue to particular difficulties (Goldstein & Wood 1989) and the use of such models is definitely problematical.

In deciding between scaling methods the point made earlier about the need to underpin scoring with a principled reward system applies equally well. Boldt (1974) puts it admirably:

> The philosophy of value that underlies the production of numbers to be compared is the philosophy of value that makes decisions about people when the numbers are used. When the decisions are made about people using different information, the scaling of the information affects the decision process and hence implements the value of that process. But values implemented by the scaling process may not be, and probably are not, those of the user. The two systems of values are not necessarily in conflict, rather they are probably unrelated. Therefore, if the user wishes his values to carry the most emphasis, he must undertake active technical steps to assure that the process that produces numbers or scores to be compared incorporates his particular interest. This is probably not accomplished with existing techniques.

The need to imbue awarding procedures with personal values is what the DAATE project is all about. The SEC researchers' approach to this issue is to advocate what they call **judgemental scaling** whereby the results of performing various statistical manipulations, like linear and non-linear scaling, are fed to examiners, who then decide whether the consequences are sensible and coherent. If they are not, fresh manipulations are requested and the process continues iteratively until someone calls a halt.

Judgemental scaling may well be the way to smooth out anomalies but at the present time there is no way of knowing. The SEC work has only scratched the surface; let us see what DAATE brings. After four years' work the project director is satisfied that the DAATE methodology has a definite future, perhaps most obviously as a routine scrutiny tool (French, personal communication). He concedes that the decision analysis side of things is unproven, but believes that the combination of interactive computing and graphical presentation will, as it apparently already has, create a powerful impact in examiners' meetings. The day when chief examiners use PCs routinely is not far off, he thinks.

References

Adams R. M. & Murphy R. J. L. (1982) The achieved weights of examination components. *Educational Studies*, **8**, 15–22.

Adams R. M. & Wilmut J. (1982) A measure of the weights of examination components, and scaling to adjust them. *The Statistician*, **30**, 263–9.

Backhouse J. K. (1976) Determination of grades for two groups sharing a common paper. *Educational Research*, **18**, 126–37.

Boldt R. F. (1974) Comparability of scores from different tests though on the same scale. *Educational and Psychological Measurement*, **34**, 239–46.

Cresswell M. J. (1987) A more generally useful measure of the weights of examination components. *British Journal of Mathematical and Statistical Psychology*, **40**, 61–79.

Forrest G. M. & Shoesmith D. J. (1985) *A Second Review of GCE Comparability Studies*. Manchester: JMB on behalf of the GCE examining boards.

French S. (1981) Measurement theory and examinations. *British Journal of Mathematical and Statistical Psychology*, **34**, 38–49.

French S. (1985) The weighting of examination components. *The Statistician*, **34**, 265–80.

Goldstein H. & Wood R. (1989) Five decades of item response modelling. *British Journal of Mathematical and Statistical Psychology*, **32**, 139–68.

Good F. J. (1988*a*) Differences in marks awarded as a result of moderation: Some findings from a teacher assessed oral examination in French. *Educational Review*, **40**, 319–29.

Good F. J. (1988*b*) A method of moderation of school-based assessments: Some statistical considerations. *The Statistician*, **37**, 33–49.

Good F. J. & Cresswell M. J. (1988*a*) *Grading the GCSE*. London: Secondary Examinations Council.

Good F. J. & Cresswell M. J. (1988*b*) Placing candidates who take differentiated papers on a common grade scale. *Educational Research*, **30**, 177–89.

Govindarajulu Z. (1988) Alternative methods for combining several test scores. *Educational and Psychological Measurement*, **48**, 53–60.

Green B. F. & Wigdor A. K. (1988) *Measuring Job Competency*. Washington, DC: National Academy Press.

McIntosh D. M., Walker D. A. & Mackay D. (1962) *Scaling of Teachers' Marks and Estimates*. Edinburgh: Oliver & Boyd.

New South Wales Department of Education (1978) *The Processing of Higher School Certificate Examination Marks – A Technical Paper*. Sydney: New South Wales.

Peaker G. F. (1971) A reply to Please. *Educational Research*, **13**, 233–6.

Petersen N. S., Kolen M. J. & Hoover H. D. (1989) Scaling, norming and equating. In Linn R. L. (ed.) *Educational Measurement* (3rd edition).

Washington, DC: American Council on Education/Macmillan Series on Higher Education.

Plackett R. L. (1976) Discussion of paper by Barnett. *Journal of the Royal Statistical Society, A*, **139**, 318–55.

Please N. W. (1971) The 1965 CSE monitoring experiment: A comment. *Educational Research*, **13**, 233–6.

Secondary Examinations Council (1987) *Decision Analytic Aids to Examining (DAATE) Research Project*. London: SEC.

Thurstone L. L. (1925) A method of scaling psychological and educational tests. *Journal of Educational Psychology*, **16**, 433–51.

Vernon P. E. (1957) *Secondary School Selection*. London: Methuen.

Wood R. (1978) Placing candidates who take different papers on the same mark scale. *Educational Research*, **20**, 210–15.

11 Reliability

This is a general treatment of reliability. Elsewhere, in the relevant chapters (*Language testing*, *School-based assessment*, *Essay questions*, *How practical work is assessed*) there is a discussion of reliability as it pertains to that topic. Reliability is concerned with the consistency of examinee performance, and the quantification of that consistency (or inconsistency) is the business of reliability analysis.

In its 1976 paper *School Examinations and Their Function*, UCLES set out, in its own words, 'certain stringent conditions which were thought to be necessary if an examination was to provide a qualification which might affect the career of a candidate' (UCLES 1976, p. 8). Four conditions were stated, of which (*b*) was this – 'The marking of answers has to be as reliable as possible.' The paper continued (p. 9):

> This is the field which causes examination boards the greatest concern and no one involved with public examinations could possibly claim that it is less important now than previously. As the number of candidates grows it becomes progressively more difficult to ensure that all examiners are marking to the same standard, and co-ordination techniques become more sophisticated. A great deal of research into different types of test, methods of marking, co-ordination of examiners' standards, and statistical analysis of results has been undertaken in recent years... It will be sufficient here to point out that all boards which at present offer certificates based upon external examinations have to take this problem very seriously if they are to maintain any credibility, and that it is probably true to say that none of them will ever completely solve it.

How interesting, but how typical, that the Syndicate should give reliability primacy above everything else. Typical, because the examination boards have paid next to no attention to validity (see the next chapter) which actually has primacy over reliability. No one has put this thought better than Feldt & Brennan (1989, p. 143):

> No body of reliability data, regardless of the elegance of the methods used to analyze it, is worth very much if the measure to which it applies is irrelevant or redundant.

It may well have been correct in 1976 to say that a 'good deal of research' on reliability had been done in the past few years. There were, after all, the Nuttall & Willmott (1972) and Willmott & Nuttall (1975) investigations; also Willmott & Hall (1975). Some 150 CSE examinations and 29 GCE examinations had been scrutinised for technical soundness. Willmott & Nuttall themselves noted (p. 3) that much of the research had concentrated on the reliability of the marking of examinations, which is only one of the factors that causes an apparent variation in a candidate's performance. Naturally, they discussed the seminal work of Hartog & Rhodes (1936) and speculated that results as depressing as Hartog & Rhodes found would be unlikely to be found today. This they put down to improvements in marker standardisation but were obliged to add that estimates of reliability of marking under these improved conditions are 'hard to come by'.

Moving on, there is no reason to doubt that UCLES (and other boards) would deny that it (reliability) is any less important now than previously. Nothing has happened to weaken the statement; if anything, it can be affirmed with greater power since qualifications affect the careers of candidates at least as much now in a time of greater unemployment than was the case in 1976, and the proliferation of examinations makes it possible to be wrongly graded in more different ways. It is therefore fair to ask whether the boards are taking the problem 'very seriously' and what indeed they are doing to make tangible such expressions of concern. It is not enough to make appeal to a recent body of work because that work has not been done. Ignoring discursive papers such as Cresswell's (1986, 1987), the last empirical work of any substance relevant to school examinations was published in 1982 (Murphy 1982). Johnson & Cohen's work on cross-moderation exercises using generalisability analysis is relevant, apart from being intrinsically interesting, but it does not throw up a great deal of information bearing directly on reliabilities across the range of subjects. At any rate, this work is dealt with later.

As long as GCE continued, the boards could plead a steady-state situation and appeal routinely to the evidence on reliability gathered in the past. Now that there is a new system, which is quite different from the last (GCSE), there seems no alternative to doing the necessary research (to establish characteristic reliability levels) or else to act quite conservatively in the expectation that at first reliability will be worse than it is suspected to be at present. This need not necessarily be so because the wider ability range of GCSE entries should, *ceteris paribus*, conduce to higher reliability estimates, although that is strictly an artefactual effect since reliability, being a correlation, is always influenced by range. In any case, the presence of untried or as yet unfathomed elements and features would point to the need for caution.

Reliability of grading

The reliability of grades is, in an important sense, the bottom line of the examining system; all other reliabilities, of markers, teachers and items, feed in to produce outcomes which are more or less reliable, and therefore just. There exist direct relationships between the reliability of the examination, which usually means the reliability of the overall marks, the number of grades on the scale, the reliability of the grades and the severity of the consequences of misclassification. If a board were able to calculate or estimate by some means the modal reliability expected, then it could choose the necessary number of grade points such that, for most examinations, any grade awarded was correct, or true, within plus or minus one grade. By acting in this way the board comes clean with the public, which is then compelled to come to terms with the awkward truth that examinations are not perfect. At the same time the board has an obligation to institute regular reliability checks on samples of its examinations so that the original formula governing the choice of grade points can still be seen to hold, or at least is not badly out of kilter. Cresswell (1986) maintains that there is no generally accepted rationale for deciding the number of grades which should be used to report examination results. He posits two schools of thought – those who say that the number of grades should reflect the reliability of the mark scale, and those who say that the loss of information incurred when a small number of relatively coarse categories is used justifies the use of a relatively large number of fine distinctions. Cresswell believes that the two schools of thought can coexist; others might say that they can be reconciled.

Work on the necessary number of grades problem goes back at least to Skurnik & Nuttall (1968). They, and others (such as Pilliner 1969; Mitchelmore 1981), took the view that the credibility of examination grades depends upon there being relatively few misclassifications. Unless an examination is perfectly reliable, some of those who lie just to one side of a grade boundary will have true scores which fall the other side of it. As a consequence no system of grades can ever have an accuracy better than ± 1 grade. Skurnik & Nuttall proposed that the reliability of an examination should be reported in terms of the number of grades which it can support, given that the grades are very probably accurate to ± 1. To the objection that differing reliabilities would mean differing numbers of grades (from exam to exam and board to board) and that this would cause chaos, Pilliner, among others, argued that the problem can be avoided by choosing a number of grades which renders the examination with the **least reliable** marks accurate to ± 1 grade. With this conservative strategy, all examinations are then accurate at least to the same margin of error and most will be considerably better.

There has been official awareness of the linkage between number of grades and reliability of marks. In 1980 the Schools Council warned users of GCE and CSE that '... research has suggested results on a six- or seven-point grading scale are accurate to about one grade either side of that awarded' (Schools Council 1980). Whether eight grades is enough for GCSE is a moot point, if it is accepted that the inclusion of untried elements points to the need for a conservative strategy. But the number of grades has never been decided on measurement grounds alone, as the JMB discovered when in 1970–1 it campaigned for 20-point scales for the ill-fated Q & F, and later for A level (JMB 1983). Too many grades to cope with has been the stock objection; also an error margin of ± 3 is too much for the man in the street to deal with. Besides, a large number of grade points suggests, in itself, that the examination is unreliable and the producers have little confidence in it.

The second school of thought identified by Cresswell says simply that, regardless of errors in estimating achievement, the finer the scale used for reporting grades, the more accurate the report will be. In other words, the grades resulting from two administrations of the same examination will be more like each other if a large number of grades is used, precisely because the reliability of grades and the reliability of marks will converge as the number of grades increases. Against that, as Cresswell notes, if the precise replication of candidates' previous results by a second assessment is considered desirable, then it makes sense to report those results in terms of a few broad categories. Although fewer will be misclassified, the penalties for misclassification will be altogether more severe.

To the extent that JMB continues to fight its corner for 20-point scales, Cresswell is right that there is no generally accepted rationale for choosing the number of grades. In that respect the GCSE solution is a compromise, not especially conservative but one which avoids the pitfall of too few categories, a strategy which would not have been supportable in the light of what is known about current mark reliabilities. The intention, now, must be to make sure that the choice of eight grades can be supported.

What research remains to be done on this topic? Cresswell (1988) discusses situations where grades, instead of marks, are combined into a final grade. This, he argues rightly, represents a double loss of information. An overall grade based upon combinations of marks will, in general, be a more reliable measure of achievement than an overall grade based upon combinations of grades. It follows, however, that as with marks, increasing the number of grades used in the mix will increase the reliability of the overall grade. Perhaps this issue will come to have practical significance.

The various kinds of reliability

A major source of inconsistency is the day-to-day variation of individuals. To capture this variation, one or more days must elapse between the several measurements or observations of each individual. To accomplish this, it is necessary to have available at least two interchangeable test forms or else it must be possible to readminister the form previously used. The use of alternate forms on different days is generally referred to as the **parallel forms** approach. Readministration of the same form is called the **test–retest** approach.

Evidently both approaches are, as Feldt & Brennan (1989, p. 11) so delicately put it, 'often incompatible with administrative realities'. The response has been to see what might be done with a single administration of a test or examination. If a test or, more generally, an assessment procedure can be split into two parts then each part can serve as a test, and test–retest or parallel forms estimation is possible; the only extra feature is the need to estimate from the half-test results what the reliability of the test or procedure would have been had it been twice as long. This is accomplished by application of something called the Spearman-Brown formula.

The trouble with the **split-half** procedure is that it is not always clear what the rule should be; dividing into odd- and even-numbered questions is, after all, arbitrary if convenient and could produce halves contaminated by dependencies. For example, split-half coefficients that are obtained from scoring odd- and even-numbered items separately could easily yield an inflated estimate for a highly speeded test (because items at the end are not reached or are answered incorrectly).

Evidently the split-half procedure can be extended to any set of items. Imagine a set of items or questions or tasks or markers or raters being formed into all possible permutations and the aggregate scores on all these forms correlated in all possible pairs. The average of these correlations is Cronbach's **coefficient alpha**. It is a measure of the **internal consistency** of responses, but that is all it is. It should not be confused with the more authentic methods of estimating reliability.

Estimating the reliability of components, singly and in combination

A multipart examination is a tough proposition when it comes to estimating reliability. Attempts at estimating parallel forms and test–retest reliabilities for whole, or even part examinations, have hardly ever been seen. Besides, it is not clear what parallel forms and test–retest mean when applied to school-based assessment. Willmott & Hall's attempt at a combined parallel forms test–retest exercise using people retaking in winter is ruled out as not genuine; in any case, the study was flawed (see their p. 145). The JMB enquiry (Hewitt 1967) was advertised as an investigation of reliability and validity, but the best it could do with test–retest was to use what was really not a parallel form (other boards' examination papers) 'soon afterwards' (p. 8). The result was more an estimate of concurrent validity.

Makers of psychological tests have been more persevering. Alice Heim, for instance, has always produced parallel forms of the AH series and has also been able to offer test–retest reliabilities (Heim, Watts & Simmonds 1978). Of course, psychological tests need to be durable, whereas with odd exceptions (such as the English Language Testing Service) any one examination does not; in fact it self-destructs after it has been sat (although it could be argued that what **is** durable is the 'shell' from which a series of similar examinations is produced). Perhaps this is why boards have not thought it worth trying to press for what would clearly be an unwelcome burden on candidates and teachers. And even if agreement could be negotiated, the test–retest and parallel forms exercises could hardly be repeated often enough to provide a secure basis for generalisation. While it would be satisfying to have even two or three authentic estimates, little could be made of them. The upshot of this is that the **internal consistency** method of estimating reliability has been favoured.

The *Standards for Educational and Psychological Testing* (APA 1985) is adamant (Standard 2·6) that coefficients based on internal consistency analysis should not be interpreted as substitutes for parallel forms reliability or estimates of stability over time, unless other evidence supports that interpretation in a particular context. Coefficient alpha signifies consistent response behaviour; it has nothing to say about day-to-day variation. Answers to questions could be quite inconsistent yet the test–retest correlation could be high simply because the inconsistent responses are reproduced. Whenever test–retest and parallel forms and internal consistency estimates are available for comparison, there are usually noticeable discrepancies, as some interesting data from the Iowa Tests of Basic Skills manual demonstrates (ITBS 1986).

The study was designed in such a way as to make possible an analysis of the relative contributions of various sources of errors in measurement across tests, year grouping (grades) and schools. The following estimates were calculated:

1 parallel forms, administered a week apart;
2 internal consistency (KR-20);

3 split-half (odd and even items);
4 split-half (equivalent forms obtained by matching items).

For (3) and (4) full test reliabilities were estimated in the usual way by using the Spearman-Brown formula.

The manual notes that parallel forms are considered superior to internal consistency procedures in that all four major sources of error are taken into account – variations arising within the measurement procedure, changes in the specific sample of tasks, changes in the individual from day to day and changes in the individual's speed of work. Internal consistency procedures take only the first two sources into account, which is why they tend to produce higher estimates than those obtained from parallel forms.

The most important result of the Iowa study was a quantification of the extent to which between-days sources of error contribute to unreliability. As predicted, the parallel forms estimates were always the lowest and split-halves were always higher than parallel forms. Differences between split-half estimates obtained in the same testing session and parallel forms estimates obtained a week or more apart constituted the best evidence on the changes in pupil motivation and behaviour across several days.

The plausibility of internal consistency estimates appears to be further compromised by the deliberate efforts made to introduce variety and heterogeneity into examinations. If the principle of inclusion in an examination is to mix modalities and skill requirements and contents so that individual opportunities to respond well are enhanced, why expect internal consistency? This was a conundrum which exercised Nuttall & Willmott. They offered two escape routes, one logical one empirical. The first – inasmuch as marks are aggregated, there must be a belief that a single trait is responsible for generating answers (somewhat dubious this; the decision to aggregate is borne out of sheer tradition, and anyway a trait is just a convenient label for the multiple determinants of responses to that particular collection of questions). The second – it is a fact that the data show a good deal of internal consistency. We may not expect or even want candidates to be consistent on apparently quite diverse tasks, but they very often are. What it is that binds performance together is not known, but it could be something which involves, in a joint way, variables like motivation, examination-taking ability and perseverance.

The resolution of the conundrum lies in recognising that Cronbach's alpha is not an index of test or examination homogeneity. Certainly high internal consistency, as indicated by a high coefficient alpha, will result when a general common factor runs through the items of the test. But this does not rule out obtaining high internal consistency as measured by coefficient alpha when there is no general factor running through the test items. Since coefficient alpha is a lower bound to the proportion of total-score variance due to common factors running through the items, one can establish high values for coefficient alpha when most of the item variances are determined by several common factors. In other words, while homogeneity implies high internal consistency, high internal consistency need not imply homogeneity. Green, Lissitz & Mulaik (1977) give a practical demonstration.

Since designers of multipart, multifaceted, multimodal examinations like GCSE are not especially interested in homogeneity, either within-part and certainly not across parts, coefficient alpha can be interpreted for what it is – an internal consistency estimate of composite test reliability. This, in fact, is the sense in which Nuttall & Willmott used it. With the help of Backhouse's analysis of variance models they calculated coefficient alpha estimates for the parts of the examinations studied, and combined these into a coefficient alpha estimate for the whole, that is the overall mark distribution.

Backhouse's particular contribution was to formulate an internal consistency estimate of reliability where a choice of questions is allowed, which is still, of course, a common feature of British examinations. Using this formula, he reported (in Nuttall & Willmott, p. 113) that the estimates obtained for an assortment of GCE examinations were 'a creditable achievement', inasmuch as most values lay in the range 0·8–0·9, and 'with such selected populations it would, indeed, be surprising to obtain a reliability greater than 0·9'.

The point about selected populations is well taken. Like all correlation measures, reliability is indeed a function of the range and distributions of the variables involved. That is why there is no point in talking about **the** reliability of a test or examination, unless it is in terms of a strictly defined population. With a greater proportion of the ability distribution entering for GCSE than for GCE and CSE combined, higher reliability estimates may be expected, at least in the long run. Even so, Willmott & Nuttall note (p. 59) that unless the inconsistencies in examining (however caused) are reduced, it would not be anticipated that the likelihood of a given candidate being misgraded by a given number of grades would be decreased in any significant way.

Willmott & Nuttall reported a range of internal consistency estimates from 0·70 to 0·93 for 29 examinations scrutinised. A vexed question is how to interpret these numbers. Take a value such as 0·75, which we might regard as on the low side and therefore unsatisfactory. But that would be to jump to conclusions. Only after a coefficient has been compared to those of **equally valid** and equally practical and time-consuming alternative tests can such a judgement be made. It is worth remembering that multiple choice tests for these populations usually produce internal consistency estimates in excess of 0·90 but they only last for one hour or so. A three-hour multiple choice test, that is one lasting as long as an examination, would be very reliable indeed, and a one-hour examination would not pass muster.

It is also necessary to remember that the reliability coefficient is a correlation coefficient and, as such, is calibrated on a non-linear scale. We may think we take this into account when comparing values, but it is doubtful if we do. A correlation is also vulnerable, as we have seen, to distortion through restriction of range and, in general, through distributional quirks such as lumpiness and outliers. It is preferable to work with the standard error of measurement, which is on a linear scale, is more stable from group to group and, for the individual, is capable of direct interpretation (see below).

Mark–re-mark estimates of reliability

By having senior examiners re-mark scripts, Murphy (1978, 1982) approached the estimation of reliability by another route. While his results for 20 GCE examinations broadly bear out the Willmott–Nuttall findings and their overall judgement, he found sufficient evidence of inconsistency at the paper level for there to be concern over how individual candidates are treated. Marking unreliability is, of course, only one of the sources of variation affecting marks.

The methodology Murphy used was to select a random sample of candidates for each of a number of GCE examinations. This selection, in each case, was made after the completion of the normal marking period. The examination scripts of each of the selected candidates were prepared for re-marking by having all previous marks and examiners' comments removed from them; it has been shown that this is vital if true variations between the marking standards of different examiners are to be revealed. Once the scripts had been prepared in this way, they were then sent for re-marking to the Chief Examiner (or in one or two cases to a Senior Assistant Examiner) who had been involved in co-ordinating the normal summer marking of the examination from which the scripts were selected. These examiners were asked to mark the scripts using the same marking scheme and standards that were agreed for the marking of the June examination.

Thus, in each case, the results were based on a comparison of the marks awarded to a random selection of scripts as a result of the normal team marking procedures applied by the AEB, and marks awarded a short time after the normal marking period by the Chief Examiner for that examination. Murphy argued, quite reasonably, that the level of agreement between the marks awarded by the Chief Examiner and the marks arising from the team marking procedures that s/he has co-ordinated give an indication of the overall level of reliability of marking of each examination.

In reviewing his results, Murphy noted that the least reliably marked examinations tended to be those that place the most dependence on essay-type questions and the most reliably marked examinations tended to be those that are made up of highly structured, analytically marked questions. He felt that the differences in the style of examining technique tended to outweigh between-subject differences, and pointed to the discrepancies in correlations between the various papers for A level Biology, French and English. The three subjects where the mark–re-mark correlations were below 0·90 were, in fact, the three where there is the greatest problem of standardising the marking and Murphy recommended that steps be taken to train new examiners.

As to the meaning of these results for the individual candidate, Murphy noted the shortcomings of the correlation coefficient and mentioned various alternatives, including the standard error of measurement. The descriptive measure he favoured was the average mark change resulting from the re-mark. This he found to vary from 0·8 to 6·7 in the subjects studied. His interpretation of these figures was that examination marks in general should only be treated as approximate measures.

A full treatment of marker variability was given in chapter 5. The conclusions can be summarised as follows:

1 A script should always be marked by two people. It does not have to be more than two.
2 The correlation between the marks awarded to the same script by the same examiner on two different occasions is usually greater than that between different markers, although not by much.
3 Markers' behaviour on one kind of question is barely predictable from that on another.
4 By switching from analytical to impression marking a candidate's result is unlikely to be any more affected than if s/he were to be marked by another examiner.

Standard error of measurement

The standard error of measurement represents a measure of the net effect of all factors producing variability in candidate performance. It is an index of the variability of the scores of candidates having the same actual ability; a measure of the discrepancy, as it were, between competence and performance on the day. For about two-thirds of examinees, the scores they obtain are 'correct' to within one standard error value; for 95% the scores are in error by less than two standard errors; for more than 99%, the scores are in error by less than three standard error values.

Methods exist to calculate the standard error from the reliability estimate, however arrived at. The important thing to note is that an increase in reliability will not necessarily bring down the standard error. Willmott & Nuttall remark on the constancy of the standard error across all subjects and observe that the increase in reliability values expected from 16+ examinations is unlikely to be accompanied by significantly altered standard errors.

One good reason for calculating standard errors is that they usually vary according to ability level; in other words, the standard error of measurement reported is an average across all levels. It has not been customary in this country to calculate standard errors by ability level (it has not been customary to calculate standard errors), but there is every reason to do so with the differentiated paper arrangements for GCSE. It would be embarrassing to have to deal with a finding that the examination was less precise at one level than at others. The Iowa Tests of Basic Skills manual reports (p. 91) that the largest standard errors tend to occur in the lower ends of the ability distributions, and the smallest occur near the medians or, with some tests and year groupings, in the upper ends of the distributions.

Generalisability analysis

The fact that the various methods of estimating reliability give different readings makes interpretation awkward, even if some of the differences are systematic. They are systematic, of course, because they take account of more or less sources of error – parallel forms is sensitive to four, internal consistency to only two. Then there are the different kinds of reliability – between-marker, within-marker, within-candidate, within-teacher. It would be altogether cleaner and more satisfying if a methodology was available which took into account all identifiable sources of error simultaneously. Such an integrated methodology is available. It is called generalisability theory, although 'theory' is something of a misnomer; analysis would be better. It replaces the one-source-of-error-variance-at-a-time approach of classical theory (Swanson, Norcini & Grosso 1987) with an integrated framework and analytical routines which enable the user to assess the influences of multiple sources of error within the desired universe of inference. The greatest gain is a better conceptualisation of reliability that ties it directly to the intended use of scores.

For the candidate unreliability hurts when s/he reflects that the judgement handed down is the result of an assessment on certain tasks on a particular day by a single assessor. Generalisability analysis provides the statistical apparatus for answering the fundamental question, 'Given an individual's performance on a particular task at a particular point in time assessed by a particular assessor, how **dependable** is the inference to how that individual would have performed across all occasions, tasks, observers and settings?' To estimate dependability, an individual's performance needs to be observed on a sample of tasks, on different occasions, at different settings and with different observers. In the examinations context, different settings might mean classroom and examination hall, tasks would mean different kinds of paper; occasions would probably have to be omitted for the reason already given, although occasions could be used for school-based assessments (see Wood 1976 for just such an application). The statistical apparatus, which is just mixed model analysis of variance with the emphasis on estimating variance components rather than effects, is then used to estimate measurement error due to inconsistencies arising from one task to another, or one setting to another. The special beauty of it is that once the important sources of error have been identified, reliability levels can be forecast for alternative assessment set-ups, such as the effect of increasing the number of markers or decreasing the number of papers.

There has been a major published application of generalisability analysis to British examinations data. Johnson & Cohen (1983, 1984) applied it to one of the comparability methods, cross-moderation of scripts, and were able to say something useful about the lack of reliability of O level French as exhibited in the inability of examiners to agree on appropriate rewards, and about the best design for future cross-moderation exercises.

Discussion

Stressing the primacy of validity is a corrective to the penchant for high reliability instruments, above all multiple choice. At the same time, pleas for greater attention to validity have to be tempered by the realisation that reliability places a limit on validity. If reliability levels fall too far, the measurement procedure becomes a shambles in which the rank order of candidates changes according to which topics they answered, which examiner marked their paper, or which school they came from. The aim should be to drive for high reliability and good validity simultaneously, which defines the measurement task in a nutshell.

Sometimes, as with so-called authentic language performance tests (chapter 19), there is prima facie evidence of validity enrichment and it is necessary to work on the reliability of the scoring even if that means compromise. School-based assessment is, in principle, the source of the most valid evidence of all, but we do not know too much about its reliability. Multiple choice is undoubtedly reliable; should we try to build up its validity? Building up validity usually means more elaborate, more expensive and time-consuming exercises, and the time element, in particular, jeopardises reliability because fewer exercises can be fitted into realistic time slots. An excellent review of medical simulation exercises (patient management problems) makes the point. Validity enrichment claims could not be substantiated and reliability values were so poor that the authors (Swanson *et al.* 1987) concluded that multiple choice tests did a better job.

Examination boards which say that they care about reliability (and which board would not) have a responsibility for carrying out reliability studies, whether of the conventional kind, or using the superior methodology of generalisability analysis. It is necessary to build up a collection of empirical results to compare with the work in the early 1970s and early 1980s. Those results are now too old to be wheeled out as comforting evidence. GCSE is sufficiently different from what has gone before, in makeup and candidate populations, to require a clean sheet.

References

American Psychological Association (1985) *Standards for Educational and Psychological Testing*. Washington, DC: APA/NCME/AERA.

Cresswell M. J. (1986) Examination grades: How many should there be? *British Educational Research Journal*, **12**, 37–54.

Cresswell M. J. (1987) Describing examination performance: Grade criteria in public examinations. *Educational Studies*, **13**, 247–53.

Cresswell M. J. (1988) Combining grades from different assessments: How reliable is the result? *Educational Review*, **40**, 361–78.

Feldt L. S. & Brennan R. L. (1989) Reliability. In Linn R. L. (ed.) *Educational Measurement* (3rd edition). Washington, DC: American Council on Education/Macmillan Series on Higher Education.

Green S. B., Lissitz R. W. & Mulaik S. A. (1977) Limitations of coefficient alpha as an index of test unidimensionality. *Educational and Psychological Measurement*, **37**, 827–38.

Hartog P. & Rhodes E. C. (1936) *The Marks of Examiners*. London: Macmillan.

Heim A. W., Watts K. P. & Simmonds V. (1978) *AH2/AH3*, 2nd edition. Windsor: NFER-Nelson.

Hewitt E. A. (1967) The reliability of GCE O-level examinations in English language. *JMB OP27*. Manchester: Joint Matriculation Board.

Iowa Tests of Basic Skills (1986) *Manual for School Administrators: Levels 5–14*. Chicago, IL: Riverside Press.

Johnson S. & Cohen L. (1983) *Investigating Grade Comparability through Cross-Moderation*. London: Schools Council.

Johnson S. & Cohen L. (1984) Cross-moderation: A useful comparative technique. *British Educational Research Journal*, **10**, 89–97.

Joint Matriculation Board (1983) *Problems of the GCE A-level Grading Scheme*. Manchester: JMB.

Mitchelmore M. C. (1981) Reporting student achievement: How many grades? *British Journal of Educational Psychology*, **51**, 218–27.

Murphy R. J. L. (1978) Reliability of marking in eight GCE examinations. *British Journal of Educational Psychology*, **48**, 196–200.

Murphy R. J. L. (1982) A further report of investigations into the reliability of marking of GCE examinations. *British Journal of Educational Psychology*, **52**, 58–63.

Nuttall D. L. & Willmott A. S. (1972) *British Examinations: Techniques of Analysis*. Slough: NFER Publishing Co.

Pilliner A. E. G. (1969) Estimation of number of grades to be awarded in one examination by consideration of its reliability coefficient. Internal research paper. Edinburgh: Godfrey Thomson Unit.

Schools Council (1980) *Focus on Examinations, No 5*. London: Schools Council.

Skurnik L. S. & Nuttall D. L. (1968) Describing the reliability of examinations. *The Statistician*, **18**, 119–28.

Swanson D. B., Norcini J. J. & Grosso L. J. (1987) Assessment of clinical competence: Written and computer-based simulations. *Assessment and Education in Higher Education*, **12**, 220–46.

University of Cambridge Local Examinations Syndicate (1976) *School Examinations and Their Function*. Cambridge: UCLES.

Willmott A. S. & Hall C. G. W. (1975) *O-level Examined: The Effects of Question Choice*. London: Schools Council.

Willmott A. S. & Nuttall D. L. (1975) *The Reliability of Examinations at 16+*. London: Macmillan.

Wood R. (1976) Halo and other effects in teacher assessments. *Durham Research Review*, **7**, 1120–6.

12 Validity and validation

Validity is a huge topic, witness Messick's 90-page chapter in the 3rd edition of *Educational Measurement* (Messick 1989). Rather than paraphrase Messick, this chapter concentrates on what is actually an underdiscussed area of validity – the British examination boards' response to it. In addition, the opportunity is taken to present an example of the multitrait–multimethod paradigm, a favourite tool of validation analysts.

The 30-year old idea of three types of validity, separate but equal, is an idea whose time has gone. Most validity theorists have been saying that content and criterion validities are no more than strands within a cable of validity argument. A favourable answer to one or two questions can fully support a test only when no one cares enough to raise further questions.

Cronbach (1988) has to be listened to, for the 30-year-old idea is his idea. It was in work with Meehl, first in 1954 on the APA committee, which produced the original 'Technical Recommendations', and then in a 1955 paper (Cronbach & Meehl 1955) that the four categories of validity – content, concurrent, construct and predictive – first surfaced. Concurrent and predictive are usually combined into criterion-related validity, giving rise to the three 'types' of validity, called by Guion (1980), in the churchy language which this topic seems to attract, the **trinitarian** view.

While it is still possible to say that in the house of validity there are many mansions, the hierarchs (Linn 1980; Guion 1980; Landy 1986; Anastasi 1986; Cronbach 1988; Messick 1989) are warning that excessive devotion to one of the three types is mistaken. As Guion puts it, it is not the case that there are these various roads to psychometric salvation and any one will do. Messick (p. 131) stresses that validity is actually a unitary concept. It always refers to the degree to which empirical evidence and theoretical rationales support the adequacy and appropriateness of interpretations and actions based on test scores. Cronbach, who did much to convey the notion that there is no such thing as **the** validity of a test, rather it is an interpretation from test scores which has to be validated

(Cronbach 1971), now prefers to talk of validity argument instead of validation research. Landy, along the same lines, prefers to think of validation as hypothesis testing:

> People who do well on test X will do well on activity Y, or Y = F(X). In null form, the hypothesis would assert that there is no relationship between test performance and activity performance. (p. 1186)

> There are not different types of validity... The question is what form of evidence the investigator will choose to test that hypothesis. (p. 1188)

For those, like examining boards, who have barely come to terms with the trinitarian view, in fact have hardly genuflected to any one of the Trinity, the revisionism which is abroad will be well nigh incomprehensible. All the more reason to ask the question 'What does validity (and validation) mean in the context of British examinations?' The situation with regard to aptitude tests is considered in chapter 17.

Validity is ultimately more important than reliability but any attempt at validation depends crucially on the reliability of the observations. If these cannot be trusted, then a misleading judgement concerning validity is likely to be reached. That must be why validity has been so much less explicated than reliability. After Hartog & Rhodes, 40 years passed before there was a published study of validity in British examinations, and then it was content validity only (Willmott & Hall 1975). Hoste (1980, 1982) tried to do justice to construct validity (chapter 15) but without producing anything substantial. What activity there has been has occurred in the predictive validity sector, perversely enough the least interesting and meaningful sector. It is, of course, a facile exercise to correlate O and A level grades, or A grades and degree class; what the results mean is quite another matter. And that is the point. Predictive validity studies are easiest to do (even if the reliabilities of predictor and criterion, especially criterion, are unknown), followed by certain kinds of reliability studies, and lastly content and above all, construct validity studies. That is why validity is so much less explicated, and understood, than reliability.

If an examining board were to be asked point blank about the validities of its offerings or, more to the point, what steps it takes to validate the grades it awards, what might it say?

If it knew the term **curricular validity**, it might be inclined to appeal to that, and perhaps nothing else. Curricular validity, a term introduced by McClung (1978), refers to the correspondence between what the examination assesses and the objectives of instruction. Since the connecting rod between the two is the syllabus, and schools and teachers are supposed to follow the syllabus, and the board is supposed to set questions on it, curricular validity ought to be assured. Specimen and past papers tighten the coupling; syllabus sampling and question spotting loosen it. The move towards unpacking syllabuses, which came on the back of the behavioural objectives movement, has certainly conduced to improved curricular validity. In Holland, where apparently syllabuses may occupy less than one side of a sheet of paper (Maas-de Brouwer 1986), and where schools are obliged to interpret freely the little they see, which was the situation in the UK pre-1970 or so, there must be doubts (let us put it no higher than that) about the curricular validity of any one centralised examination.

McClung also introduced the notion of **instructional validity** which he defined as the correspondence between what a test demands and what the instruction preceding it provided. Although it can be virtuous by dint of issuing clear instructions and guidelines to schools, there is not a lot more an examining board can do about instructional validity. It is for schools to provide students with instruction appropriate to the test or examination. Disputes about instructional validity have arisen in the USA where schools have been accused of not providing instruction necessary to enable students to meet statewide minimum competency requirements (*Debra P.* vs. *Turlington* 1981). Obviously, the concept of adequacy of preparation is central. Yalow & Popham (1983) maintain that it is not to do with validity at all, and that the measurement community is almost totally unfamiliar with the nature of how to establish whether preparation is adequate, about which there is no argument.

Content validity, by contrast, is a matter for the board and the board alone. It is a function of the success with which the board translates what the syllabus says into an operational examination. If the content is not validly selected, then score interpretations are liable to distortion. It might be thought that a board could rest its case fairly and squarely on content validity, without reference to any other validity arguments. But, as noted elsewhere (chapter 7), that can never be enough. The board might be like the AEB, which sets a basic skills test (Skillcheck) and therefore has a duty to explain what it means by 'basic skills', and to validate their measurement. Any board (which means all boards) which certificates something called 'Practical' has a construct validation obligation. Then there are all the varieties of, say, mathematics arising from modularised, pick-and-mix arrangements. Is this mathematics different from that mathematics, and so forth? Content validity, in the sense of fidelity to a blueprint, is neither here nor there when it comes to answering questions of meaning. Worrying about whether content validity is a property of test forms or of person responses (as it ought to be if validity is truly a unitary concept – see Messick, p. 41) is of little consequence when content validity only goes so far.

Fidelity to the blueprint, or content–objectives grid, was what the Schools Council researchers (Willmott & Hall) decided to check, and they did what they could in the circumstances, scrutinising a broad range of CSE and GCE examinations. There are essentially mechanical methods of ensuring tight item–objective congruence, based on the item sampling paradigm (see chapter 1), but these have never found favour in Britain. As a general rule, it can be said that the less information is provided about tests or examinations the greater the doubts about content validity, and about validity in general. In the discussion at the end of chapter 1 it was noted how, in effect, test constructors cover their tracks so well (without necessarily meaning to) that other parties would experience great difficulty trying to reproduce what they came up with. In this regard, Cronbach's (1971) suggestion that the same blueprint be interpreted by two independent teams, who then compare the tests or examinations they produce, is worthy of serious consideration. An instance where something like this was done is reported in chapter 1.

Where the only interest is in the relationship between a test or examination and an external criterion, content validity could be seen as strictly irrelevant. If test or examination results are used pragmatically to make predictions, then it is the ones that 'work' best which will be preferred. It is possible to imagine a perverse experiment in which the cells of grids are swapped around and an examination produced which is a distortion of what should have been, and yet for the results to predict as well (or as poorly) as the genuine article. It is fair to assume that a good number of the examinations which appear in Britain are not at all what they ought to be in content validity terms. The saving grace is that, leaving aside any aptitude tests they produce, the examining boards do not see themselves in the business of maximising prediction of results further down the educational road.

In fact, content validity has not been abandoned in prediction work. Once judges in the US courts fastened on to the notion of content validity, employers who had used tests as the basis for hiring people took a fearful hammering from interlocutors who insisted that they show 'point-to-point correspondence' between the contents of the test, item by item, and the contents of the job, task by task (Wigdor 1982). No longer could Chicago policemen or Pittsburgh firemen be rated for promotion on the basis of a writing test alone. Attempts in Britain to show that, for instance, the point-to-point correspondence between O level English Language (and, naturally, it depends which English Language) and the job requirements for Administrative Assistant in the Civil Service is too weak to be taken seriously, have so far failed to impress the courts and industrial tribunals (Wood 1987). Experts for the Civil Service have clung to the highly dubious validity argument that O level English Language and O levels generally tap, in sufficient measure, into a construct or constructs which are sufficiently relevant to what the most junior level in the Civil Service needs now, **and** in the future, for it to be worth persisting with these O levels as screening devices. No supporting data other than plain correlations over time have ever been brought forward. That such correlations lend themselves to opportunism and are always subject to quite severe methodological limitations, seldom seems to be realised.

The appropriate methodology for investigating construct validity is the multitrait–multimethod paradigm, invented by Campbell & Fiske (1959), and used, for instance, by Hoste (chapter 15) and Marsh & Ireland, de Glopper and Lehmann (chapter 5). The idea is that measures of the same trait by different methods should correlate more highly than measures of different traits by the same method. **Convergent validity** is demonstrated when a measure of a single trait correlates at a low level with a conceptually different trait measured via a similar method. But, as Cronbach (1988) notes, the Campbell–Fiske correlational check is not subtle. A substantial correlation of trait 1 with trait 2 does not make the 1–2 distinction untenable; rather the correlation puts the advocate under pressure to create conditions under which the variables pull apart. This is what happened to Hoste when he hoped that 'theory' and 'practice' would separate. It is the same with different aspects of writing which cannot be pulled apart. High correlations are the bugbear of construct analysts (nor are low correlations open and shut; unreliability may be to blame). Just because two components of an examination correlate highly is no reason to drop one or the other. Recall Cronbach's neat trick (chapter 4) of calculating correlations at higher levels of aggregation, such as at school or class level, before jumping to that sort of conclusion, if ever. It may be that the correlation of school means for the two components is quite different, indicating that the extent to which schools concentrate on one component or the other is liable to be uneven, in which case remedial work is indicated.

The matter of **predictive validity** is something the examining boards really ought not to be concerned with. Examinations index achievement over a specified period of time and, as such, are essentially backward looking. That others take the results and attempt to use them for forward looking predictive purposes is strictly not the boards' affair. There are, in any case, structural problems with any predictive study. The first is the truncation of the joint distribution of predictor and criterion (restriction of range) brought about by the attrition of individuals at the selection thresholds (O to A level, A level to university and so on). Such attrition invariably results in lower estimates of the predictor–criterion correlation than would otherwise occur if the population had remained intact. The second is the unreliability of the criterion, the extent of which is usually unknown; who knows anything about the reliability of degree awards? You know where you stand with an unreliable test (you need a better test); when the criterion is unreliable, the test may or may not be valid and there is no way to tell until a better criterion is found (Green 1981). The same point applies to the use of other tests for validating (concurrent validity); sometimes even less is known about such tests than the one being validated. Neither of these dangers is sufficiently appreciated.

Despite all this, the question of the predictive power of O and A levels has proved a seductive topic for statistical dilettantes. Foy & Waller (1987) provide a more or less up-to-date review. Their own work, based in pharmacy, can be largely discounted. Studying the relationships between 31 variables with only 80 individuals is unwise, to say the least. It is evident from the Foy & Waller paper that the results reported are such a mixed bag that the only way to evaluate the research is to examine closely the size and composition of the samples and the range of scores on the predictor (O and A level) and criterion variables (first- and second-year undergraduate performance and degree class). The only solid finding seems to be that A levels correlate particularly well with early parts of the course, weakening afterwards, but that is really only an empirical statement of the obvious proposition that the closer the temporal proximity of observations, the higher the correlation between them. Foy & Waller are certainly not entitled to this conclusion (p. 697):

> The above study lends little support to those who would downgrade the importance of A levels and rely instead on aptitude and intelligence tests, interviews, personality traits and headteachers' reports.

The examining boards have been lucky not to have been engaged in validity argument. Unlike reliability, validity does not lend itself to sensational reporting. Nevertheless, the extent of the boards' neglect of validity is plain to see once attention is focused. Whenever boards make claims that they are measuring the ability to make clear reasoned judgements, or the ability to form conclusions (both examples from IGCSE Economics), they have a responsibility to at least attempt a validation of the measures. The failure to validate Bloom's *Taxonomy*, from which so many of these abilities have been derived, is instructive, but on no account should it be used as an excuse for inaction. The boards know so little about what they are assessing that if, for instance, it were to be said that teachers assess ability (intelligence) rather than achievement, the boards would be in no position to defend themselves.

Validation work is unglamorous and needs to be painstaking but has to be done. As long as examination boards make claims that they are assessing this or that ability or skill, they are vulnerable to challenge from disgruntled individuals. Following Hoste, there is plenty of scope for construct validation work using the preferred multitrait–multimethod methodology but remembering that it is not subtle. Examinations use several methods and are certainly trying to measure several constructs, whether the boards realise it or not. There is a good example in the literature which demonstrates rather neatly the sort of validity study which could be done. It is also a good example of how to assimilate and then extend a line of previous research.

An example of a validity study

Taking as his point of departure the adequacy of objective spelling tests as measures of spelling ability, Croft (1982) set out to investigate the validity of spelling tests, or rather to ascertain the most valid measure of spelling ability. Croft starts by acknowledging that the relationship between the quality of spelling in written language, and performance on a test of spelling is not immediately obvious, especially when that test is in a multiple choice format. Here the task is one of **recognition** (of a mistake), as opposed to the **production** of correct spelling. This suggests that the criterion ought to be an estimate of spelling performance in a sample of writing, which in fact is what Croft opted for.

Three tests with differing formats were constructed. Test A was a proofreading/correction test in which the respondents were required to read three short paragraphs, identify misspelt words and spell them correctly. Credit was given when the error was rewritten in its correct form, or when the lines containing no errors were identified as correct. Test B followed a multiple choice/cloze format, the respondents being required to complete a short sentence by choosing the correctly spelt word from five alternatives. The emphasis was different from that of the typical multiple choice test in that the respondents were required to recognise a correctly spelt word and not an incorrect one, or a 'no mistakes' option. Test C was an example of a traditional dictated word test following the word–sentence–word format.

Because the reliabilities of the tests and the language samples were as low as 0·78, it was necessary to correct the correlation estimates for attenuation. The correct estimates came out as follows:

Test A 0·80
Test B 0·74
Test C 0·79

In each case, the estimate is the median for four language samples (the criterion). The intercorrelations between A, B and C were:

$$r_{AB} = 0{\cdot}79$$
$$r_{AC} = 0{\cdot}82$$
$$r_{BC} = 0{\cdot}84$$

Evidently this was not a full-blown multitrait–multimethod analysis; rather a monotrait–multimethod analysis. The results show that the tests emphasising production or recall skills have a more positive relationship with spelling in written language than the test emphasising recognition skills. If recall and recognition are viewed as differing processes, which they surely are, it follows that the three tests were probably measuring different aspects of spelling. Perhaps it was a multitrait analysis after all. However, the high correlation between the tests indicates, thought Croft, that the process being tapped is probably secondary to knowing how to spell a particular word.

Croft felt able to report that, despite methodological differences, broad agreement existed between the results of his study and previous studies going back to 1936. He concluded that spelling tests emphasising the production of correct spelling are a more valid measure of the ability to recognise correctly (or incorrectly) spelt words. He was thus reproducing the general objection to multiple choice testing and drawing attention to its validation weakness. He was also able to demonstrate that a proof-reading and correction test was superior, albeit marginally, to the traditional dictated word test which is the preferred test of production skills in spelling. Croft's may seem a rather modest study but this is precisely how advances in instrumentation are made.

Psychological tests and validity

With psychological tests the emphasis is rather more on construct validity than content validity because there are usually implicit construct claims made in the name of the test and, ipso facto, a great deal more arbitrariness about content. Also predictive validity is of more interest and value than is the case with examinations.

The research literature on validity with respect to psychological tests is so voluminous that it is impossible to summarise except in a glib way. Every other issue of the journal *Educational and Psychological Measurement* has a thick section devoted to validity studies. No one study can illustrate all the aspects of validity argument, but Meier's study of 'burnout' is quite illuminating and it does have the merit of demonstrating a proper multitrait–multimethod analysis. One major difference from the spelling exercise is that the constructs involved are altogether more diffuse (unless spelling is a good deal more complicated than we imagined).

Meier (1984) defined 'burnout' as a state of lowered expectation for

Multitrait–multimethod correlation matrix[a]

	(*a*) Multi-point			(*b*) True–False			(*c*) Self-ratings		
Method	1	2	3	1	2	3	1	2	3
(*a*) Multi-point									
1 Burnout (MBI)	(88)								
2 Depression (CCD)	57	(88)							
3 Order (CPS-O)	−18	−13	(87)						
(*b*) True–false									
1 Burnout (MBA)	<u>61</u>	65	−09	(76)					
2 Depression (MMPI)	57	67	−13	69	(80)				
3 Order (PRF-O)	−17	−17	74	−14	−23	(86)			
(*c*) Simple self-ratings									
1 Burnout	<u>65</u>	53	−14	<u>63</u>	59	−12	(73)		
2 Depression	55	62	−12	54	63	−13	60	(57)	
3 Order	−14	−23	70	−12	−20	73	−10	−13	(60)

[a] Decimal points have been omitted.

obtaining valued work reinforcement. He sought to distinguish it from 'depression' which was defined rather similarly as what happens when individuals experience a low rate of positive reinforcement. So as to get a measure of discriminant validity, Meier introduced 'orderliness', a trait which assesses the need for routine, neatness, cautiousness and organisation. There is no reason to suppose that orderliness will relate to burnout and depression. Including contrast variables like this is a necessary step in multitrait–multimethod analyses. Three methods were used: multipoint scales, true–false scales and simple self-ratings. With three methods and three traits, all the data needed are shown in the table (Meier's table 1).

Convergent validity is demonstrated when different measures of the same trait correlate highly. Three convergent validity coefficients for burnout (underlined in the table) are displayed in the table. These high correlations, uncorrected for reliability, the estimates of which are shown in brackets, indicate strong convergent validity in the measures of burnout.

For evidence of discriminant validity, each validity coefficient should exceed the correlations in the corresponding row and column in its multitrait–multimethod block; in other words, each validity coefficient should be higher than the correlations between that trait and any other trait having methods in common with those assessed in the convergent validity coefficient. There are 12 such comparisons, of which 11 meet the criterion, the sole exception being the correlation between the MBA and the CCD (0·65), which exceeds the correlation between the MBI and the MBA (0·61).

The second discriminant criterion states that each validity coefficient should be higher than the correlation between that variable and different traits which employ the same method. Again there were 12 possible comparisons, with 10 of 12 meeting the criterion. The exceptions were that the correlation between the MBA and the MMPI-D (0·69) exceeds the correlation between the MBA and MBI (0·61) and between the MBA and burnout self-rating (0·65).

The third, and most stringent, criterion for evidence of discriminant validity is that the same pattern of trait interrelationships can be demonstrated. This is checked by examining the rank order of correlations within the monomethod and multitrait–multimethod triangles. Thus, in the nine triangles found in the matrix, six of the rankings were identical, with the correlation between burnout and depression the highest, followed by the depression–order correlation and the burnout–order correlation. In two of the triangles the burnout–order correlation exceeds the depression–order correlation and in one triangle they are equal.

Although claiming strong support for the convergent validity of burnout, Meier was obliged to acknowledge that measures of burnout correlated highly with depression, thereby weakening support for burnout's discriminant validity. Considerable overlap exists between burnout and depression measures despite the ability of the burnout measures to largely meet Campbell & Fiske's requirements for construct validity. In addition, the table shows that burnout meets roughly the same number of validity and reliability criteria as do the constructs of order and depression. Meier takes this to mean that to the extent that depression and order have gained acceptance as constructs, burnout appears to merit similar treatment.

In discussing the limitations of his study, Meier makes an important point which has general application. Campbell & Fiske's approach to construct validity centres on **tests** of constructs. Thus, improved measures of burnout and depression could very well result in improved convergent and discriminant validity. This was probably what Hoste was struggling with in trying to separate 'theory' and 'practice', and what made Marsh & Ireland (chapter 5) despair when their markers were only able to distinguish 'mechanics'.

References

Anastasi A. (1986) Evolving concepts of test validation. *Annual Review of Psychology*, **37**, 1–15.

Campbell D. T. & Fiske D. W. (1959) Convergent and discriminant validity in the multitrait–multimethod matrix. *Psychological Bulletin*, **56**, 81–105.

Croft A. C. (1982) Do spelling tests measure the ability to spell? *Educational and Psychological Measurement*, **42**, 716–23.

Cronbach L. J. (1971) Test validation. In Thorndike R. L. (ed.) *Educational Measurement* (2nd edition). Washington DC: American Council on Education.

Cronbach L. J. (1988) Five perspectives on validity argument. In Wainer H. & Braun H. (eds.) *Test Validity*. Hillsdale, NJ: Lawrence Erlbaum.

Cronbach L. J. & Meehl P. G. (1955) Construct validity in psychological tests. *Psychological Bulletin*, **52**, 281–302.

Debra P. vs. Turlington (1981) 644 F.2nd 397 (5th Cir.)

Foy J. M. & Waller D. M. (1987) Using British school examinations as a predictor of university performance in a pharmacy course: A correlative study. *Higher Education*, **16**, 691–8.

Green B. F. (1981) A primer of testing. *American Psychologist*, **36**, 1001–11.

Guion R. M. (1980) Content validity – the source of my discontent. *Applied Psychology*, **11**, 385–98.

Hoste R. (1980) The construct validity of some CSE biology examinations: The evidence from multitrait–multimethod matrices. *Journal of Biological Education*, **14**, 41–8.

Hoste R. (1982) The construct validity of some CSE biology examinations: The evidence from factor analysis. *British Educational Research Journal*, **8**, 31–42.

Landy F. J. (1986) Stamp collecting versus science: Validation as hypothesis testing. *American Psychologist*, **41**, 1183–92.

Linn R. L. (1980) Issues of validity for criterion-referenced measures. *Applied Psychological Measurement*, **4**, 547–62.

McClung M. S. (1978) Are competency testing programs fair? Legal? In the *Proceedings of the National Conference on Minimum Competency Testing*. Portland, OR: Clearing House for Applied Performance Testing.

Maas-de Brouwer T. A. (1986) The use of reporting and assessment data with regard to the Dutch final examinations. *Studies in Educational Evaluation*, **12**, 351–4.

Meier S. T. (1984) The construct validity of burnout. *Journal of Occupational Psychology*, **57**, 211–20.

Messick S. (1989) Validity. In Linn R. L. (ed.) *Educational Measurement* (3rd edition). Washington, DC: American Council on Education/Macmillan Series on Higher Education.

Wigdor A. K. (1982) Psychological testing and the law of employment discrimination. In Wigdor A. K. & Garner W. R. (eds.) *Ability Testing: Uses, Consequences and Controversies*. Part II. Washington, DC: National Academy Press.

Willmott A. S. & Hall C. G. W. (1975) *O-level Examined: The Effects of Question Choice*. London: Schools Council.

Wood R. (1987) Discrimination through assessment with special reference to ethnic minorities. Report to the Manpower Services Commission.

Yalow E. S. & Popham W. J. (1983) Content validity at the crossroads. *Educational Researcher*, October, 10–14, also 21.

13 Differentiation

At the present time the research on differentiation in the GCSE context resides almost wholly in the reports of the SEC project on Novel Examinations at 16+ (Good & Cresswell 1988*a*). Rather than evaluate that work in detail, this chapter concentrates on dealing with the underlying issues, and also introduces some testing procedures used in the USA which are certainly appropriate for producing differentiation.

When the Schools Council report on the 16+ feasibility studies distinguished between **grade–range** systems of differentiation and **content–method** systems (Schools Council 1975, p. 20), it was, in effect, positing two distinct rationales for differentiation. In the first, achievement at 16+ is seen as quantitative in character; individuals are strung out on some single dimension and for those who have more of it (or less of it) than others, extra 'harder' (or 'easier') papers are needed to measure what they have accurately. In this realisation, achievement is treated as interchangeable with ability, or even intelligence, and what has been called the 'strength' model of attributes is taken to apply. Along with this goes the stronger notion of ability as essentially fixed; a notion which is necessary to justify allocating individuals to different papers, something Radnor (1988), among others, has noticed.

The second rationale for differentiation is quite different, because achievement is now seen as essentially qualitative in character, meaning that it varies in kind, not in extent. It is acknowledged that people will vary in their interests and skills (without specifying which comes first) and that continuous interaction between the two will lead to diversity. This implies a multi-dimensional view of achievement in which some skills and areas of study are strongly emphasised and others are barely exercised.

All that we know about the achievement texture of young people (which is not much) suggests that the second view of achievement conveys the way things are for most 16 year olds, even for those who appear to be uniformly excellent or dull. For the unidimensional view of achievement to be more plausible, a curriculum would need to be **developmentally** driven, and the GCSE curriculum does not appear to be so, nor were GCE and CSE before it.

By developmentally driven is meant the enterprise of building up an integrated structure of knowledge and skills over time. If we distinguish between 'experts' and 'novices', it is the expert who, over years of learning practice and application, has built up such integrated structures, while the novice possesses knowledge which is varied, incomplete and incorporates a number of misconceptions (Glaser & Bassok 1989). Lesgold *et al.* (1988) provide a particularly interesting application. Without a developmentally aware instructional regime, the syllabus becomes one huge cafeteria in which students (and their teachers) are given carte blanche to pick and mix. With fragmentation dominant, instead of progression, the result is an achievement texture which is bitty and incoherent. Writing of the Assessment of Performance Unit (APU) science surveys, Murphy (1988) observed that they 'indicate that most pupils possess fragmentary knowledge which is only usable in narrow context and content-specific instances...Pupils apply the simplest of strategies across investigations irrespective of the solutions required'. But then pupils are just that, novices; they have to be weaned off what di Sessa (1988) has called the 'knowledge in pieces' view of learning. What needs developing are the executive skills and deep conceptual understanding which characterise the expert.

Once the bitty and undeveloped nature of achievement is assumed, various findings become quite explicable. Radnor (pp. 42–3) comments on the low correlations between common and extension papers and wonders how the examination is graded if people do better on the extension paper but cannot benefit because of a hurdle on the common paper. The fact is that people can do better on a 'harder' paper because it is not harder for them (this is implicitly recognised in the Southern Examining Group's decision to award the better of the two grades for those who take common and extension papers; see Owen 1988). The breakdown of the notion of hardness, a group concept, when applied to individuals appears to dash hopes of building inclines of difficulty, that is to say stepping questions and papers so as to produce differentiation in a common papers format. The SEC project described some of the problems of arranging the parts of a question in order of difficulty. These include the questions having a natural order which does not correspond to the (group-defined) facility order; the same order of difficulty not holding for all candidates (some find recall easy, some prefer other types of question); and the difficulty of understanding examiners' cues in essay questions.

Practising grade limitation implies a 'strength' model of achievement but there are no grounds for supposing that for 16 year olds this model conforms at all. Testing for achievement is not at all the same as testing for intelligence where you can always get a distribution on one dimension. What in fact happens is that, even when grade limitation is applied, the nature of achievement is such that specialisation will occur and something which is more appropriate to the 'content–method' system emerges. The problem with the content–method system is that it is merely a vehicle for accommodating pick-and-mix arrangements on a large scale. With achievement fragmented rather than progressively calibrated, there arises the vexatious problem of establishing parity of esteem and accreditation for all the various offerings, something the MEG project on grading modular systems will have to address.

It is instructive to relate the principles and practices of **graded assessment** to differentiation. It could well be argued that graded assessment is actually the appropriate method of doing what differentiation is supposed to do – cater for individuals progressing at different rates (see, for instance, Radnor, pp. 43–4). What graded assessment does is to do the sorting over an extended period of time. Moreover, by emphasising progression and acknowledging the variation in developmental timetables, it actually helps to promote mastery, and therefore has the effect of stringing people out on what can be more obviously treated as a unidimensional continuum. Graded assessment also removes the need for grade limitation, which is such a bothersome issue. Instead of someone deciding whether an individual tries something corresponding to grades C–G instead of, say, A–E, that individual waits until ready to try C–G, and if successful, that is gains C or D, goes on to try A–E, or it might be A–C, except of course that the assessments would not be represented in those terms.

Multilevel testing

In the United states, differentiation is implemented through the concept of **multilevel testing**, as for instance by the Iowa Tests of Basic Skills programme, and by two-stage testing, as for instance by the National Council of Medical Examiners in Philadelphia (this last application is very recent). Both assume achievement to be unidimensional in character. Neither is likely to be readily applicable to the British situation, although an adapted form of two-stage testing could be implemented if the administrative consequences could be handled.

In multilevel testing, candidates are directed to where out of a continuous run of questions (always multiple choice) they should start to work, and where they should cease. Allocation is invariably on a grade basis, thus all grade 7s may be asked to start at item 110 and continue to item 180. However, 'out of grade' testing is permitted and so a clever grade 7 might be invited to start at item 150 and work to item 225.

Individual estimates of achievement are arrived at by entering all the item responses, in what is an incomplete data matrix, into a large-scale latent trait estimation program such as LOGIST, and solving simultaneously for individual values. Naturally, use of such programs is predicated on achievement being a unidimensional construct, always an arguable supposition.

Multilevel testing has some of the features of graded assessment in that it is progressive, but otherwise it suffers from being too age-bound (although that could be modified), and too multiple choice bound. It also depends on a strict incline of difficulty holding up in practice. Graded assessment can do the same job without needing to collect the whole sequence of assessments between two covers.

Two-stage testing

Two-stage testing works by assigning or routing individuals to a second test on the basis of their performance on a first test (see, for example, de Gruitjer 1980). It therefore has the advantage that individuals settle their own fate by virtue of their performance alone. To work in the GCSE context the first paper would need to be marked very quickly so that in the following week, say, it would be possible to assign the appropriate second paper to candidates who would have been instructed to attend a session in any case. Such an arrangement presupposes two second papers, one 'easy' and one 'hard', but it might be feasible to have only a 'harder' paper, in which case some means would have to be found of telling the relevant proportion of candidates not to attend.

The objection to this scheme would be that candidates would not know which second paper to study for, or whether to study for a second paper at all. The answer to this is that they should study the whole syllabus, the very advice which has generally been ignored in favour of syllabus sampling or specialisation. What two-stage testing might be able to do is to fulfil more closely the injunction to give candidates the opportunity to demonstrate what they 'know, understand and can do'. If there were two second papers, these could be used to give candidates, strong and weak, the chance to deliver more than they were able to do in the first paper. That, of course, triggers the objection that on the first paper they were being judged, rather conclusively, on insufficient evidence of positive achievement. To the extent that the first paper is usually conceptualised as being as short as measurement desiderata allow, this objection would become more serious. However, there is no reason why a first paper, or perhaps a battery of two or three papers, should not be moderately long in duration, although the more papers there are the harder it will be to mark them quickly and come up with a decision rule for assigning candidates at stage two.

Two-stage testing has some appeal and is not automatically ruled out for application in British examining conditions. However, it is a system for examining in more or less one fell swoop. It is most suitable for selecting a smallish number from a large number of candidates presenting themselves at one particular time, such as doctors in hospital training. Where school students are concerned, there seems no good reason why they should not be spared assignments or rejection and instead graduate over time, starting from what would amount to the lower-level second paper and perhaps missing out the first paper which would in any case need to be redesigned if it were to be used as an intermediate assessment.

Differentiation within papers

The problem of creating inclines of difficulty, and therefore of stepping questions and parts of questions, has already been remarked on. This is likely to be a permanent problem as long as students' achievement textures are so heterogeneous and the nature of what they know so incoherent. The alternative to stepping is differentiation by outcome, where the most common applications are in essay-type questions and coursework. Some ULSEB work (Stobart 1988) claims that essay writing in itself requires higher level skills and does not provide the intended 'neutral stimulus'. For many candidates this format inhibits rather than encourages positive achievement, a theme developed by Wood & Power (1987); also Wood (1976), who wrote of a deadlock between examiners, candidates and teachers (see chapters 3 and 5).

The ULSEB study also looked at the capacity of coursework to supply differentiation. The conclusion from studying nine subjects was that coursework was neither an easy source of marks nor a poor discriminator (as commonly supposed). In addition, coursework discriminated well in most subjects, offering a wider range of marks than the examination papers. These findings need corroboration, but for the time being they present an interesting corrective to conventional wisdom. It may be that coursework assessment, being over an extended period, works more like graded assessment and so produces a stringing out effect; it may also constrain achievement to be more homogeneous than is the case with examinations, which will also enhance differentiation. The other significant point about coursework is that of all techniques it is the one most likely to elicit 'positive achievement', perhaps too much so if the stories about students (and teachers) spending far too long on assignments are well founded. An SEC pamphlet is quite explicit on this – 'teachers will not only be able to match students to assignments but also to select optimum performances which best illustrate positive achievement' (SEC 1986, p. 2).

Differentiation between papers

The ULSEB paper suggests that there may be a tension between discrimination and differentiation. The DES seems not to have been aware of it. Paragraph 16 of the *General Criteria* (DES 1985) states that 'All examinations must be designed in such a way as to ensure proper discrimination so that candidates across the ability range are given opportunities to demonstrate their knowledge, ability and achievements...'. It is the 'so that' which is puzzling. The statement is obviously not referring to discrimination in the technical sense. It must mean that discrimination will be built in a priori, by sorting candidates before they even sit papers. Be that as it may, the ULSEB argument is that if targeting of questions is done well, and if positive achievement is elicited (both big 'ifs') then the result should be higher mark levels, especially for those who are bracketed as low achievers. Such a result would tend to weaken discrimination (in the technical sense), especially if the 'tail' of the distribution is 'rolled up'. The ULSEB paper reports that on easier papers offering lower grades the average marks were often low, and that it is these low marks which are providing the necessary 'good spread' of marks, and therefore maintaining discrimination.

Question targeting presents a big challenge to examiners who have been accustomed to a 'suck it and see' approach to question setting, and who have always had the comfort of knowing that statistical manipulation was there as a long stop. Partington (1988), himself a moderator, argues that the current moderation process sets out usually to ascertain that questions are *acceptable* (his italics). Moderators tend not to grapple with the principles of what makes a question hard or easy. At the moment, he says, we have no answer to the question, 'What are the unique linguistic characteristics of a test item which is targeted on candidates (for example) of C grade or better?'

Evidently, the tension between differentiation and discrimination, if there really is one, hangs on what positive achievement turns out to be. At present no one knows what the relationship will be between **optimum** performance and typical, or restricted, performance. It is instructive to think of what the result of applying mastery learning strategies might be. The purpose of such strategies is to get most individuals to the point of mastery, which is to say, to the point of displaying positive achievement (how do we indicate degrees of this?). If the strategy is successful then, except for the few stragglers, there is on the face of it no discrimination. (The flaw with this argument, of course, is that mastery learning thresholds tell you nothing about what more those above the threshold can do.)

Grade limitation

By its very name, the practice of **grade limitation** is objectionable in that it appears to place a limit on the demonstration of achievement, which does not sit well with the emphasis on positive achievement. If the intention behind it is that 'candidates should be examined at a level in which they can demonstrate success' (Tattersall 1983, p. 43), then a more felicitous term would be desirable. If, on the other hand, grade limitation is a device for expressing a belief in the fixity of ability, and therefore of achievement, then positive achievement can only be some kind of window-dressing. At best it could be seen as the upper bound of some slight oscillation around a fixed point.

Grade limitation is bothersome, not only because it turns students and their teachers into gamblers, but because it stores up all sorts of grading problems for examiners. It could be argued that these shortcomings are so serious that grade limitation really ought to be viewed as a last resort.

Perhaps the most serious difficulties occur with those schemes which ask candidates (and/or their teachers) to choose between obtaining something in the grade range of A–E + ungraded, and something in the range C–G. Presumably the ungraded is there to put off individuals who might fancy their chances of picking up an E by merely turning up on the day. What it will do is pick up the grade C or D who is having a bad day, and therein lies the objection. The objection against the grade C–G scheme is of another kind. What does grade C mean in this connection? It could be a true C, but it could also be a B or an A. The same objection which was levelled at mastery learning thresholds applies here, for that is precisely what grade C is. It is no use saying that As or Bs should not have been entered when it is part and parcel of positive achievement rhetoric that in principle, no one, including the candidate, quite knows what s/he is capable of when the right questions are put. The emphasis on positive achievement is, or ought to be, at odds with schemes which invite deterministic judgements on what individuals are capable of. The fact that teachers seem well able to enter candidates appropriately for differentiated papers (Good & Cresswell 1988*b*) hardly validates grade limitation.

In any case, as Good & Cresswell note, the major problem is likely to be that examiners will find it difficult to make mark levels on different papers commensurable, or, what comes to the same thing, keep the standards required for the overlapping grades the same at all levels of an examination. To be precise, will examiners be able to agree that 70% on one paper is equivalent broadly to 45% on a tougher paper? The suggestion is that they will resist the equivalence and want to believe that the 70% indexes a superior performance. This immediately creates problems for scaling, should that be desired; scaling, that is, to place all marks, wherever they derive from, on one mark scale prior to drawing grade boundaries.

Scaling is discussed in general, and with reference to this particular problem, in chapter 10. At this point in time, there is no reason to disagree with Tattersall (1983, p.97):

> Research in Britain and America suggests that none of the known statistical methods – scaling, ranking or regression – is sufficient in itself to equate marks from options of varying difficulty. Each method appears to disadvantage one or other of the groups of candidates; this is borne out by decision-making theory in relation to the preference of individuals [She has in mind French's work – see chapter 10]. ... It is not recommended, therefore, that the grading of differentiated options should be carried out statistically; statistics may, however, support professional judgements.

There seems little doubt that examiners will need to be provided with statistical data to aid the judgemental process. Such data would tell them when they might be getting out of line in terms of parity of grade boundary placement between papers, and they would in effect be invited to give good arguments as to why they should persist with their judgements.

The results are not yet in to allow conclusions to be drawn about the efficacy of differentiation. Yet the verdict ought not to be decided on empirical grounds alone. An appreciation of the nature of achievement at age 16 as we see it now should indicate that the expectations surrounding differentiation are unlikely to be met. The best guess at the moment is that differentiation will fail as a system; and in particular will not provide the opportunity for candidates to demonstrate 'positive achievement'. Indeed the failure to define properly what is meant by this term almost certainly means that it will go by default.

References

de Gruitjer D. N. M. (1980) A two-stage testing procedure. In van der Kamp L. J. Th., Langerak W. F. & de Gruitjer D. N. M. (eds.) *Psychometrics for Educational Debates*. London: Wiley.

DES (1985) *GCSE General Criteria*. London: HMSO.

di Sessa A. (1988) Knowledge in pieces. In Forman G. & Pufall P. B. (eds.)

Constructivism in the Computer Age. Hillsdale, NJ: Lawrence Erlbaum Associates, 49–70.

Glaser R. & Bassok M. (1989) Learning theory and the study of instruction. *Annual Review of Psychology*, **40**, 631–66.

Good F. J. & Cresswell M. J. (1988*a*) *Grading the GCSE*. London: Secondary Examinations Council.

Good F. J. & Cresswell M. J. (1988*b*) Placing candidates who take differentiated papers on a common grade scale. *Educational Research*, **30**, 177–89.

Lesgold A. *et al.* (1988) Expertise in a complex skill: Diagnosing X-ray pictures. In Chi M. T. H., Glaser R. & Farr M. J. (eds.) *The Nature of Expertise*. Hillsdale, NJ: Erlbaum.

Murphy P. (1988) Insights into pupils' responses to practical investigations from the APU. *Physics Education*, **23**, 330–6.

Owen S. (1988) Marksmanship for the GCSE. *Education*, 6 May.

Partington J. (1988) Towards a science of question-setting in the GCSE. *British Journal of Language Teaching*, **26**, 45–9.

Radnor H. (1988) GCSE – does it support equality? *British Journal of Educational Studies*, **36**, 37–48.

Schools Council (1975) *Examinations at 16+ : Proposals for the Future*. London: Methuen Educational Ltd.

Secondary Examinations Council (1986) *Differentiated Assessment in GCSE. Working Paper 1.*

Stobart G. (1988) *Differentiation in Practice: A Summary Report*. London: University of London School Examinations Board.

Tattersall K. (1983) Differentiated examinations: A strategy for assessment at 16+? *Schools Council Examinations Bulletin*, No. 42. London: Methuen Educational Ltd.

Wood R. (1976) Barking up the wrong tree? What examiners say about those they examine. *Times Educational Supplement*, 18 June.

Wood R. & Power C. N. (1987) Aspects of the competence – performance distinction: Educational, psychological and measurement issues. *Journal of Curriculum Studies*, **19**, 409–24.

14 Bias

It is easy to agree with Humphreys (1986, p. 327) that bias is an emotionally loaded word for which **difference** ought to be substituted. Even so, the term has currency and will not go away just yet. Humphreys is exercised because he believes that what is vulgarly called bias, group differences in item difficulties, are not only small and ubiquitous, but are actually intrinsic to the construction of good tests. For him, writing from a prediction point of view, causes of differences in **criterion** performance of different groups is the core of the problem. In this, he is surely right. Perhaps he would concede that bias is always unjustifiable, whereas differences are only unjustified when due to bias.

Once outside prediction, other considerations apply. Where certification is an end in itself, and group membership is irrelevant, it matters greatly whether constituent parts of tests are put together in such a way as to disadvantage one group or another. The question then is, having noted differences, should they be allowed to persist? That in turn means coming up with a defence of why certain questions should be included or why an examination should be compiled in a certain way. The subject of bias (and differences) in the achievement testing sphere has to be treated very differently from the aptitude testing sphere.

The groups concerning which bias is imputed are the conspicuous ones, that is gender-defined and race-defined, to which the disabled is increasingly added. Why other definable groups should not be invoked is unclear. Why not left-handers and right-handers or, as Lorge (1952) once joked, ectomorphs and endomorphs? Writing in the context of 11+ selection, Goldstein (1986) asks why one should stop at adjusting for gender differences when selecting. If the practice is justified in terms of maturity, why not use household size as a grouping (there being evidence that children in larger households mature earlier)? More to the point, why not use social class? Mean differences on ability tests for males and females are generally smaller than those between high and low socio-economic status (SES) groups. When differences in social circumstances are taken into account Macintosh (1986) has shown that most of the reported differences in IQ between black and white children in this country are removed. Social circumstances or class overrides the power of race, and certainly gender, to determine life chances.

Bias in relation to achievement tests including examinations

In the context of British examinations, bias is usually discussed solely in terms of gender and revolves on three kinds of data or evidence:

- differences in item or question difficulty;
- differences related to the method or format of examining;
- alleged stereotyping via the scenarios on which questions are built.

Data of the first kind usually come to the surface through post-examination item analyses. This leads to further analysis and probing, which may extend to other subjects. For instance, analyses of O level Mathematics multiple choice papers set by the London Board revealed that, with the exception of items involving map scales, solid geometry and graphical distance–time relationships, it was four simple probability items which differentiated the genders more sharply than any others; this for boys and girls taught together (Wood & Brown 1976). Although average marks on the 60-item paper differed by 7% in 1973 and 6% in 1974 in favour of the boys, the average difference on the four probability items set in the two years was 17% in favour of the boys (the actual percentage differences were 17, 16, 15 and 20). A necessary qualification when interpreting gender differences is that there is always far more within-gender variability than between-gender, but a figure of 17% for the numbers involved is significant, and not only statistically.

The wider analysis of which this was part (Wood 1976) found (as did a later American analysis – Doolittle & Cleary 1987) that geometry and maths reasoning items (especially solid geometry and scaling and probability) are relatively more difficult for female examinees and the more algorithmic computation-oriented items, such as matrix manipulation and algebraic operations generally, are relatively easier. Put another way (Englehard 1990), gender differences tend to become more favourable toward boys as the level of cognitive complexity increases and also as the content changes from arithmetic through algebra through geometry.

Gender differences, especially in mathematics, are now a hot research topic (and, dare one say, over-researched compared to some neglected topics). The recent spate of papers, mostly authored by women, have generally concluded that gender differences in mathematics performance are small, once differential performance of the kind just mentioned is acknowledged (Friedman 1989; Hyde, Fennema & Lamon 1990; Linn &

Hyde 1989*a*). The conclusion must be correct given that individual differences within gender are always going to exceed between-gender differences. All the same, Hyde *et al.* are concerned about the lower performance of females in problem solving that is evident in high school. Not surprisingly, Linn & Hyde reject biodeterministic explanations and urge instead that learning environments be redesigned to promote gender equity.

A modest test of cultural influence is to look at differences across schools, and this Wood did. There were cases where the gender differences between schools were greater than those in the sample as a whole, but also cases where the differences vanished or were even reversed. Whether this was because of selection or not, was impossible to say. It has been suggested (such as Jones 1973) that the general teaching methods used in a school and the general ability of the students have a greater effect on the methods a student uses to answer questions than does the gender of the student. This seems entirely plausible. After differences between schools had been allowed for, there remained palpable differences between the sexes on linear scale items and on distance–time graphs. It is interesting that an analysis of the Swedish Scholastic Aptitude Test found that a test called 'Interpretation of diagrams, tables and maps' produced (along with a logical reasoning test) the biggest differences in item difficulty between males and females (Stage 1988).

The question remains of how to deal with such differences in terms of practical action. In the annals of intelligence testing the issue of gender differences is either ignored or is resolved by legislating the differences out of existence through deliberate selection of so-called unbiased items or by including enough different types of items known to favour each sex so that overall differences are equalised. The absurdity of selecting items just because they show no gender differences or any other kind of difference was pointed out by Lorge. He took the view, which I share, that genuine differences should be allowed to reveal themselves, the important thing being to have a watertight defence for including items in a test. In this regard, Dwyer's (1976) claim that in the early 1970s ETS 'balanced' test scores for SAT-Verbal, but never balanced for SAT-Math, is particularly instructive.

The consequences of letting the chips fall where they may is that scores for the two sexes should be treated separately for predictive and reporting purposes on the understanding that a systematic deficit for either sex does not have a stigma attached to it. This position has interesting implications for achievement testing, in particular school examinations where no systematic predictive use is made of results and reporting is in absolute terms without reference to separate norms for the sexes (although separate norms may exist). This means that any bias will have an insidious effect which will be to all intents and purposes undetectable, with unfortunate consequences for those affected.

What makes the whole issue peculiarly difficult is the fact that the content of any examination is only a sample of what could be asked and that the choice of material is always liable to be controversial. Returning to O level Mathematics, take, for instance, the topic of scaling or proportion. Did it really warrant two items out of 60, three if a pie chart item is included? Or the calculation of a mean from a frequency distribution, of which there were three examples in 1973, albeit in different forms? Argument about these and other matters would or should occur even if there was no such phenomenon as gender difference; the point is that the extra knowledge gleaned about gender differences can and should inform the final composition of a paper, not by veto but as a moderating influence. This is particularly true of papers which offer a choice of questions; Wood's work showed how girls could be disadvantaged by being 'forced' into a restricted choice.

The issue of what to include, and in what weight, is dramatised by a subject like English Language where there is no syllabus as such with the consequence that examiners have more latitude than usual when it comes to selecting material for inclusion in tests. Having studied the contents of O level English Language multiple choice tests set by the London Board, Wood (1978) decided that there was prima facie evidence of gender-related stereotyping which would show itself in the item statistics. Analysis of item responses revealed that boys did better than girls on items relating to a passage about a man looking back to a boyhood spent near a railway and girls did better than boys on a passage about a girl's ordeal at a dinner dance. Investigation of another test found girls doing better on a passage about a 14-year-old girl and boys doing better on a passage about the Crimean War. Wood argued that the association was no coincidence and that examiners may have favoured one gender or the other without realising it.

Some years earlier, Coffman (1961) had noticed that women perform better on SAT-Verbal items geared toward human relationships and personalities, while men score higher on items with technical or mechanical terms. P. Murphy (1989) found the same with APU science questions. 'Ask about the interpretation of data and talk about flowers, girls will respond ... but if the data concern traffic flow, or talks about bolts or washers, boys will respond better.' In the same vein, Linn & Hyde (1989*b*) report that women do better on math problems concerning aesthetics, interpersonal relationships and traditionally female tasks, such as sewing, and men do better at questions involving measurement, sports and science. But another American study was not so forthright. McLarty, Noble & Huntley (1989) examined the effects of gender-related item-wording changes on the performance of male and female examinees. Mathematics word problems and English Language items were created in neuter, male and female versions. None of the three gender versions appeared consistently more or less difficult than the others. They did, however, note some methodological and statistical problems which may have affected their results. Incidentally, the favoured procedure for estimating item bias – the Mantel-Haenszel method and its derivatives – is liable to be seriously flawed in certain applications (Wood & Johnson 1990).

Although both males and females are able to identify items as being oriented toward males and females, they cannot readily identify items that give rise to gender differences in student performance. That was the conclusion of Wedman & Stage (1983). Scheuneman (1987) made the same point, observing that what the results flag up as possible bias is often not spotted by judges. She thought this would be more true for race-related than gender-related differences. In an American study where black and white teachers were asked to rate items for perceived racial favouritism, the correlation between actual performance differences and favouritism ratings was −0·10 for the white teachers and −0·11 for the black teachers, suggesting little or no relationship (Hieronymus & Hoover 1986, p. 157).

The reconciliation of these various findings would appear to hinge on how obvious the gender or race typing was. McLarty *et al.* talk of 'fairly superficial' manipulations of content; in my case (Wood 1978) the gender typing could be said to have been overt. Wedman & Stage did note that, where the content was of a kind considered traditionally male or female, prediction of differences was likely to be good. Bateson & Parsons-Chatman (1989) are correct to say that researchers should not assume the gender content of items to be obvious.

What does this mean for examiners? Evidently, they cannot be held responsible for the existence of gender differences, and apparently they cannot be expected to anticipate the more subtle manifestations of gender-related bias, but they can at least avoid giving undue advantage to one gender or the other. English Language examiners are peculiarly exposed because theirs is the one subject to which candidates bring, in a direct way, their experiences with language to date.

The implications for corrective action are quite different for Mathematics and English. For Mathematics the question was, 'Do you leave the suspect items there because they are too important to leave out, and how many do you leave there?', whereas for English it is much less problematical, 'Do you remove the suspect items altogether, or at least modify them?'

It is certainly possible to apply *reductio ad absurdum* reasoning to alleged item bias. After all, if differences in interest and motivation are considered to be biasing factors, all tests or assessment methods may be said to have a certain amount of bias (Hieronymus & Hoover 1986). A reading passage or a language item might be more interesting and motivating for a girl than a boy (even when overtly gender-related material is removed) or for one who is sports minded, or for someone who is interested in science as opposed to someone who is interested in literature. Examples of these subtly slanted situations are all much easier to find than items that favour one ethnic group over another, or one sex over the other.

If bias is regarded in this light, it is difficult to conceive of a test that does not present some advantage for a given student or group of students. But if all 'bias' of this kind were to be removed, it would likely result, so Hieronymus & Hoover argue, in the elimination of all that is interesting, clever, novel, challenging and creative. Such a test would be bland, uninteresting and irrelevant for everyone. It would be the culture-fair test taken to the limit. That is the *reductio ad absurdum*. A tempered view would be that group differences for groups as conventionally defined should always be looked at for what they might say about the teaching of the subject or test construction strategies, and that material which is liable to be significantly correlated with group performance, and which need not appear in that form, should be removed.

Gender differences related to technique of assessment

While doing the English Language study, Wood noticed that the difference in pass rates (percentages) at O level for the London Board narrowed from 22·2 (in favour of the girls in 1971) to 10·0 in 1977, with the biggest single reduction coming in 1972. What was special about 1972? It was the year in which the multiple choice comprehension test was introduced into the examination, replacing a written comprehension paper. This was not just happenstance. Investigation of other subjects revealed that when multiple choice is introduced into an examination, the boys' pass rate nearly always improves noticeably relative to the girls' pass rate, which may even decline. Murphy (1978, 1982) confirmed this observation from AEB data. It does appear that multiple choice both favours boys and disadvantages girls and that essay tests have the opposite effect. Girls may still do better on the multiple choice paper, but the margin of superiority would almost certainly be greater were the paper to be written.

As to the explanation of these effects Murphy (1982) was inclined to settle for the evidence pointing to female superiority in written language skills or, more generally, linguistic adeptness, a superiority which has been attributed to gender-related asymmetry in the brain's hemispheres. Murphy also mentioned neatness of handwriting, again more strongly marked in females, which in at least one study has been shown to have a significant effect on the marks students are awarded in examinations (chapter 5). It has also been shown (Linn *et al.* 1987) that girls are more reluctant to guess on multiple choice questions than boys who, by overestimating their likelihood of success, are rewarded in the multiple choice format. Grandy's (1987) finding that women are more likely to leave items blank than men is in the same vein. Is it the case, asked Murphy, that objective tests remove a bias in examination marks that is caused by the neat handwriting of female candidates?

The work by Wood, and by Murphy and the other studies, have perhaps congealed into conventional wisdom. Now a study has appeared which provokes some re-evaluation of this wisdom, at least where English Language as a subject is concerned. Bell & Hay (1987), noting Wood and Murphy's remarks that general life experiences may be partially responsible for any differential performances of the sexes on different English Language examination formats, concluded that candidates should be compared, not just in terms of gender but in terms of other subjects studied by them. (This would seem to miss the point, since Wood, at any rate, was referring to experiences outside school, but no matter.)

The data were from the Australian Tertiary Admissions Examination. The ability range was almost certainly narrower than an O level range and, of course, the multiple choice test was different from those studied by Wood and Murphy. Female students scored higher in all three components of the examination, but since the difference was least for the multiple choice test there was still evidence to back the relative disadvantage hypothesis.

Bell & Hay were inclined to think that similar studies be undertaken in situations such as university entrance where such tests are used for selection, with a view to determining whether any candidates have been disadvantaged by the format or mode of examination questions. They also called for more research to define more precisely the effect of question format. Do short answer questions share some of the qualities of multiple choice questions and some of those of extended response questions? What precisely are the differences and biases that could be expected in such cases?

The idea of determining whether **any** candidates have suffered, given their simultaneous membership of many groups, is something of a Pandora's Box. The research Bell & Hay suggest should certainly be undertaken. Otherwise the general practical strategy should be that recommended by Murphy (1982), which is that schemes of assessment that include a variety of assessment techniques may well be the best way of minimising any unwanted biases that may be associated with certain techniques of assessment. Incidentally, we know next to nothing about how school-based assessment might stand on the bias issue, although studies which report teacher preferences for females or good-looking pupils or compliant pupils are suggestive (chapter 6).

Stereotyping as carried by content

'The most frequently occurring sexism, and the easiest to identify, is the overpoweringly masculine flavour of the papers.' (*Exams for the Boys*, Fawcett Society 1987, p. 38). The Fawcett Society's report is an attempt to establish whether changes in society indicative of a relaxation of traditional gender-roles are reflected in examination papers. Casual reading of the 1983 papers of some of the boards suggested that this was not the case, so the Society wrote to the English and Welsh boards to ask them what they were doing about it. From the replies, the Society gathered (p. 4) that only the London and Oxford boards were concerned about the situation. A study of a sample of 1985 papers suggested little progress. On the few occasions when girls or women appeared in the texts or questions, they tended to be portrayed as flighty, inadequate, domesticated or servile. The Society decided that it must undertake a much more comprehensive and detailed study of the 1986 papers.

By their own choice, the authors eschewed statistical description, so the report, based on a reading of over 1000 papers, relies on verbatim quotation and strong commentary. It is therefore difficult to represent its contents and to evaluate the commentary, although the report does enough to establish that there is a problem.

Seven types of discrimination were identified. Note that there is no reference to technique of assessment, although the report shows an awareness (p. 13) that 'girls are known not to perform as well as boys in this type of test', also apropos English Language, that 'research suggests that boys in fact do rather better in this sort of answer than in continuous prose' (p. 19).

The types of discrimination were:

1 the overall effect of a paper can be biased, because reference is made predominantly to one sex;
2 the presentation of men and women in the paper is stereotyped – men are admirable, women frivolous;
3 questions about subjects of interest only to boys;
4 the assumption that people are male, and so is the genotype – girls and feminine pronouns go into brackets, if they appear at all;
5 the authors of texts are almost exclusively male;
6 passages chosen for criticism and comment have a strong male bias;
7 an opportunity to mention an eminent woman has been missed (such as a physics question naming Pierre Curie, but not Marie).

The distinction is made between explicit and non-explicit sexism. In the first, men or boys make most or all of the appearances in the papers, or are the ones shown using maths in an intelligent way, or else women and girls appear in frivolous or stereotyped roles. With non-explicit sexism examiners have tried to use what could be gender-neutral terms, but which may not work as such.

The Modern Languages papers appear to have contained as much explicit sexism as any, but then they are more firmly anchored in the social world. To start with, the set books are almost entirely by male authors, so it is always a male view of the world which is presented to candidates. This is particularly so with German. The examiners, who are also likely to be mainly male, compound this effect in their choice of material for comprehension passages. In a German translation, Helmut gets drunk in Cologne, and is taken back home by a helpful person. The action revolves around him. His wife is not named, just referred to as 'his wife'. Stereotypical male behaviour, drunkenness, would not be acceptable if it were from a woman. Here, the report says, it is portrayed as quite an endearing feature. Men are portrayed as having power, and their weaknesses are treated gently.

The report is keen to point out (p. 24) that there were some good papers, and some good questions, and from most boards. This is what we would expect; the point is that while questionable material continues to be published there is corrective action to be taken. The report takes a constructive line in suggesting what might be done. Even in Religious Studies where, as the report notes, there is inevitable 'bias' introduced by the fusing of deity with male, efforts could be made to at least recognise the existence of two sexes and the roles and contributions of both in religious life and practice.

On non-explicit sexism, there is a reprimand for boards which refer to feminine forms in brackets (or she), when there is a simple method, he/she or s/he, of conveying the dichotomy without implying any differential value. Nor are the sometimes rather clumsy efforts to balance a question by excluding gender-specific pronouns always effective. In this culture, the mention of a manager, a worker, a nurse or telephonist, conjures up, the report says, a vision of a person of a particular sex. Unless a question specifically includes a pronoun that contradicts this expectation, no balance has been achieved. In order to balance exam questions properly, genders have to be explicit.

The Fawcett Society report goes beyond sexism to consider a number of other issues which probably lie outside the scope of this survey. Talking of mathematics and physics, it asks (p. 39) 'What sorts of people are being excluded by the impersonality of these subjects? We know that girls are put off subjects that seem to have little relevance to life and people.' Perhaps examination content is not the chief culprit here. The gender-related performance gap in physics has plausibly been attributed to the very different leisure activities of young boys and girls out of school (Johnson & Bell 1987). Besides, there is recent evidence that, while the familiar tendency for girls to choose biology in greater numbers than boys and for boys to choose physics and the technological sciences in greater number than girls persists, the traditional polarisation of science subject choice may be weakening, mainly because of the slowly increasing popularity of physics and chemistry among girls (Johnson & Bell). On this last point, there is an interesting little piece of work by two teachers on how girls fare with chemistry (Love & Wild 1989). Girls, they say, do not do well in competitive situations with boys, especially where there is a practical slant to the work; whereas boys seem inclined to accept material in any form, girls are deeply influenced by format and presentation. Finally, girls are thought to peak earlier, and the suggestion is that they should be entered for GCSE at the end of the fourth year.

Bias in relation to aptitude tests

The discussion of bias in relation to achievement tests or examinations has been wholly in terms of relative gender disadvantage. It would be possible to have a discussion in terms of ethnic minority disadvantage, and no doubt this will come, but not so far. When the subject of attention is aptitude tests, it is the latter bias, or **cultural bias**, which takes centre stage, although gender bias still comes into the reckoning.

The cultural test bias hypothesis contends that commonly used aptitude tests are biased in content, procedure and usage against students coming from disadvantaged minority backgrounds. Group differences are believed to stem from characteristics of the test, which are in turn due to flawed psychometric methodology, and to be unrelated to differences in the psychological trait being measured. Consistent cultural group differences in scholastic aptitude, either at paper or item level, are interpreted directly as cultural bias. Consequently, all sorts of aptitude tests are said to be inappropriate for the assessment of minority candidates' scholastic aptitude or for the prediction of their academic performance, or for aspects of their work potential.

How easily test producers can be thrown back on the defensive when challenged is illustrated by the case of the Civil Service Commission, who, faced with black–white differences on its Qualifying Test, announced that it was doing further analyses 'to help assess whether the disparity is due to cultural bias in the test' (Civil Service Commission 1987, p. 9). To be fair, the Commission did add that it was looking at an alternative explanation which was that there might be differences in the attributes of the candidates they are currently attracting from the white and ethnic minority groups.

Ranged against the cultural bias proponents is what might be called the psychometric position, which is founded on an examination of the empirical research. This says that there are differences, but no bias. It is not the case that different traits are being measured for different groups. The regression of criterion measures, such as first-year grade point average on scholastic aptitude test scores as predictors, are not heterogeneous across groups. Every study has found that the Law School Admissions Test (LSAT) is about as good a predictor of first-year law-school grades for blacks or Hispanics as it is for whites (Kaye 1980, p. 453). When the regression systems do differ by cultural group, the locus of the difference is found mainly in the intercept, with the minority group intercept falling slightly below that of the majority group (Linn 1982). This would normally result in the **overprediction** of the former group's criterion performance, given the common regression lines; in other words, people are prophesied to do better than they actually do. Macintosh (1986) has reported overprediction for West Indian children in this country; they did worse on reading and maths tests than their IQ scores might lead one to expect. Zeidner (1986) has reported the same phenomenon for Arab students in Israel. But there are also instances where the regression line for an ethnic minority is already at a parity with whites, for example Chicanos (Linn, p. 37), or can become so. Macintosh demonstrated that five years of British schooling can increase Asian children's scores on the supposedly culture-fair Cattell's or Raven's tests by 20 points or so.

There is a methodological angle. Systematic errors of prediction may occur purely because of the unreliability of the aptitude test, given a common regression line (Jensen 1980). Zeidner observes that reducing the amount of measurement error in the predictor would have concomitantly decreased the amount of overprediction of Arab scholastic achievement. There is also the possibility, quite strong, that the criterion measure may also be what the critics call culturally biased as well as being unreliable. Criterion and predictor may well offer the same handicaps. An obvious example is people who have trouble reading. They will be uncomfortable with any sort of test. Here is an example of a factor which is not so much culturally biased as culture-bound, as must be the case. And this is the thrust of the psychometric position. The relationship between impaired performance on a predictor and impaired performance on a criterion is liable to be the same as that in groups where there is not the same impairment.

The culture-fair test is a chimera. In principle, a test could be tinkered with by inserting material thought favourable to the disadvantaged group until equal average scores were produced and adverse impact cancelled out, but what would such a test say about future job performances, or even potential, given that the job is most certainly culture-**based** and cannot be tinkered with in the same way? The obvious conclusion is that minority groups have to develop and then apply to aptitude tests the same attributes which conduce to good performance on the culture-bound criteria. At the same time, the claim that people who have low scores on a test are apt to perform poorly on a job must be supported by evidence. It does not logically follow that, because such a claim can be supported for one group, it can also be supported for another. And even if it can be supported that is no reason to acquiesce in the situation. If we think people are doing as well as expected, even if they are doing poorly, it is easy to forget about them. Studies like that of Kaye (1980) are regularly seized upon by those who wish to defend test use unconditionally, but the risk of inducing or encouraging complacency is obvious. The possibility that tests may be differentially valid for members of different groups and that they may have different predictive meanings is central to the discussion of fair test use (Linn, pp. 366–7).

What must never be overlooked is that relationships between test scores and criterion measures, such as supervisor ratings, are typically modest. The modal correlation might be about 0·25. Thus there is every likelihood that disproportionately large numbers of **able** members of minority groups will be selected out when a decision rule based on test scores is applied (Hartigan & Wigdor 1989).

Gender differences

The size of gender differences on cognitive variables changes as a function of age. Studies have generally found few or no gender differences in quantitative abilities for young children. Differences in quantitative scores begin to appear in adolescence and to increase during the secondary school years. Gender differences in spatial abilities begin to appear at about ages 6–8 and to increase with age through secondary school. Female superiority in verbal ability has been observed for very young children. The difference appears to diminish for a time and then increase again after about age 11. There is, however, fresh evidence (Feingold 1988) that the gaps between the sexes are closing on a whole range of skills; see also work reported in Stage (1988) and in the papers referenced earlier.

Norms are presented separately for boys and girls on a number of standardised ability tests. For the Differential Aptitude Tests (DAT) (Bennett, Seashore & Wesman 1974) the larger group differences occur on the more specialised aptitudes, such as mechanical reasoning (favouring boys), clerical speed and accuracy (favouring girls) and spelling (favouring girls). It follows that if people were selected from the DAT norm groups on the basis of high scores on the mechanical reasoning test, fewer girls than boys would be selected. That is, the mechanical reasoning test would be expected to have an adverse impact on girls. Adverse impact requires that the evidence of test validity be given close scrutiny, which might involve investigations of differential validity and prediction. In a Canadian court case (*Action Travail des Femmes* v. *Canadian National Railways*) a group of women claimed, successfully, that use of the Bennett mechanical comprehension test discriminated against them (Cronshaw 1986). A more surprising instance of bias, again involving mechanical comprehension, occurred with Protestant and Catholic engineering apprentices in Northern Ireland where the Catholics suffered adverse impact for reasons to do with previous syllabus provision (Johnson, Wood & Hall 1990).

There is differential prediction, as discussed, and differential validity, as indexed by differences in correlations between predictors **and criteria**. Differences in correlations suggest that the groups differ in the magnitude of non-systematic errors of prediction that are typically made. They say nothing about possible systematic errors of prediction for members of an identifiable subgroup when a single equation is used to make predictions for everyone. Correlations between SAT scores and freshman grade-point average (GPA) are usually higher for women than for men, and the standard error of estimate is generally smaller for women than for men, which would follow. A similar result has been reported for British data in respect of the (aborted) Test of Academic Aptitude (TAA) when used for predicting degree results (Choppin *et al.* 1973, pp. 34–5). It has also been shown that the use of SAT scores as predictors underpredicts the actual GPA of women. These results apply also to the LSAT. This has been put down unequivocally to 'gender-bias' (Rosser 1989).

In trying to discover whether bias might be present, the point of departure is the regression of the criterion on the predictor and any differences in slopes and intercepts between groups. Differences in slopes between groups are always undesirable. There is no doubt that a test on which a criterion has a different slope for blacks as compared to whites is biased. Since slopes are affected directly by the discrimination statistics of the items, the opportunity is there to control this bias through careful test construction practices. Tests designed to measure individual differences in a heterogeneous population should discriminate equally well among individuals in all subgroups of the population (Humphreys 1986).

Eliminating intercept differences, that is abolishing over- and underprediction, is more problematical; Humphreys calls it unrealistic and counterproductive. His argument is that discarding those items which are relatively most difficult for blacks (on the supposition that these are automatically biased) will only increase overprediction of black performance. If these items are also average or better than average measures of the dominant factor common to the predictor and criterion, then discarding them will also act to reduce the predictive validity of the test. The controversy in the USA concerning the so-called Golden Rule is directly relevant. Golden Rule states that within groups of equally valid items in the same content areas, test publishers must select those items that display the smallest differences between the correct answer rates of minority and majority test-takers. Its advocates, such as Weiss (1987), say that questions that maximise differences between high- and low-scoring students may really be measuring test-takers' knowledge of irrelevant, culturally specific information, as in the following, unfortunately rather daft, SAT item:

RUNNER: MARATHON

(a) envoy: embassy
(b) martyr: massacre
(c) oarsman: regatta
(d) referee: tournament
(e) horse: stable

53% of the whites, but just 22% of the blacks, gave the wanted answer (C) (Donlon 1982). Clearly, says Weiss, this item does not measure students' 'aptitude' or 'logical reasoning ability', but instead knowledge of an upper middle-class recreational activity.

To this, Humphreys would presumably respond that such an item cannot be tapping strongly into the dominant factor common to the predictor and criterion; but that there are other items difficult for blacks which do, and those should not be discarded.

In any case, overprediction means that blacks are not discriminated against; rather the reverse. Underprediction for females is more injurious. There the pressure is on the test constructor to find a measure of the missing qualities that will reduce bias. If the measure is found and added to the existing predictor, the predictor will now show a gender difference favouring females, but it will be more valid than the original predictor, which is what is wanted. What Humphreys is saying is that mean differences can sometimes be reduced by sound professional practices, but intercept differences can be increased by those same practices. The important thing is the correlation of the item or question with the dominant factor, not the small residual correlations with race or sex. Harking back to the earlier discussion on O level Mathematics items, this is just another way of saying that items which are testing something which should be tested should not be thrown out just because there is a discrepancy in their difficulties between the sexes.

Conclusions

There is such a thing as bias; it is a difference which cannot be defended. In examinations it occurs when too much reliance is placed on techniques which favour (relatively) one group or the other. Quite a lot is known now about how multiple choice and free response stand in this respect to gender bias, but there is room for more enquiry, such as into short-answer questions. Little is known about how school-based assessment stands; in fact the Fawcett Society concluded its report thus: 'But we shall also need to find out how the boards plan to monitor for sexism in continuous assessment'.

Bias can also occur as a result of representing the genders in stereotypical or patronising ways. This can show up at the item or passage level, or even permeate papers. Boards need to make their examiners more aware of how they may introduce bias when compiling questions. The Fawcett Society suggests that boards might show some commitment to the outcomes of educational research by circulating summaries of relevant research. A better idea would be to convene meetings to discuss how to produce balanced papers.

Any board involved with aptitude tests will find itself challenged by the commonplace findings of overprediction for blacks (and other groups, such as Arabs in Israel), and underprediction for females. Brute force solutions, such as throwing out all items which are relatively difficult for blacks, are not the answer. For females there is apparently a need to build into the aptitude test experience something of the demands which produce relatively superior achievement later.

References

Bateson D. J. & Parsons-Chatman S. (1989) Sex-related differences in science achievement: A possible testing artifact. *International Journal of Science Education*, **11**, 371–85.

Bell R. C. & Hay J. A. (1987) Differences and biases in English Language examination formats. *British Journal of Educational Psychology*, **57**, 212–20.

Bennett G. K., Seashore H. G. & Wesman A. G. (1974) *Fifth Edition Manual for the Differential Aptitude Tests*. New York: The Psychological Corporation.

Choppin B. L. *et al.* (1973) *The Prediction of Academic Success*. Slough: NFER Publishing Co.

Civil Service Commission (1987) *Annual Report for 1986*. Basingstoke: CSC.

Coffman W. E. (1961) Sex differences in responses to items in an aptitude test. *18th Yearbook, National Council on Measurement in Education*, 117–24.

Cronshaw S. F. (1986) The status of employment testing in Canada: A review and evaluation of theory and professional practice. *Canadian Psychology*, **27**, 183–95.

Donlon T. F. (1982) The SAT in a diverse society: Fairness and sensitivity. *College Board News*, **122**, 12–16.

Doolittle A. E. & Cleary T. A. (1987) Gender-based differential item performance in mathematics achievement items. *Journal of Educational Measurement*, **24**, 157–66.

Dwyer C. A. (1976) Test content and sex differences in reading. *The Reading Teacher*, May, 753–7.

Englehard G. (1990) Gender differences in performance on mathematics items: Evidence from the United States and Thailand. *Contemporary Educational Psychology*, **15**, 13–26.

Fawcett Society (1987) *Exams for the Boys*. London: Fawcett Society.

Feingold A. (1988) Cognitive gender differences are disappearing. *American Psychologist*, **43**, 95–103.

Friedman L. (1989) Mathematics and the gender gap: A meta-analysis of recent studies on sex differences in mathematical tasks. *Review of Educational Research*, **59**, 185–213.

Goldstein H. (1986) Sex bias and test norms in educational selection. *Research Intelligence*, May, 2–4.

Grandy J. (1987) Characteristics of examinees who leave questions unanswered on the GRE general test under rights-only scoring. *ETS Research Report*, **87-38**. Princeton, NJ: Educational Testing Service.

Hartigan J. A. & Wigdor A. K. (eds.) (1989) *Fairness in Employment Testing*. Washington, DC: National Academy Press.

Hieronymus A. N. & Hoover H. D. (1986) *Iowa Tests of Basic Skills: Manual for School Administrators, Levels 5–14*. Chicago: Riverside Publishing Company, 156–8.

Humphreys L. G. (1986) An analysis and evaluation of test and item bias in the prediction context. *Journal of Applied Psychology*, **71**, 327–33.

Hyde J. S., Fennema E. & Lamon S. J. (1990) Gender differences in mathematics performance. *Psychological Bulletin*, **107**, 139–55.

Jensen A. R. (1980) *Bias in Mental Testing*. London: Methuen.

Johnson C. E., Wood R. & Hall J. P. (1990) How what is taught in schools can affect job chances: The case of engineering apprentices in Northern Ireland. *British Journal of Education and Work*, **3**, 69–77.

Johnson S. & Bell J. F. (1987) Gender differences in science: Option choices. *School Science Review*, **69**, 269–76.

Jones D. A. (1973) An investigation of the differences between boys and girls during the formative years in the methods used to solve mathematical problems. Unpublished M.Phil. thesis. University of London Institute of Education.

Kaye D. (1980) Searching for truth about testing. *The Yale Law Journal*, **90**, 431–57.

Linn M. C. & Hyde J. S. (1989*a*) Gender, mathematics and science. *Educational Researcher*, **18**, 17–19, 22–7.

Linn M. C. & Hyde J. S. (1989*b*) Male/female test differences narrow – except on SAT. *Fair Test EXAMINER*, Spring, 10.

Linn M. C. *et al.* (1987) Gender differences in National Assessment of Educational Progress science items: What does 'I don't know' really mean? *Journal of Research in Science Teaching*, **24**, 267–78.

Linn R. L. (1982) Ability testing: Individual differences, prediction and differential prediction. In Wigdor A. K. & Garner W. R. (eds.) *Ability Testing: Uses, Consequences and Controversies, Part 2.* Washington, DC: National Academy Press.

Lorge I. (1952) Difference or bias in tests of intelligence. In Anastasi A. (ed.) (1966) *Testing Problems in Perspective.* Washington, DC: American Council on Education.

Love R. M. & Wild B. (1989) A case study on the relative performance of girls and boys in chemistry. *School Science Review*, **70**, 112–16.

Macintosh N. J. (1986) The biology of intelligence. *British Journal of Psychology*, **77**, 1–18.

McLarty J. R., Noble A. C. & Huntley R. M. (1989) Effects of item wording on sex bias. *Journal of Educational Measurement*, **26**, 285–93.

Murphy P. (1989) Quoted in 'The nuts and bolts of prejudice'. *Independent*, 9th February, 19.

Murphy R. J. L. (1978) Sex differences in examination performance: Do these reflect differences in ability or sex-role stereotypes? *Educational Review*, **30**, 259–63.

Murphy R. J. L. (1982) Sex differences in objective test performance. *British Journal of Educational Psychology*, **52**, 213–19.

Rosser P. (1989) *SAT Gender Gap.* Washington, DC: Center for Women Policy Studies.

Scheuneman J. D. (1987) An experimental exploratory study of causes of bias in test items. *Journal of Educational Measurement*, **24**, 97–118.

Stage C. (1988) Gender differences in test results. *Scandinavian Journal of Educational Research*, **32**, 101–11.

Wedman I. & Stage C. (1983) The significance of contents for sex differences in test results. *Scandinavian Journal of Educational Research*, **27**, 49–71.

Weiss J. (1987) The golden rule bias reduction principle: A practical reform. *Educational Measurement: Issues and Practice*, **6**, 23–5.

Wood R. (1976) Sex differences in mathematics attainment at GCE ordinary level. *Educational Studies*, **2**, 141–60.

Wood R. (1978) Sex differences in answers to English Language comprehension items. *Educational Studies*, **4**, 157–65.

Wood R. & Brown M. (1976) Mastery of simple probability ideas among GCE Ordinary level mathematics candidates. *International Journal of Mathematical Education in Science and Technology*, **7**, 297–306.

Wood R. & Johnson C. E. (1990) Detecting item bias: Problems with the use of Mantel-Haenszel procedures and DIF statistics. Unpublished paper, Psychometric Research and Development Ltd, St Albans.

Zeidner M. (1986) Are scholastic aptitude tests in Israel biased towards Arab college student candidates? *Higher Education*, **15**, 507–22.

15 How practical work is assessed

A 1973 report on the assessment of attainment in sixth-form science (Schools Council 1973) had this to say:

> *About the integration of practical and written work*
>
> Also apparent is a move towards a much wider variety of practical work, its integration with the factual and theoretical basis of science ... (p. 20)
>
> *About the lack of clear statements defining objectives of practical work*
>
> In the absence of such statements, any attempt at assessment of attainment in practical work can be nothing more than a shot in the dark. (p. 20)
>
> *About the inadequacy of the practical examination*
>
> On a single occasion it is simply not possible reliably to examine attainment in more than a fraction of the objectives, techniques and subject matter of a whole sixth-form practical science course. (p. 35)
>
> *About the virtues of teacher assessments*
>
> Direct observation by teachers extends the range of student attributes which can be assessed beyond those which are assessed on written evidence alone. (p. 28)

The report might have hoped that the traditional practical examination was on its last legs, but that has not turned out to be the case, although in the CSE there was certainly a decline (Lock 1988). Boards still offer it, alongside teacher-assessed options. That said, there has been a drive to at least supplement measures of product with measures of process, and the various reforming projects, like the Oxford Certificate of Educational Achievement (OCEA), have been in the van. Interestingly, however, teachers in OCEA (and presumably elsewhere) are apparently still focusing more on skills than on process, with the criteria becoming more atomistic in nature than had originally been intended (Lock & Ferriman 1989). The atomistic or separatist approach is currently under attack, notably by Woolnough:

It is not at all evident that the ability a pupil demonstrates on a skill test which has been 'purified' to separate it from other interacting skills is in any way related to the ability that will be shown in a different context. (Woolnough & Toh 1990, p. 128)

As to statements of objectives, these are now ten a penny. Whether they are yet sufficiently unpacked is doubtful. Writing about the OCEA Science component, Josephy (1986) suggests that the following list is probably a fair representation of the areas widely felt to be important. Note that these objectives are not, nor do they need to be, expressed in Bloom *Taxonomy* language. It was Wyatt (1973), in a list which may have shaped Josephy's, who demonstrated that a clear approach to defining what we want students to be able to do, unencumbered by Bloomian categories or any others, was perfectly feasible.

Here is Josephy's list:

The student should demonstrate ability to:

1 handle apparatus;
2 make measurements;
3 make observations;
4 handle data;
5 record results;
6 make inferences, discern patterns and draw conclusions;
7 formulate problems;
8 plan experiments and investigations;
9 select and suggest appropriate equipment;
10 modify a plan as necessary;
11 work effectively, either independently or as a member of a team.

Items 1–6, says Josephy, are commonly assessed in practical work, while 4 may be included in some written papers. Items 7–11 are rarely assessed at all, he claims, although they are increasingly seen as important. A 'set piece' practical test is an unsatisfactory way of assessing most of these objectives. Although possible for items 1–6, it takes them out of context and separates them from their purpose. For items 7–11 it is difficult to see how reliable assessment could be carried out in a set piece. The very nature of an investigation means that time is needed to try out different approaches, that different skills cannot be practised in isolation; they only make sense as part of the whole activity.

It can be concluded, said Josephy, that assessment of these objectives should be in the context in which skills are practised, that is during laboratory coursework.

So much for the ideology, with which it is hard to take exception. On psychometric grounds alone the one-off practical test or examination is desperately weak. And who will take issue with the American physicist who asserted that 'it is impossible to measure certain neuromuscular laboratory skills by means of paper-and-pencil tests. A student might get a perfect score on written tests but not be able to handle apparatus in the laboratory' (Kruglak 1958)? Not the APU science team, who wrote that 'Pupils are able to perform tasks in a practical situation which they are unable to perform mentally in response to a written question' (DES/APU 1984).

The empirical research work in this area is largely (and typically) of the correlational kind. Citing other workers, Hofstein & Lunetta (1982) reported that a low correlation exists between laboratory-based practical examinations and written paper-and-pencil tests. But what if the correlation had been high? Would it be argued that practical examinations be scrapped? And might that not extend to laboratory work itself? One of the few studies of the construct validity of examinations (Hoste 1982) found that for CSE Biology examinations the correlation was persistently high and that it was not possible to isolate practical ability as a distinct mode of performance. There is clearly an overlap, said Hoste, between the abilities tested by practical and theory papers. In order to answer both papers, candidates must have the verbal skills to be able to read the question papers; they need biological knowledge and understanding to comprehend the questions together with other verbal skills to write down the answers. Hoste concluded that these shared aspects of performance may have swamped the practical skills tested in the examinations.

But suppose that purer measures of practical skills could be devised. The remarks above notwithstanding, there would be no guarantee of low correlations between 'practical' and 'theory' scores. All interpretation is conditioned by the deeper methodological problem (endemic in all construct validation enterprises) that while 'practical' and 'theory' are recognisably different constructs which perhaps ought not to be related, if it so happens that those who are strong (weak) on one are strong (weak) on the other, the sought-for differentiation cannot be established. What is true is that abilities tend to differentiate with practice (Anastasi 1970) and this is the key to thinking constructively about the whole issue.

The neuromuscular or sensory–motor aspects of practical work are but one objective; number 1 in Josephy's list – handling apparatus. The remainder of the objectives, and practical work itself, have a strong cognitive orientation. Farmer & Frazer (1985), writing of Revised Nuffield O level Chemistry, reckoned that the majority of practical tasks play a key role in only a small proportion of the experiments. Might not a paper-and-pencil test suffice to assess those, notwithstanding the exhortations to avoid set-piece and one-off assessments of product? Another Israeli piece of work (Finegold & Meyer 1985) cites other work, including friend

Kruglak, as demonstrating that cognitive laboratory skills can be assessed 'with relative ease' by means of paper-and-pencil tests.

It was certainly customary for A level Science papers of the 1970s to include a sprinkling of questions intended to measure practical skills (Lock 1988). The University of London A level Chemistry papers and the Nuffield A level Chemistry papers studied by Wood & Ferguson (1975) were just such examinations. Wood & Ferguson were interested in the relationships between the results of a practical examination, teachers' assessments of up to eight experiments over the duration of the course, and marks on the written papers, especially the one with a sprinkling of practically oriented questions.

For the teachers, practical skills were defined as **A** = manipulative skills, **B** = observational skills, **C** = interpretation skills and **D** = creative skills or devising and planning of experiments; thus **B**, **C** and **D** had a cognitive orientation. It was noticeable that **A** produced the lowest correlations with the two written papers – of the order of 0·30. More significantly, all correlations involving the practical examination were low (0·22–0·31); in fact there was as little agreement between the external and internal practical assessments as between the written papers and the practical assessments.

The highest correlations between any skill category and the written papers involved **C**, which is not unexpected given that **C** was the most 'literary' of the categories. There was enough of a relationship (0·60) between the total teacher assessment and the paper with the sprinkling of practically-slanted questions to suggest that the latter might serve as a suitable moderating device for the total teacher assessment.

Especially interesting to Wood & Ferguson was the fact that this 'moderating' correlation rose with the number of teacher-assessed experiments, or rather the number cumulated. No doubt it was a manifestation of an effect familiar to test constructors; as with items in a test, the more measures are added the richer the composite becomes and the greater the criterion variance is accounted for. From plots they made, Wood & Ferguson deduced that the correlation between the cumulative teacher assessment based on **two** (any two) consecutive experiments and the practically-oriented written paper was in the region of 0·3, of the same order as that between the same paper and the practical examination, **which just happened to consist of two experiments**. They concluded that the practical examination had the measurement characteristics of any two teacher-assessed experiments combined. Teachers, however, were commonly assessing seven or eight experiments. If seven or eight experiments can be regarded as a working definition of what constitutes an adequate sampling of practical skills (note Wood & Ferguson), it follows that the practical examination is inadequate. The low correlations with other measures must then be taken as reflecting this inadequacy, compounded by unreliability, rather than signifying a distinctive and reliable assessment of practical skills.

The broader conclusion from the Wood & Ferguson work would be that practical work could be suitably assessed by a combination of paper-and-pencil tests (for the cognitive skills) and continuous assessment of performance in the laboratory (for the motor skills). As a matter of fact, the objections against a one-off paper-and-pencil test are precisely the same as for one-off practical examinations. If performance in the laboratory is to be the subject of continuous assessment, then it had might as well encompass all skills and all objectives.

Quite how many assessment occasions there should be is undetermined. The seven or eight experiments mentioned by Wood & Ferguson will not necessarily serve as a yardstick. Treatment of this question falls neatly under the generalisability paradigm (chapter 11). In their investigation of a particular instrument for assessing sensory–motor coordination, Finegold & Meyer (1985) demonstrated that the main contribution to the total variance was, by some margin, the Occasion–Rater interaction. The same examiner gave the same examinee different scores for the same performance on different occasions, and different examiners gave the same examinees different scores for the same performance on the same occasion. In short, examiners' ratings were not stable. Importantly, it was not the type of experiment which mattered. Finegold & Meyer were moved to observe that examinees' claims such as 'It's a pity that I had to do Newton's second law and not Ohm's law' have no foundation at all.

The coefficient of generalisability (conventional reliability where individual differences are concerned) is defined as the fraction of the total variance represented by the true variance of the population. All sources of variance are divided by the number of times they are sampled. Where an examinee performs an experiment on one occasion and is rated by one examiner only, there is no dividing by sample size, and the generalisability coefficient is bound to be low. The trick is to increase sample size for one or more of the factors. If an examinee is assessed over and over again, even by the same examiner (his/her own teacher), all the contributions to the variance resulting from the occasion factor and its interactions with other factors will be divided by the number of occasions. That is the justification for repeated observations.

Further evidence that the assessment of practical work lacks stability comes from Hubbard & Seddon (1989*a*). This particular exercise (involving 15-year olds in Norwich) required the students to prepare a salt by the reaction of an oxide with an acid, and the points of assessment concerned the production of the salt and the performance of a filtration at an intermediate stage. The results showed a significant change in both the marking standard and the reliability for two of the four points assessed (those which required the judges to inspect the filtrates and residues). A puzzling feature of the results was that the change occurred **for girls only**. Hubbard & Seddon had no idea why, but they did say that 'the observed bias almost certainly arose due to the fact that the judges knew the sex of each student', and that the bias occurred because on those particular two tasks, the judges, men and women, experienced most initial uncertainty in deciding whether or not the girls' performance was satisfactory. It is hardly an explanation, but Ebbutt's (1981) suggestion that what distinguishes girls' science from boys' science is that the former is product-oriented may be relevant insofar as the judges' confusion was greatest on intermediate process assessment points.

Observing performance in groups

Chapter 16 deals with the problem of assessing students when working collaboratively in groups. The problems of assessing students in groups while working independently (or ostensibly so) are not quite so acute, but the matter of how many students to assess simultaneously is vexatious. Intuitively, it would seem that the difficulties in making the assessments are going to increase as the number of students increases; with any task there is bound to be a number of students above which it is physically impossible to observe each student carrying it out, and to do the necessary recording. It may be that the appraisal is so rushed that the quality of the assessments with large numbers of students is significantly worse than that achieved with small numbers.

Little or no work has been done in this area but Hubbard & Seddon (1989*b*) have made a start. Eight teachers were allocated randomly and evenly to two panels, one of which assessed a random group of 5 students and then a group of 20, while the other worked with different randomly selected groups of the same size, but in the different order (to take care of order effects). Each student worked independently using a work sheet which gave the necessary instructions. There must always be doubt whether students ever work truly independently as long as they stand alongside each other in full view, but then again the covert look is a long way from active collaboration. Presumably, the more difficult the task the more collaboration is needed and these were not difficult tasks (heating test tubes to produce residues and precipitates).

There were 64 comparisons of five-group and 20-group results. In 61 of the comparisons, there was no loss of standard or reliability of marking for groups of 20 students compared to five students. Realising that teachers might still find it administratively difficult or inconvenient to handle up to 20 students simultaneously, Hubbard & Seddon suggest that it may well be possible to arrange for subgroups of, say, five to stagger their commencement of the different operations within a schedule which allows the teacher to observe every student perform every task. If the teachers quoted by Fairbrother (1987) are right about the magnitude of the assessment task entailed by GCSE – **ten** assessments for each pupil on **six** criteria – then larger group sizes will have to be entertained. Whether teachers can actually cope in these circumstances, bearing in mind the increased safety risks, is open to doubt.

There is an issue over what kind of scoring scheme to use when assessing process, whether students present in groups or singly. An example of a checklist (Gott 1987) is discussed in chapter 16 where marks can be gained for three kinds of apprehension. The virtues of this scheme (for teachers) is that the problem is clearly stated for the students; an apparatus list is given and there is a marking scheme which produces a numerical score for the students. Hubbard & Seddon chose the straightforward atomistic way of awarding one point for each recognisable stage of the experiment without worrying about whether the points were commensurable, such as one point for using a blue flame for heating, one point for obtaining an orange precipitate, one point for returning the test tube to the rack at the end of the exercise. Again there are doubts about the practicality for teachers of handling checklists for a number of students simultaneously. Singer & Lock (1984) reported 'a difficulty in operating up to 17 checklists at one time in the laboratory'(!). Asking students to produce their own reports takes the weight off the teacher, apart from having intrinsic value for the student. Whether students will take kindly to the elaborate recording systems used by OCEA, and recommended by Lock himself (Lock & Wheatley 1989), is open to doubt. A more acceptable method may be that proposed by Toh & Woolnough (1990) which, in keeping with Woolnough's holistic inclinations, tries to hold a balance between an open-ended (uncued) form of reporting and a specifically cued reporting style.

These exercises were, as noted, of the simplest kind, and the skills required to do them were developed in most students. This itself has attracted criticism. Hodson (1990), in the course of an onslaught on the value of practical science as presently conducted, complains that pupils are doing little more than following recipes. Woolnough & Toh assert that too much emphasis on assessing basic skills can trivialise science. What, though, if the skills required to make a success of more demanding practical work have not been acquired? If pupils are unable to get their experiments to work properly, then they obtain little insight into the chemical phenomena that the experiments were designed to illustrate. The Farmer & Frazer enquiry concluded, on the basis of a detailed analysis of performance of key tasks in the Revised Nuffield syllabus, that there is a mismatch between the practical capabilities of secondary pupils and the experimental demands of the chemistry courses that they follow. Is it not possible, they say, to organise the structure and sequencing of the pupils' experiments so that the practical tasks required for their exertion are not only fewer in number but repeated more often? Hodson (p. 36) makes a slightly different point. It is not that practical work is necessary in order to provide children with certain laboratory skills. Rather, it is that certain skills are necessary if children are to engage successfully in practical work. These criticisms are reminiscent of what Shayer (1972) had to say about the old Nuffield O level Physics syllabus. Teachers, he said, were too inclined to present material prematurely, or pitch it at too high a conceptual level, omitting the intermediate steps. Some recent Scottish work bears this out; in S4, after three years of science teaching, many 'basic skills' have clearly **not** been mastered by substantial numbers of pupils (Bryce & Robertson 1985, p. 4). Some APU findings were along the same lines: 'knowledge of some of the basic practical skills is not as widespread as might have been anticipated' (DES/APU 1982, 1984).

Discussion

Following an article called 'The assessment of observation in science', for the *School Science Review* (Gott & Welford 1987), a Belfast schoolmaster took the authors to task for begging the very question posed by the title – 'for as long as I have been teaching, questions have been set claiming to test one skill while actually testing others' (Oxlade 1988). By observation, teachers mean all sorts of things, said Oxlade. How interesting, then, that OCEA researchers should find observing to be the skill most often assessed by teachers (Lock & Ferriman 1989).

In making this charge, Oxlade put his finger on the crux of the matter where assessment of practical (and other) work is concerned. It is what Gagné called 'distinctiveness of measurement' (chapter 4). It was the lack of it which Hoste ran up against when trying to separate 'practical' from 'theory'. What makes matters worse, said Oxlade, is that setting questions which are not a valid test of the skill they are aimed at has two unfortunate effects. It teaches pupils that other skills are more useful than or can substitute for the one in question, and it penalises those pupils who attempt to answer the questions literally. If we are to encourage and develop observation as a science skill in our pupils it will be necessary to develop both assessment tasks which genuinely test the skill and mark schemes which reward the observant without rewarding the simply knowledgeable or conceptually advanced. In my experience, Oxlade concluded, the distribution of good powers of observation amongst pupils bears little relation to the pupils' overall performances and 'it is for this reason that I don't expect to see real tests of observation put into common use. It would go too much against the grain to find pupils who scored high on observation tasks but who were theoretically ignorant'.

Asking people to say or write down what they would do in practical situations is a surefire way of blurring the assessment. They have to be watched doing it and practicable ways have to be found of judging performance on several students simultaneously. Above all, it is necessary to have clear working definitions of what it is (reverting to Josephy's list) to handle data, to make measurements, to make observations, to modify a plan as necessary and so on. Here is where the greatest effort is likely to be needed, and where examiners may be found wanting. There is no great confidence that they can write questions targeted on particular skills, especially if Partington (1988) is right that they are more concerned with writing questions that are **acceptable**, that is get by, than enquiring into what makes a question work and whether it measures the targeted skill(s).

References

Anastasi A. (1970) On the formation of psychological traits. *American Psychologist*, **25**, 899–910.

Bryce T. G. K. & Robertson I. J. (1985) What can they do? A review of practical assessment in science. *Studies in Science Education*, **12**, 1–24.

DES/APU (1982) *Science in Schools: Age 15, Report No. 1.* London: HMSO.

DES/APU (1984) *Science in Schools: Ages 13 and 15, Research Report No. 3.* London: HMSO.

Ebbutt D. (1981) Girls' science: Boys' science revisited. In Kelly A. (ed.) *The Missing Half*. Manchester: Manchester University Press.

Fairbrother R. W. (1987) Problems in assessing practical work for the GCSE. *Education in Science*, **124**, 11–12.

Farmer A. & Frazer M. J. (1985) Practical skills in school chemistry. *Education in Chemistry*, **22**, 138–40.

Finegold M. & Meyer J. (1985) Assessing students' skills in the physics laboratory. *Studies in Educational Evaluation*, **11**, 321–6.

Gott R. (1987) The assessment of practical investigations in science. *School Science Review*, **68**, 411–21.

Gott R. & Welford G. (1987) The assessment of observation in science. *School Science Review*, **69**, 217–19.

Hodson D. (1990) A critical look at practical work in school science. *School Science Review*, **70**, 33–40.

Hofstein A. & Lunetta V. N. (1982) The role of the laboratory in science teaching: Neglected aspects of research. *Review of Educational Research*, **52**, 201–18.

Hoste R. (1982) The construct validity of some Certificate of Secondary Education Biology examinations: The evidence from factor analysis. *British Educational Research Journal*, **8**, 31–42.

Hubbard J. I. & Seddon G. M. (1989*a*) Changes in the marking standard and reliability of successive assessments of practical skills in science. *British Educational Research Journal*, **15**, 53–60.

Hubbard J. I. & Seddon G. M. (1989*b*) Comparison of the standard and reliability of the assessments of practical scientific skills using groups of different sizes. *Research in Science and Technological Education*, **7**, 45–9.

Josephy R. (1986) Assessment of practical and experimental work in physics through OCEA. *Physics Education*, **21**, 214–20.

Kruglak H. (1958) Evaluating laboratory instruction by the use of objective type tests. *American Journal of Physics*, **26**, 31–2.

Lock R. J. (1988) A history of practical work in school science and its assessment, 1860–1986. *School Science Review*, **70**, 115–19.

Lock R. J. & Ferriman B. (1989) OCEA – the development of a graded assessment scheme in science. Part 3: School trials. *School Science Review*, **70**, 103–12.

Lock R. J. & Wheatley T. (1989) Recording process skills and criterion assessments – student systems. *School Science Review*, **71**, 145–50.

Oxlade E. L. (1988) Rejoinder to Gott & Welford. *School Science Review*, **70**, 832–3.

Partington J. (1988) Towards a science of question-setting. *British Journal of Language Teaching*, **26**, 45–9.

Schools Council (1973) Assessment of attainment in sixth form science. *Examinations Bulletin No. 27*. London: Methuen Educational.

Shayer M. (1972) Conceptual demands in the Nuffield O-level physics course. *School Science Review*, **54**, 26–34.

Singer B. W. & Lock R. J. (1984) Assessment of practical skills in A-level chemistry. *Education in Chemistry*, **21**, 51–3.

Toh K-A. & Woolnough B. E. (1990) Assessing, through reporting, the outcomes of scientific investigations. *Educational Research*, **32**, 59–65.

Wood R. & Ferguson C. M. (1975) Teacher assessment of practical skills in Advanced level Chemistry. *School Science Review*, **57**, 605–8.

Woolnough B. E. & Toh K-A. (1990) Alternative approaches to assessment of practical work in science. *School Science Review*, **71**, 127–31.

Wyatt H. V. (1973) Examining examined. *Journal of Biological Education*, **7**, 11–17.

16 Assessing individuals working collaboratively in groups

The thought at first was to subsume this chapter under another. After all, it is bound up with school-based assessment, with the assessment of practical work, with oral assessment and, as Bain (1988) points out, with pupil self-assessment. Although some teachers may connive to avoid the problem altogether, others are certain to encounter it (those doing OCEA Science, for example). OCEA Science assessors are directed categorically to assess students working collaboratively. How, though, are individuals to be assessed? A separate chapter seemed to be called for, however slim the material.

There is, in fact, little in the way of research on this topic; perhaps the most solid is the work by Denvir & Brown (1987). Otherwise, there are accounts of what people have tried or suggest should be tried, such as Gott (1987). No one pretends to have ready answers.

Bain's little experiment captures the predicament facing assessors. Groups of four teachers discussing a mathematical topic were asked to try to assess the individual input into the activity of each member of the group by splitting 40 marks between them. In one group they split the marks 7, 10, 10, 13. The teacher who had 7 felt she had not input much. Two of the others, however, felt that her limited inputs were of greater value than their many and that by saying little but being involved she had empowered them, so to speak, and so they each gave her two of their marks. The other member could not see this. 'We can only assess what is said, not what is thought or not said.' The discussion could have gone on for a long time, remarked Bain. Here were four adults negotiating a distribution of marks between themselves. The task faced by the teacher assessor is a good deal harder, especially if pupils are not allowed to negotiate.

Presumably the problem of distinguishing between individual contributions is greatest when pupils work in pairs, except for large groups (six or more?) where it will be impossible, not so much because of the numbers but because some of the pupils will not register at all. With groups of three, four or five, the increased number of pairwise discriminations possible makes it that much easier to 'place' students. An instance in science practical work where it was impossible to distinguish the contributions of any one individual in a pair has already been reported (Gott 1987). The exact number of pairs assessed simultaneously was not given, but it is likely to have been nine or ten. Gott calls this a 'relatively large numbers of pupils' and thinks that distinguishing between pairs may be possible with reduced numbers.

Gott proposes an assessment method for individuals carrying out investigations which could, in principle, be used to assess individuals working jointly. Based on APU science testing at ages 13 and 15 (APU/DES 1988) it entails a short checklist to record pupils' investigations, the record of what they do, the pupils' records of their results, their subsequent write-up of their investigation and questions to individuals as a 'back stop' in case the rest of the data prove ambiguous.

Gott says that the key to the assessment is the checklist. He discusses a checklist for the 'Squash' investigation (investigating the bounciness of a squash ball at different temperatures).

Gott wrestles with the problem of how to produce a mark. One obvious way is to allocate one mark to each checkpoint and add them up. Another would be to allocate more than one mark to some of the more important checkpoints to weight the total. A third way, and one worth considering in more detail because of its lack of familiarity, is criterion-related. For an example of how this might work, suppose it was decided that to get one mark pupils would be expected to at least know what the investigation was supposed to be about – they know they were supposed to be measuring something about the bounciness of the ball at different temperatures but failed to devise an appropriate method of altering the temperature perhaps. In other words they had put an investigation into practice which contained the bare elements that define the problem – the variables to alter and to measure.

For their second mark pupils would be expected to put these variables into practice effectively (checkpoints under the second heading) and perhaps to have considered some of the variables that must be controlled if their investigation is to be a fair test. The third mark would be concerned with the validity (scale and accuracy) of the data they collected. To get this final mark pupils would not only have to have defined the investigation correctly and collected appropriate data, but also have ensured that the data would allow them to reach a valid conclusion.

These principles could be applied to all the investigations, giving a set of criteria common to them all. This is not to say that pupils could be expected to do any investigation well if they had done one successfully; it is not criterion-referencing in the strict sense. In some investigations, such as 'Springs' for example, fewer pupils will be able to cope with the complexity introduced by the two independent variables of diameter and number of coils. In others, the marks for effectiveness and validity will be harder to obtain.

When Gott tested these various methods on a (limited) sample, there were no changes to the rank ordering of pupils. What the exercise did do was to allow some sensible description to be made of what the 'mark' represents. Evidently, more complex versions of this approach can readily be devised.

It is obvious that the 'back-stop' interviewing of individuals to clarify contributions will always produce discrimination, according to the depth and duration of the questioning. If, as seems likely, the interview will produce better-quality information, then it would seem to be imperative, but, of course, it is time-consuming. A report on an SMP group investigation (Bloomfield 1987) is instructive. Bloomfield concluded that assessment by written work alone did not provide a satisfactory method of assessment. Talking to individual students will soon determine what mathematics they have made their own and how involved they were in the process of investigation. When students write up their work, Bloomfield says, they select the information they want to present. Bloomfield illustrates his point with two examples. Student A, who had appeared very confident working in a small group situation, was hesitant throughout the interview. She was unable to develop rules and when asked about a particular situation commented, 'I don't know because my friend did that one. I just copied it off the paper'. Student B, by contrast, was able to classify her rules and extend them. She was clearly familiar with the work she had written up and was able to extend her ideas beyond this.

What is significant here is that student A had been ranked and graded above student B consistently on the basis of written work. Bloomfield remarks that ranking and grading would have had to have been reversed had the information from the interviews been taken into account. 'From my knowledge of the class alone I would not have made such a reassessment, nor would their usual mathematics teacher', which makes an interesting comment on the inviolability of the teacher's rank order of students (chapter 6). The interviews took approximately 10 minutes. Bloomfield accepts that the problem of assessing joint work does not seem capable of easy resolution given the constraints on teachers' time.

The contrasting of written work and individual testimony was taken further by Denvir & Brown (1987; also papers referenced there); the context was again mathematics, this time in the primary school. The aim of the study was to investigate the extent to which a group assessment instrument would yield reliable diagnostic information about individual pupils' mathematical understanding (chapter 8). Three types of instrument were available – norm-referenced written tests, criterion-referenced written tests and practical/interview observation schedules to use with individuals or small groups of pupils.

Fourteen skills were singled out for assessment, with between one and six items to assess each skill. Although every effort was made to ensure that the same skills were being assessed, there were some slight differences in the way that items were presented in the class assessment and in the interview. Many of the differences in posing the questions were a direct result of the individual interview protocol which permits more detailed probing of children's understanding. For example, in an item which assessed children's ability to appreciate multiplicative structures presented as arrays, the strategy in the class assessment was to display a picture for a length of time which was adequate for correct enumeration of a row and column, but was not long enough for each item to be counted one by one. But in the interview it was possible simply to present the picture and leave it until the child had counted because the strategies available could be discovered through observation and questioning.

In terms of results, performance on every skill except the hardest one was higher in the interview than the assessment. There was a total of 76 out of 448 (17%) pupil-skills on which performance differed in the class assessment and the interview; 65 passed in the interview and failed in the class assessment and 11 failed in the interview and passed in the class assessment. Denvir & Brown comment that of the 32 pupils in the interview sample, six would have been significantly misplaced in the sense that they would have been wrongly assessed on at least 25% of the 14 skills by taking their score in the written test rather than their performance in the interview as a measure of their attainment in number. For each of these six pupils their performance in the written test underestimated their understanding of number.

Why the discrepancies? Eleven reasons were given by Denvir & Brown, of which the most significant would appear to be as follows:

Learning: in resolving inconsistencies in the interview, the pupil arrives at or stumbles on the required answer, whereas in the group test the situation and time constraints limit the response.

Prompting and clarification: in an interview, interviewer and pupil will attempt to agree about what is meant by a question. This is not generally possible in a group test. Prompting can also stimulate quite different thinking, which will produce different, probably better strategies and therefore answers.

Anxiety: as would be predicted, most pupils were more anxious with the class assessment than with the interview. Even so, some undoubtedly felt more anxious under close questioning.

Inability to see, hear or attend in the class assessment: these possibilities are reduced to a minimum in the interview.

Correctly guessing or estimating the answer in class: in the interview guesses are revealed as such because they cannot be backed up either by a logical justification or by certainty about the answer. This produces an overestimate of performance in the class assessment.

The interview would appear to be the preferred method for ascertaining what students 'know, understand and can do'. Denvir & Brown choose not to see it quite that way. Performance in the interview may supply the most veridical information about attainments, and therefore can serve as criterion, but since it was generally the case that if pupils were successful on a skill in the class assessment they were successful in the interview, then the class assessment must be deemed acceptable as an initial assessment of number understanding, from which pupils needing further diagnostic assessment can be identified. It is possible that Denvir & Brown may have arrived too easily at the last part of this conclusion. Those who get by on guessing also need help.

Discussion

More can always be learned about someone providing time is taken. But time is rationed and has to be cut off, or has it? Josephy (1986), writing about OCEA Science assessment, emphasises that it is not necessary that the teacher comes to a decision for any student **on a particular occasion** (his emphasis), only that such a decision is reached **over a period of time**. In this respect it is different from conventional formal testing, where, for better or worse, the result of the assessment **must** be recorded.

When there was no requirement that positive achievements be sought, the restricted achievement sample occasioned by time limits, and by inappropriate questions and lack of opportunity for clarification and so on, was the norm, even if its shortcomings were widely recognised. With the introduction of the notion of positive achievement, such arrangements will not do. Mass group testing, with or without differentiation, is not well conditioned to produce positive achievement.

No one knows exactly what positive achievement means, but suppose it is defined as that which is elicited by helpful probing and clarification, or more generally by what have been called **elaborative** procedures. Quite how mass group testing might accommodate procedures which are characteristic of 1:1 interviews was something Wood & Power (1987) struggled with, without arriving at operational solutions. They noted the shortcomings of multiple choice (too prone to give false positives through guessing **and** false negatives through reading too much into the item and anyway not indicative of positive achievement in an elaborated sense) and of essays (marking bias leading to false negatives, poorly worded questions leading to false negatives, bluffing the examiner leading to false positives) and concluded that school-based assessment offered, in principle, the best opportunity for **actualising** competence simply because the time is there to establish current limits of performance.

Once the interview method is decided upon, the problem of how to assess individual contributions to joint work merely turns into the more general problem of how to get the most veridical assessment of an individual's achievement to date. Since elaborative procedures are out of kilter with the extremely formal apparatus of British external examining, it is predictable that they will continue to be resisted even though the ambition is to release positive achievement. With school-based assessment, realities may force a different outcome. Here is Josephy again:

> Suppose that, during movement around a class, the teacher notices that student A has successfully assembled an electrical circuit from a diagram. This is recorded as indicating 'Performing' criterion $2b_2$ and 'Communicating' criterion $2a_2$. Student B is having considerable difficulty, and requires a good deal of help to do it properly. The teacher gives the help, and decides that student B is not yet meeting these criteria. Student C appears to be 'stuck', but encouraging noises and a judicious prompt from the teacher, enable her to complete the circuit. The teacher may decide that this, together with previous observations, indicates that student C *is* meeting the criteria even though some teacher input was needed.
>
> Many teachers may feel uneasy about this, brought up as they are on the supposed high reliability and validity of formal tests. We should remember though that in the real world we do depend on interactions with others, we do have 'blocks' and we do make mistakes. This does not necessarily mean we are not operating effectively. Also, consider how unsatisfactory a wrong answer in a formal test is. It *may* mean that the student is unable to do the task required; but it could instead mean that she/he misunderstood the question, made a trivial error, needed only a little more guidance, or was simply having a 'bad day'.

These remarks serve to dramatise the always imminent collision between progressive educational practice and rigid examining practice. In chapter 8 it was noted how it is impossible simultaneously to carry out successfully grading and genuine diagnostic work. Talk of positive achievement only finesses the fundamental problem of assessment, which is how do we ascertain the limits of an individual's capacity to achieve?

References

APU/DES (1988) Assessment of Performance Unit *Assessing Investigations: Ages 13 and 15*, Science Report for Teachers, No. 9.

Bain D. M. (1988) The assessment of group work. *Mathematics in School*, January, pp. 10–11.
Bloomfield A. (1987) Assessing investigations. *Mathematics Teaching*, **118**, 48–9.
Denvir B. & Brown M. (1987) The feasibility of class administered diagnostic assessment in primary mathematics. *Educational Research*, **29**, 95–107.
Gott R. (1987) The assessment of practical investigations in science. *School Science Review*, **68**, 411–21.
Josephy R. (1986) Assessment of practical and experimental work in physics through OCEA. *Physics Education*, **21**, 214–20.
Wood R. & Power C. N. (1987) Aspects of the competence–performance distinction: Educational, psychological and measurement issues. *Journal of Curriculum Studies*, **19**, 409–24.

17 Aptitude testing

The *Standards for Educational and Psychological Testing* (APA 1985) defines an aptitude test as follows (p. 89):

> A test that estimates future performance on the other tasks not necessarily having evident similarity to the test tasks. Aptitude tests are often aimed at indicating an individual's readiness to learn or to develop proficiency in some particular area if education or training is provided. Aptitude tests sometimes do not differ in form or substance from achievement tests, but may differ in use and interpretation.

Writing of the American scene, Jencks & Crouse (1982, p. 34) had this to say:

> Universities in other countries rely on what psychometricians call 'achievement' tests rather than what they call 'aptitude' tests to help them make admissions decisions. They do this because they assume that the best single predictor of how much a student will learn from studying something in a university is how much he or she learned from studying something similar in secondary school.

A ready rejoinder to the last point would be that there are higher education subjects not studied at school. Law is a prime example, and that is why the Law School Admissions Test (LSAT) came into being.

There is a conceptual distinction to be made between aptitude and achievement but it has proved difficult to sustain operationally. We might say that achievement tests are sensitive to recent learning while aptitude tests are sensitive to cumulative learning but, of course, that recent learning will be heavily conditioned by the quality of past learning and so on. The distinctions Schwarz (1971, p. 314) makes are as keen as any. The aptitude test differs from the achievement test in that the items may be based on skills not explicitly taught in school, and from the intelligence test in that the content is derived from the characteristics of the specific outcome to be predicted. But, says Schwarz, the assumptions of the three rationales are entirely compatible and, under certain circumstances, the identical test item can logically appear in all three types of test.

Do scholastic aptitude tests like the Scholastic Aptitude Test (SAT) actually succeed in placing applicants for college education from secondary schools of varying quality on a more equal footing than achievement tests do? Do race and socio-economic status affect conventional achievement scores as strongly as they affect SAT scores? The available data are too thin to permit any firm conclusions but, from what there are, it has been argued (Jencks & Crouse) that SAT scores appear to be just as dependent on home environment and school quality as scores on conventional achievement tests, and that the latter predict success in college and adult life just as well (or poorly, chapter 18) as the SAT or other aptitude tests do: '...for those concerned with equality of opportunity the choice between so-called aptitude tests and conventional achievement tests is a toss-up' (Jencks & Crouse). It is the case, however, that SAT scores and high school rank together provide better prediction of college performance than does rank alone (Gottfredson & Crouse 1986).

For a British audience there is some irony in the fact that Crouse favours replacing SAT with a battery of standardised achievement tests; irony when one thinks how often examinations (batteries of achievement tests, although not standardised) have been the object of attack. Amusingly, the arguments for preferring examinations to, say, intelligence tests have been rediscovered. Rather than improving admissions decisions, the aim is to improve education. Achievement tests may be no better at predicting college success than the SAT is, but at least they oblige students to engage in learning and encourage diligence at school (Crouse & Trusheim 1988).

A further irony is that while aptitude tests are under challenge in the US, there is some interest in the UK in introducing them, such as the British version of LSAT administered by UCLES and, now, the Academic Aptitude Profiles. The last time anything like the Academic Aptitude Profiles was mooted was the Test of Academic Aptitude (TAA), which did not survive the feasibility study (Choppin *et al.* 1973; Choppin & Orr 1976). Just as the Academic Aptitude Profiles resemble the LSAT, so the TAA was modelled on the SAT. This itself is interesting as the LSAT is more taxing and more sophisticated than the SAT.

The credo espoused by the Educational Testing Service for the SAT might be held up for the other tests mentioned – 'previous experience or training...is assumed to be constant for all individuals' (ETS 1980, p. 9). The TAA exercise, however, demonstrated unequivocally that this assumption would not stand up in practice. Among social sciences courses, in particular, the degree of mathematics content was crucial in determining TAA scores profiles. Psychologists and economists had clearly higher TAA Mathematics scores than sociologists and law students, and the highest Verbal scores were obtained by students of psychology and law (Choppin *et al.*, p. 18). When individuals are competing against each other for places in a department this may not matter very much, but when they are competing against each other for places in a university it does. The constancy assumption is clearly unrealistic.

To obtain equally accurate predictions of the identical skill for such different groups as boys and girls, or Asians and Europeans, different test exercises, consistent with their different experiences, may have to be used (Schwarz, pp. 313–14). As with the TAA, unless these different groups are to be compared with each other, there are no special problems. Schwarz argues that international organisations that use a standard set of aptitude tests everywhere, simply because the target skills are identical at all locations, are not taking full advantage of the flexibility afforded by this rationale.

Predictive or criterion-related validity

An aptitude test is judged ultimately on its ability to predict future outcomes. The same applies to other instruments like biodata (chapter 18) and the same cautions about the temptations of 'mindless empiricism' hold. An aptitude test must look appropriate (face validity) and it must incorporate samples of the specific skills which underlie effective performance later; in other words there should be point-to-point correspondence between predictor and criterion. If strong associations are revealed, then it should be possible to explain through a plausible causal narrative why they occur, even if the narrative relies on structural regressive phenomena, such as existing practices among educators and employers that reward academic ability.

Predictive validity calculations are always attended by methodological problems, notably the unreliability of predictor **and** criterion and the restriction of range problem, all of which typically attenuate product moment correlation estimates (chapter 12). It is therefore always possible to argue that reported correlations could and should have been higher but, of course, such special pleading can easily get out of hand. Uncorrected correlations (validity coefficients) in the 'thirties' (0·30–0·39) for reasonable sample sizes are usually as good as you can expect to get. When it comes to comparing competing instruments there is often not much daylight to be seen, because so many are operating in this band, or in the upper 'twenties'. That said, the NFER evaluators of the TAA were able to see enough daylight between the mathematical and verbal parts of the TAA and mean A level grade to be able to declare that mean A level grade was quite clearly the best single predictor of first year assessment in college

(Choppin *et al.*, p. 29). Validity coefficients ranged from 0·17 for History to 0·49 for Mechanical Engineering. The respective range for TAA-M was −0·07 (Economics) to 0·30 (Psychology), and for TAA-V −0·13 (Economics) to 0·22 (History).

It was results like this which gave people like Foy & Waller (1987) the confidence to argue that A level results should not be lightly discarded for admissions decisions and that aptitude tests should not be allowed to supplant them. That was said, it should be stressed, against a background where A level and degree class are far from the 'cleanest' variables imaginable. Sear (1983) found it necessary to list eight further kinds of analysis which would be required to investigate properly the relationship between these two variables.

A study similar to that of Foy & Waller, but in the medical education context, reported as its most striking finding that an applicant's O level performance correlated with performance throughout the entire medical course. Performance was measured in terms of score on 8 O levels and the correlations were 0·21, 0·12 and 0·11 for Parts 1, 2 and 3 respectively. Montague & Olds (1990) believe that these lowish correlations 'emphasize the importance of academic criteria in the medical student selection process'. It could be argued that O levels look more influential than they really are because they are the first substantial measure of academic ability and possess a special status on that account. The pertinent question to ask here is what happens after Parts 1, 2 and 3. An American commentary (McGaghie 1990) asserts that modest aptitude–achievement correlations drop dramatically as medical students move from the lecture hall to clerkships to clinics and beyond. Medical school achievement is predictable for only a short time span. Grades predict grades, test scores predict test scores, ratings predict ratings, but attempts to demonstrate scientific convergence among indicators of professional competence have not been successful.

Where there is no intention of supplanting A levels, and any aptitude tests which are introduced will coexist alongside, the simple correlation between predictor and criterion is less interesting than the **multiple correlation** between several predictors, considered simultaneously, and the criterion (or it could be multiple criteria, in which case multivariate analysis is required). The TAA evaluation looked into this and was able to estimate the value of TAA scores as supplementary information. The conclusion was that TAA scores contributed little; in particular, they added very little to the predictive information supplied by the school assessment and the number of O levels passed. An interesting side finding was that TAA, singly and in combination, predicted better for women than for men. Summarising several American studies, Seashore (1962) found the same thing and later work with LSAT data (chapter 1) has confirmed it. A plausible causal narrative explaining this result is yet to emerge. It may well have something to do with artificially induced restrictions of range for female data arising from limited opportunities to date.

The NFER evaluation wished to give TAA proponents what it called a paradoxical crumb of comfort (Choppin *et al.*, p. 30). When all the undergraduates were considered together the correlation of the mathematics aptitude subscore with performance shrank almost to zero. This is because of the differential requirements for mathematical ability in the various courses. When the courses were divided into their major groupings, the predictive efficiency of TAA scores increased. Similarly, the correlations for all science courses pooled together were less than that of the individual subjects considered separately. All this suggests, said the NFER report, that the more carefully we delineate the groups of students for whom predictions are sought, the better those predictions will be.

In the worlds of the SAT and the LSAT there has been active curiosity about what happens to prediction at different levels of aggregation. A study of the LSAT (Boldt 1986) established that about 70% of the apparent variation in LSAT validities among law schools is because of the statistical artefacts of sampling error, differences in these score ranges and differences in criterion reliability (this is special pleading wrapped up, but no matter). A similar study of the SAT (by the same author) came up with slightly lower figures (53% for SAT-V and 45% for SAT-M). The interesting statistic, however, was the ratio of the validities of SAT-V to SAT-M which turned out to be nearly the same across all colleges, suggesting that the factors associated with institutional uniqueness, whatever they may be, tend to operate about equally on SAT-V and SAT-M.

Coffman's little history of the SAT from 1926 to 1962 reveals that it was the intention of the College Board, almost from the outset, to request data from institutions on a regular and continuing basis (Coffman 1963, p. 5). As experience accumulated, it became clear that the best predictions could be made if the weights applied were developed specifically for each institution. Out of that was established the policy of encouraging continuous study by the colleges of the validity of the test for their own students. In 1927 there appeared validity data for nine college groups, and since then, reported Coffman, there have been literally thousands of studies.

The LSAT has been monitored in the same way since its introduction in 1948. An account of the major research efforts of the Law School Admission Council over the years (Hart & Evans 1976) is notable for the breadth of work undertaken, although this is true also of the SAT (a recent paper discusses the effect of time limits on students disabled in various ways). Validity studies of the LSAT are conducted for each individual school on a regular basis if the school wishes them. These validity studies have two purposes – (1) to determine how well the predictors are, in fact, predicting and (2) to develop a multiple regression (prediction) equation for each school showing the weights to be given the predictors in order to obtain the optimum predictions for applicants to the school. For the validity studies completed for 99 schools in 1972–3 the correlation coefficients between the best combination of two predictors, LSAT and undergraduate grades (UGPA) and first-year law school grades, ranged from approximately 0·18 to approximately 0·73 (Hart & Evans, p. 2). The median coefficient for all 99 schools was 0·43.

The Council also sponsored a number of studies looking at particular aspects of the use of the standard predictors. For example, in 1966 the Council funded the first of three so-called discrepant predictor studies. Prior to these studies, some admissions officers believed intuitively that applicants showing wide discrepancies between their undergraduate grade-point averages and LSAT scores should be treated differently from those whose LSAT and UGPA scores were similar. For example, a multiple regression equation might predict the same law school first-year average for an applicant with a 700 LSAT score and a bare C undergraduate average, and for another applicant with a 575 LSAT score and a B undergraduate average. Admissions officers doubted whether these two applicants showed the same promise. The first two discrepant predictor studies addressed themselves to this question. Both studies showed that the predictors of applicants whose LSAT and UGPA were discrepant should be treated no differently from those with consistent scores. These studies were replicated in 1970 using validity study data. The conclusion of the replications confirmed those of the earlier studies, that is applicants whose UGPA and LSAT were discrepant should be treated no differently from those with consistent scores.

In 1972 the Council sponsored two studies in the general area of the use of the traditional predictors. One study investigated the desirability of deriving and reporting part scores from the tests. Traditionally, the LSAT has been reported as a single score, but it was thought that validity might be improved if the single LSAT score for the norming test were to be divided into parts such as reading comprehension and legal reasoning ability. However, the conclusions of the study were that part scores would not result in improved prediction over a single LSAT score.

The other study was designed to explore whether the relationship between predictors and law school grades is linear or non-linear. Normally, validity studies assume that the relationship between predictors and first-year averages takes the form of a straight line. It is possible, however, that the progression may not be linear. For example, it may be that at the higher end of the predictor scale there is a tailing off so that once a particular index or predicted first-year average is reached, everyone at or above that predicted first-year average would be expected to do equally well even though there is a difference in the prediction index. A pilot study suggested that the relationship may be non-linear, but when a broader study was undertaken the results did not support its findings. Therefore, it was concluded that the use of non-linear regression techniques would not enhance the prediction of first-year law performance. This is the sort of study which needs to be done from time to time.

Research on item types

Whatever point-to-point correspondence is achieved between the demands of the aptitude test and the demands of the performance to be predicted, the lack of definitive content and the artificial nature of the test means that there is indeterminacy in the choice of test format which can only be negotiated by the experience and insight of the test constructor. At this crucial stage, remarks Schwarz (p. 314), test development is as much an art as a science. It follows that choice of item types is critical.

The record shows the College Board to have been quite prolific in the choice of item types. Prior to 1960, 36 different item types were tried at one time or another in the SAT (Loret 1960). French (1953) reported a study in which 11 additional item types were studied in a special experimental administration.

Coffman's judgement in 1963 was that, in general, new experimental tests, when included in a multiple correlation with SAT-V, SAT-M, the College Board Achievement Tests and High School Record, had failed to add significantly to the prediction of college performance. More recently, it was reported that a test of spatial ability had been included but was then dropped, apparently for lack of any predictive contribution (Bejar, Embretson & Mayer 1987). The SAT content has been stabilised for some time now.

The steady-state outcome is not surprising. Introduce any four or five item types and the positive manifold effect (chapter 13) will ensure that the best part of the available variance is scooped up. Even so, there may be scope for fine tuning the balance between item types. It has been suggested that if the SAT-V were to be revised, more reading comprehension items should be added to obtain a more unique reading score than currently reported (Dorans & Lawrence 1987). More sentence completion items should also be included as this item type appears to be the most efficient of all verbal item types. It also takes less time than analogy items which may be the most expendable item type.

It is also the case that certain item types are more susceptible to practice or to the application of 'test-wiseness' than others, and are therefore to be less preferred than others, and may even be discarded on the basis of research. There is an example in chapter 2.

One contemporary view of the state of research on the SAT regrets that there is no research to speak of on the quantitative items, and that the sentence completion item has been totally ignored (Bejar *et al.*). However, dimensionality analyses of SAT-M have indicated that the test is unidimensional and would not benefit from subskill differentiation and reporting (Dorans & Lawrence). This should not necessarily be taken as the last word.

The history of the LSAT with respect to item type stability and experimentation parallels closely that of the SAT. A significant number of item types were tested to determine which were the most useful as predictors, and the test quickly assumed the basic form that it had until 1974. Before 1974 the last significant change had occurred in 1971 when the figure classification and organisation of ideas item types were dropped, and the editing portion of the writing ability test was reduced from 30 minutes to 20 minutes (Hart & Evans, p. 21). Several experimental item types were tried out in the early 1970s including (1) a common word item type, (2) an extended reading recall item, (3) a quantitative comparison item type, (4) a logical reasoning item type, (5) a practical judgement item type and (6) a new approach to the principles and cases item type. Extensive validation studies showed that several of the experimental items increased prediction significantly (showing that it is possible to create more between-individual variance) and these were then phased into the test which now consists of the three broad item types, that is reading comprehension, logical reasoning and analytic reasoning, plus a 'variable' section (used for pretesting items and for pre-equating) and the writing sample.

Speededness

The LSAT is designed to be an 'unspeeded' test. A benchmark that is used in the testing industry is as follows – at least 75% of persons who take the test should be able to finish 95% or more of the questions on the test. This benchmark serves as a design objective of the LSAT.

There is, at present, no way to **guarantee** that this objective is being achieved because candidates are encouraged to enter guesses for items they are unable to answer. However, the Law School Admission Council/Law School Admission Services (LSAC/LSAS) monitors speededness in two ways. First, it collects operational data on how frequently candidatės fail to complete the test. Although this is an imperfect measure (because candidates are encouraged to complete the test by guessing), some percentage of test takers invariably fails to complete each test; if this percentage is unusually high, it can signal a potential problem. The second method used for monitoring speededness is built into the item quality control process; item reviewers simulate the process of taking the test, flagging items that cannot readily be answered within the time constraints imposed by the LSAT (LSAC 1988).

The SAT was conceived of as a measure of power in the use of the languages in learning, not as a measure of speed. In an early report on the SAT (1927) a study was reported which indicated that a pure speed test did not measure the same ability as a test of the same kinds of questions chosen so that each candidate had an opportunity to answer every question for which he knew the answer. Therefore, in the third form of the test, 'an effort was made to provide much more liberal time limits, the compensation in total time being made by reducing the number of tests from nine to seven' (Coffman 1963). Loret (1960) presents a graphic record of the gradual reduction in the number of items per unit time. The successive test analyses demonstrate that the reduction in the number of questions has not been accompanied by a comparable reduction in reliability. By choosing questions on the basis of experimental try-out, and allowing time for candidates to answer all questions they are capable of answering correctly, reliability has been maintained, although test forms contain fewer questions (Coffman, p. 14).

A consequence of insisting on power tests is that the total test administration is protracted and may be burdensome to some or most candidates. Asking them to work at a high level on a test for three hours may be asking too much. The problem is magnified when tests are administered for a whole day, as happens when candidates take College Board achievement tests as well as the SAT. Coffman reports several studies of performance and fatigue and suggests that the finding of one particular study is typical. Seven 30-minute verbal sections and seven 20-minute mathematics sections were administered in balanced patterns in a full day of testing and there was no evidence of any lowering of performance on the later sections. Apparently, at least for periods as great as seven hours with a one-hour period in the middle, students are able to maintain a constant level of performance on tests.

Tailored testing

Should it be thought too burdensome to expose candidates to seven hours of testing in one day (and one old College Board study can hardly be taken as definitive) then there is the prospect of using tailored or adaptive testing where the presentation of test items is made contingent upon the responses of individual examinees to the preceding items. The savings in time can obviously be considerable and there is the certainty of improved measurement at the extremes of the ability range, if that is needed. Administration needs to be by computer, given the statistical computation required to select items at each step. There was, in fact, an exploratory study carried out back in 1968 (Linn & Carlson 1968) when tailored or branched testing, as it was called then, was just being developed. The results of that study were negative in the sense that a branched test was no more valid than a conventional test. The results, however, may have been due to the fact that conventional test items were used for the study instead of a test designed specifically to be used as a branched test (Hart & Evans, p. 22).

The concern these days is in ensuring that, in addition to controlling item difficulty, the blend of the different components of difficulty is maintained from one examinee to the next. By focusing on difficulty alone as a means of selecting items, we may end up choosing items that differ widely in their vocabulary load, in effect making the adaptive test for that individual a vocabulary test. In practice, items are also selected on the basis of discrimination, the higher the better. This, too, can store up problems, as when attempts are made to diversify the item pool by introducing new and different material. Since new items will tend to have relatively low item–test biserials, they will tend not to be selected. As Green (1988) says, item response theory methods of item calibration are more efficient than conventional methods in driving out the new and different, and computer-administered testing is even better. One way of dealing with this problem is to partition off item types from each other and calibrate within segments.

Discussion

In supporting Crouse's proposals to replace the SAT with achievement tests, Humphreys (1986, pp. 430–1) identified the one situation where he believes the SAT is needed. For high schools that do not fit the average pattern of quality of intake and quality of graduate the test information is crucial. A university high school, for example, tends to be highly selective. Rank in class is highly ambiguous for low-ranking students. Mean grades are little better, says Humphreys, because teachers tend to give a range of grades no matter how much information they have about their students. This seems to constitute an argument for having an aptitude test like the SAT. If the argument is sound, and it probably is, then it applies with greater force to international candidatures where achievement credentials have little or no comparability. That, however, ushers in a fresh problem which is the one of variable experiential histories Schwarz referred to. It takes a bold decision to use the same content on students from, say, Singapore, Nepal and the USSR. That said, if the SAT works most efficiently with localised weights calculated by institution, then presumably any aptitude test used with an international candidature would work best with weights adapted to the institution (or even department) **and** to the candidate country of origin.

It is this kind of validation work on a continuing basis which constitutes the main part of the research programme which must be associated with any serious aptitude test. Beyond that there is the absolute need to monitor how the various item types are functioning, and to bear in mind that change may be necessary even if, as it appears, new item types rarely make any additional predictive contribution.

References

American Psychological Association (1985) *Standards for Educational and Psychological Testing*. Washington, DC: APA/NCME/AERA.

Bejar I., Embretson S. & Mayer A. E. (1987) Cognitive psychology and the SAT: A review of some implications. *ETS Research Report*, **87-28**.

Boldt R. F. (1986) Generalization of SAT validity across colleges. *ETS Research Report*, **86-24**.

Choppin B. *et al.* (1973) *The Prediction of Academic Success*. Windsor: NFER Publishing Co. Ltd.

Choppin B. & Orr L. (1976) *Aptitude Testing at 18 plus*. Windsor: NFER Publishing Co. Ltd.

Coffman W. E. (1963) The scholastic aptitude test – 1926–1962. *College Entrance Examination Board Test Development Report* **TDR-63-2**.

Crouse J. & Trusheim D. (1988) *The Case Against the SAT*. Chicago: University of Chicago Press.

Dorans N. J. & Lawrence I. M. (1987) The internal construct validity of the SAT. *ETS Research Report*, **87-35**.

Educational Testing Service (1980) *Test Use and Validity: A Response to the Charges in the Nader/Nairn Report on ETS*. Princeton, NJ: Educational Testing Service.

Foy J. M. and Waller D. M. (1987) Using British school examinations as a predictor of university performance in a pharmacy course: A correlative study. *Higher Education*, **16**, 691–8.

French J. W. (1953) Validation of new item types for the SAT. *ETS Research Bulletin*, **53-19**.

Gottfredson L. S. & Crouse J. (1986) Validity versus utility of mental tests: Example of the SAT. *Journal of Vocational Behaviour*, **29**, 363–78.

Green B. F. (1988) Critical problems in computer-based psychological measurement. *Applied Measurement in Education*, **1**, 223–31.

Hart F. M. & Evans F. R. (1976) *Major Research Efforts of the Law School Admission Council*. Princeton, NJ: Law School Admission Council.

Humphreys L. G. (1986) Commentary. *Journal of Vocational Behaviour*, **29**, 421–37.

Jencks C. & Crouse J. (1982) Should we relabel the SAT – or replace it? In Schrader W. (ed.) *New Directions for Testing and Measurement: Measurement, Guidance and Program Improvement*, no. 13. San Francisco: Jossey-Bass.

Law School Admission Council (1988) *Specifications for the LSAT*. Newtown, Penn.: Law School Admission Council/Law School Admission Services.

Linn R. L. & Carlson A. B. (1968) Exploratory LSAT branched testing study. *Annual Council Report*. Princeton, NJ: Law School Admission Council.

Loret P. (1960) A history of the content of the SAT. *CEEB Research and Development Report*, **60-1**.

McGaghie W. G. (1990) Perspectives on medical school admission. *Academic Medicine*, **65**, 136–9.

Montague W. & Olds F. C. (1990) Academic selection criteria and subsequent performance. *Medical Education*, **24**, 151–7.

Schwarz P. A. (1971) Prediction instruments for educational outcomes. In Thorndike R. L. (ed.) *Educational Measurement* (2nd edition). Washington, DC: American Council on Education.

Sear K. (1983) The correlation between A level grades and degree results in England and Wales. *Higher Education*, **12**, 609–19.

Seashore H. G. (1962) Women are more predictable than men. *Journal of Counselling Psychology*, **9**, 261–70.

18 Personnel selection and assessment

This chapter reviews the work on the assortment of methods and procedures which are available for use in selecting personnel.

The list is headed by what Cook (1988) calls the 'classic trio', or 'we've always done it this way'. They are:

application forms;
interviews;
references.

To these can be added:

educational qualifications;
experience, seniority and age;
realistic job previews;
cognitive tests including basic skills tests;
work samples including trainability tests.

Personality tests, although widely used, are excluded because the state-of-the-art makes it risky to use them for front-line employment recruitment (Schmitt & Noe 1986). That said, Cook is undoubtedly right (p. 155) when he says that selectors still lack a good way of identifying people who could do well, but won't, because they are too anxious, because they don't get on well with people, because they are inconsistent or distractible, or because they don't like being told what to do.

The trio is classic because of its ubiquity. Two-thirds of major British employers always take up references; only a handful never do (Robertson & Makin 1986). Robertson & Makin's survey of top UK employers, taken from the *Times 1000,* found only one who never interviewed. All employers use application forms, although they differ widely in what they ask for. The Industrial Society surveyed 50 British application forms; name, address, date of birth, previous employers and reasons for leaving last job were the only constants (Cook, p. 14). Only half asked for age, and only 4% asked the bureaucrat's classic – mother's maiden name. Surprisingly few forms asked about hobbies and leisure interests. 40% wanted to avoid nepotism, and asked if the applicant had any relatives working for the company. Two-thirds asked for an educational history, and 26% about details of membership of professional bodies.

There have been efforts to make more powerful the basic application form, the interview and the references request, but in terms of reliability and validity the interview and references remain deeply suspect.

Application form

By dint of scoring the responses, and through some restructuring, the common or garden application form can be turned into what used to be known as the weighted application blank but is now known increasingly as **biodata**, also biographical inventories. Biodata works on the principle that the best predictor of the future is past behaviour, and the easiest way of measuring past behaviour is what the applicant writes on the application form.

Developing a scoring key for biodata is a thoroughly empirical affair, mindlessly empirical in the eyes of its critics. It doesn't matter **why** an item differentiates successful estate agents from unsuccessful, only that it **does** (Cook, p. 82). This offends psychologists who like to feel they have a theory. Some psychologists use factor analysis to attempt to quantify composites of items that measure an interpretable set of constructs, and to discover 'psychologically meaningful personal history variables' (Mitchell & Klimoski 1982), but these are really only fishing expeditions, one step removed from mindless empiricism.

Biodata does work, however, providing it is of the 'hard' variety (factual, verifiable) and not 'soft' (the sort of attitudinal data which might be obtained from personality tests). This much was discovered in Civil Service Commission research (Johnson 1986). Biodata has been used successfully to predict success as sales/research engineer, oil industry research scientist, pharmaceutical industry researcher, bus driver and police officer (Reilly & Chao 1982). Although biodata appears to be colour-blind, it is sometimes necessary to use different scoring keys for males and females (Cook, p. 96).

Biodata is not much used in Britain although there are signs that it is catching on. Robertson & Makin's survey found 5% of major British employers using biodata for selection. British Airways use one for cabincrew. Blue Arrow plc, the High Street recruitment people, uses biodata in its branches for hiring its own staff. One factor which restricts its use is the need for large throughputs of people so as to be able to derive a scoring key empirically. Only employers like the Civil Service Commission are really able to take advantage and, in fact, they have installed biodata in the Inland Revenue and the DHSS. Some recent research from its own Recruitment Research Unit (RRU) recommended that biodata be introduced into the selection procedure for appointments-in-administration alongside the cognitive tests which have hitherto been used exclusively (Bethell-Fox, Cureton & Taylor 1988). Candidates with high biodata scores, but with test scores below the threshold, performed as well at the Civil Service Selection Board (CSSB) as other candidates invited on the basis of satisfactory test scores. The RRU report suggests that this is because biodata picks up interpersonal skills and non-cognitive intrapersonal characteristics, such as motivation, which the test scores cannot do. It concludes that further development of the biodata instrument might focus on measures of spare-time interests and organisational activities as well.

The Civil Service Commission is on record as saying that biodata is much less likely to produce stereotypes than subjective paper-based sifting (CSC 1987). Even so, it will be evident that biodata uses items such as age, sex, race and marital status which are potentially contentious and could be the subject of litigation if it could be shown that a selection decision hinged on them. It is also the case that biodata can be faked, but then that is true of application forms generally. What the faker can never be quite sure of is whether the particular lies told are advantageous or not.

References

British 'references' are usually letters saying what the referee feels like saying about the candidate, in whatever form s/he feels like saying it. According to Cook (p. 15), very few British employers ask for ratings, or for any structured or quantified opinion of the candidate. US employers are more likely to use structured reference forms. A very early (1923) survey, described by Moore (1942), found most reference writers said:

> they always gave the employee the benefit of the doubt;
> they only said good things about him/her;
> they didn't point out his/her failings.

Cook makes the point (pp. 70–1) that if referees **are** reluctant to say anything unkind, references are clearly a poor source of information and can never demonstrate predictive validity, because the range will be very severely restricted. What research there is confirms this pessimistic conclusion. In Mosel & Goheen's (1959) enquiry, nearly all referees said 'Yes' to 'Would you employ him?'.

Interviews

This ubiquitous method of selection gets pasted time and time again but refuses to lie down. All the experts are agreed – the employment interview has poor validity. But everyone gets interviewed. In part this is because recruiters do not know that interviews have poor validity, but also because, irrespective of validity considerations, employers believe face-to-face contact to be a necessary condition for matching between individual applicant and individual organisation to occur (Herriot 1988, p. 389). For the applicant, too, the interview is indispensible; 'most people have faith in the process'. The interview is the place to 'put your best foot forward... If you can just get in to see the interviewer you can tell your whole story' (Hakel 1982). As Cook says (p. 53), interviews **look** fair, especially when they are grand and elaborate. The reality, as most recently revealed by Edwards, Johnson & Molidor (1990), is that interviewers are often biased in terms of their rating tendencies (for instance, leniency or severity) and in terms of an applicant's personal characteristics (sex, race, appearance, similarity to the interviewer and contrast to other applicants).

Ultimately, validity is low because the interview is trying to predict the unpredictable. The interviewer's judgement is compared with a 'criterion' that defines a good employee. This criterion is never perfect and is often another person's judgement, which may be just as fallible as the interviewer's judgement. Supervisors' ratings, one commonly used criterion, have fairly good reliability (around $r = 0{\cdot}60$); one supervisor agrees fairly well, but far from perfectly, with another. For training grades and also promotional progress (Meyer 1987) a better outcome can be expected, but another study found that interviewer ratings of officer cadets in 'a national defence organisation' failed to correlate at all with training grades after 6 and 12 weeks (Zedeck, Tziner & Middlestadt 1983).

Herriot (1989) believes that the purpose of the interview needs rethinking (see also Harris 1989). The model whereby selecting is something somebody does to someone else needs to be reconceptualised, as much as anything because a buyer's market has become, to a large extent, a seller's market. What is needed now is a model which represents both parties as exchanging information and coming to decisions. It must, says Herriot, imply a dynamic social process rather than an assessment of static applicant attributes. In this realisation, the interview is the vehicle for sharing information. It is removed from the front line of selection, where suspect validity and reliability make it a menace, and placed instead at the end of the recruitment or selection procedure, or indeed the promotions procedure. In this position the interview is used strictly as a medium for negotiation with those with whom the organisation wishes to discuss future employment. For those who want it, the interview still occurs, but the sting is taken out of it; no more trying to guess whether someone can do the job on the basis of answers to a few desultory questions, and no more intimidating behaviour. There is clear evidence that applicants decide whether or not to accept job offers partly on the basis of the behaviour interviewers exhibit towards them (Harn & Thornton 1985).

If the interview is to stay in the front line, then it must be structured. The structured interview questions should be based on formal job-analytic information, there should be sample answers to help evaluate responses and a panel of interviewers should be used, all of which should lead to improved reliability and validity (Wiesner & Cronshaw, 1988; Edwards, Johnson & Molidor 1990). The so-called situational interview is merely an example of the structured interview whereby the results of systematic job analyses are used to produce job-related incidents. The incidents are then turned into interview questions in which job applicants are asked to indicate how they would behave in a given situation. The study by Arvey *et al.* (1987) produced encouraging validity coefficients, perhaps because, as Robertson & Smith (1989) suggest, the interviews were functioning as surrogate work-sample tests.

So, what becomes of the 'classic trio' is this. The application form is converted into a biodata form with multiple choice questions requesting hard data, the reference is also given structure or abandoned altogether, and the interview has its teeth drawn but assumes the valuable function of negotiation, or else is given a structure.

If selection is a sequence of episodes, then, at the front end of the sequence, along with the application form and the references, is the sifting process. There are two kinds of sifting, including in (by the employer) and opting out (by the applicant). For the former, the most popular sifting devices are **educational qualifications** and **job experience**, or **seniority** generally; for the latter, the **realistic job preview** can help the applicant decide whether s/he wants the job.

Educational qualifications

Educational qualifications (EQ) have long been favoured as a strong sign of potential success. It is believed that early academic endeavour must translate itself into later occupational endeavour. The absence of any compelling evidence in support of such a belief has done nothing to dampen it. American college grade-point averages were found to correlate moderately with training grades, but hardly at all with supervisor ratings (O'Leary 1980). This suggests that better-educated individuals make a better impression but do not necessarily perform any better. Harrell *et al.* (1977) found MBA grades predicted earnings after five years very well, and earnings after ten years quite well. Reilly & Chao (1982) warn, however, that these correlations may be an artefact; quite often grades set initial salary and so initiate a self-fulfilling prophecy. A quantitative synthesis of 35 studies of the association between academic and occupational performance (Samson *et al.* 1984) concluded that 'the overall variance accounted for makes academic grades or test scores nearly useless in predicting occupational effectiveness and satisfaction'.

All the work referenced so far is American. There is next to no British work. The best we have to go on is a re-analysis of the National Child Development Study (NCDS) data which indicated that educational qualifications (EQ) in the population at large had a distinct association with a measure of occupational attainment at age 23 (Elias & Blanchflower 1987). Such a result is to be expected, if only because of the operation of EQ as an excluding device and therefore as an initiator of self-fulfilling prophecies. There will always be an irreducible (if small) relationship between EQ and occupational performance. But that relationship should never be taken, in and of itself, to support EQ as a front-line selection method.

A justifiable challenge to EQ is to ask why they are necessary to do the job in question. Sometimes the case can be made, as when it can be shown that what, say, a civil engineer studies, and the projects s/he undertakes, are directly relevant to what an engineer has to do in early career (RRU 1985). In other circumstances the point-to-point correspondence between predictor and criterion seems not at all obvious, or compelling. A hotel in Oxford advertised for bar staff, specifying two O levels in Maths and English. When asked why O levels were needed, the manager told the Commission for Racial Equality (CRE) that he received fewer, better calibre applicants, although he conceded that possession of O levels was not necessary (Coussey & Whitmore 1987). The cases *Roy vs. DHSS* and *Dattani vs. DHSS* have dramatised the problem the EQ requirement poses for ethnic minorities and for other groups of unqualified people. The Treasury Solicitor has, in fact, accepted that O level English can have adverse impact for such people. The Civil Service has now reviewed its policy and has decided to accept English Language qualifications from countries where the main official language is English or where the candidates can provide evidence that their medium of instruction was English (Civil Service Commission 1987, p. 9). It may still be asked whether an O level equivalent from Malaysia is necessary to tend bar.

The interesting feature of the Oxford case was that the hotel keeper wanted EQ, not as a sign of potential since there was no career to follow, but as an insurance that he would get competence now, or else that he would need to do little or no training. This attitude may be widely shared.

Sometimes the necessity for EQ is argued in terms of risk. EQ may not be especially job-related, but the job requires such a high degree of skill and the economic and human risks involved in mis-hiring are so great that a fairly high EQ threshold must be insisted upon. It is a kind of belt-and-braces argument. Airline pilots are often cited in this connection, and in fact the US courts in *Spurlock* vs. *United Airlines* upheld a college degree requirement for airline pilots. Against that, other US court decisions have struck down college degree requirements for the following – medical technologists, systems and traffic analyst, case worker/social worker – strictly on the grounds that the job specification in question did not support the degree requirement (Wigdor 1982). The US court decisions can be seen as a corrective to credentialism.

Experience

Experience has very moderate predictive validity for supervisor ratings, and zero validity for training grades (Hunter & Hunter 1984). **General experience**, in supervising people or selling, has no predictive validity. According to Cook (p. 92), research on air traffic controllers found that experience was only used when it was directly and specifically relevant. Having used a radio or flown an aircraft did not predict efficiency as an air traffic controller, but experience in instrument flying did. The suggestion is that job experience has a greater impact on job knowledge and job performance for low-complexity jobs than for high-complexity jobs because it has to compensate for the relative lack of educational preparation at the low end (McDaniel, Schmidt & Hunter 1988).

The principle of 'Buggin's Turn' is often used to decide who gets promoted. There is no reason to expect seniority to be related to efficiency; the epithet 'time-server' was not coined for nothing. Research on this subject is very thin; Gordon & Fitzgibbons (1982) found seniority quite unrelated to efficiency among female sewing machine operators. Schmidt *et al.* (1988) note that the question of the joint relationship of ability and job experience to job performance is a critical one for personnel psychology, both for validity and utility, and urge further research.

Age

Hunter & Hunter (1984) reviewed over 500 validity coefficients and found that age alone has zero validity as a predictor, whether the criterion is supervisor rating or training grade. A more recent study (McEvoy &

Cascio 1989), also based on meta-analysis, came to the same conclusion. Age does predict turnover; younger employees are more likely to leave (Muchinsky & Tuttle 1979). Cook (p. 94) makes the point that age can distort biodata scoring in that older people tend to have more dependants, higher living expenses, to belong to more organisations and to have held more positions of responsibility than younger people, so a biodata form using age-related items for applicants with diverse ages could give misleading results.

It is fair to conclude from this review of the methods the employer uses to sift applicants that the capacity for excluding people who might well be able to perform, were they given the chance, is great. That being so, equity is better served if applicants take the decision themselves to drop out. Providing them with a realistic job preview may lead to that outcome.

Realistic job preview

The realistic job preview trades on the reasoning, 'Show me the job and if I think I can handle it, I probably will be able to. If not, I'll opt out, which will save you money'.

Recent American work suggests that the match between self assessment of individual preferences may be a valid indicator of job performance and satisfaction (Schmitt & Noe 1986; Wanous 1989). Job previews may be of the **enhancement** type, designed to enhance overly pessimistic expectations, or the **reduction** type, designed to reduce overly optimistic expectations. Meglino *et al.* (1988) showed that the previews presented in combination increased perceptions of trust and honesty, and that the reduction preview worked as intended in dampening anticipated job satisfaction.

With sifting complete and short lists drawn up, it remains to find out who, among the applicants, will do the job best. There may be other considerations such as 'will stay in the job' or 'will go on to greater things' but the competence to do the job in hand ought to be the overriding consideration. It is when organisations try to look for too much that selection goes awry, a good example being the Civil Service insistence on looking for 'potential' even in the lowest grades. On the understanding that interviews are best left to the end, the choice of method boils down to **cognitive tests** and **job** or **work samples**.

Cognitive tests

In 1918 Link published a validation study of 139 assorted munitions workers using a battery of nine tests, including an unidentified intelligence test. Some tests predicted hourly output well; the Woodworth Wells Number Checking Test correlated well for some employees, but not for 'shell gaugers' and 'paper shot shell inspectors' ($r = 0{\cdot}02$ and $-0{\cdot}19$).

Card sorting and cancellation tests, as well as general intelligence, also had some predictive value. Link probably published the first validity coefficient.

American research during the 1950s is reviewed by Super & Crites (1962), who include the extensive wartime researches with the Army General Classification Test. The Classification Test predicted success in training in 37 different military roles, and was also used to grade civilian occupations by average intelligence. Occupations with low average intelligence were miner, farm worker, lumberjack and teamster; occupations with high average level were accountant, personnel clerk, and students of medicine or mechanical and electrical engineering.

Herrnstein (1973) took the position that intelligence is **necessary but not sufficient** for productivity. He presented data showing that few accountants had IQs more than 15 below the accountant average, whereas quite a few lumberjacks had IQs well **over** their average of 85. Assuming the latter had not always wanted to be lumberjacks, the data imply they could not or did not use their ability to find more prestigious work.

The fact that (except for very large samples) there is less predictive power in a tailored composite battery of aptitude tests than in a measure of general cognitive ability (Hunter, 1986; Thorndike, 1986), coupled with the renewed finding that general cognitive ability predicts equally well over very broad categories of occupation (Pearlman, Schmidt & Hunter 1980), has led to a new interest in general intelligence or *g*. Quite why ability tests predict productivity so well, in such a wide range of jobs, is the subject of recent research, including work by Jensen (1986) whose 1969 *Harvard Educational Review* article (and the racist motives attributed to him) made him the villain of the piece and led to a devaluation of *g*. Not everyone accepts the limitation on differential prediction and the primacy of *g*; for a dissenting note see Hartigan & Wigdor (1989, p. 146).

The causal linkages between *g* and work performance may go something like this (following Hunter 1986). More intelligent people are better workers primarily because they learn more quickly what the job is about. In high-level work this may mean learning scientific method, scientific techniques and a specific body of knowledge. In low-level work it may mean only learning where to find the raw materials, what to do with them and where to put the finished product. Hunter found the 'paths' between Ability, Work Sample, and Supervisor Ratings weaker in military samples than in civilian ones. He suggests that this reflects military emphasis on training and drill. Soldiers are not left to work things out for themselves, or to devise their own ways of doing things; performance reflects training more than individual differences in cognitive ability.

The further suggestion is that Experience also improves Work Sample performance, and leads to better Supervisor Ratings through improved

Job Knowledge. This implies that Experience can 'substitute' for General Mental Ability; less able workers will learn enough about the job to work productively, but will take longer to do so. Meanwhile they cost the employer money by being less productive than their more able colleagues. Research has not yet directly confirmed the 'substitution' hypothesis. The broader interpretation of this line of work is that the initial advantages conferred by higher ability are maintained over time (Schmidt *et al.* 1988).

Meanwhile, the increased use by industry of so-called **basic skills tests** for filling low-level jobs, such as Skillcheck (AEB 1987), is indicative not so much of a belief in the necessity for minimum or acceptable literacy and numeracy levels, whatever those terms mean, as a demand for some brainpower, or nous, however the sentiment is expressed in public.

Not that British industry has gone overboard for cognitive ability tests. The Robertson & Makin survey found that 71% never use cognitive tests. That said, there are grounds for thinking that tests are recovering from the bad press they received in the 1970s and that test use is on the increase. Even so, there may be applicant resistance to be overcome. One study discovered that applicants far prefer work sample exercises to psychometric tests, considering them fairer, clearer, and of a more appropriate level of difficulty (Schmidt *et al.* 1977). The work sample is indeed attractive; what could possess more validity than actually trying to do aspects of the job being applied for?

Work sample tests

Cook (p. 174) puts the case for work sample or 'hands-on' tests this way:

> Intelligence tests assess the applicant's *general* suitability and make an intermediate inference – this person is intelligent so s/he will be good at widget-stamping. Testing the employee with a real or simulated widget-stamper makes no such inference (nor is widget-stamping ability quite such an emotive issue as general intellectual ability).

The general principle is that the tighter the point-to-point correspondence between predictor and criterion, the stronger the validity and the less scope there is for legal challenge as, for instance, those US court cases of the 1970s where someone like a Chicago fire officer would complain that promotion should not depend on the results of a writing test. How do you test who will be a good policeman, asked McClelland (1973)? Follow him around, make a list of his activities, and sample from that list in screening applicants.

Cascio & Phillips (1979) describe 21 work samples for municipal employees in Miami Beach, covering a wide range of manual, clerical and administrative jobs, from electrician's helper (mate) to parking-meter technician, from library assistant to concession attendant. Applicants for concession attendant were tested on site, out of hours, counting cash, giving change, completing revenue reports, making announcements and dealing with irate customers. It seems that the tests were very convincing to the applicants. If applicants for electrician had completed the wiring test correctly the light lit up; if the wiring was faulty the bulbs failed to light, and the applicant could not deny s/he had made a mistake. Some of the tests had 'realistic job preview' built in; quite a few applicants for the post of sewer mechanic withdrew after being tested in an underground sewage chamber. According to Gordon & Kleiman (1976) applicants tested by work sample are better motivated to accept the job than those tested by cognitive ability tests.

'Classic' work samples can only be used if the person already has the skills to do the job; it is clearly pointless giving a typing test to someone who cannot type. This suggests that work sample tests would be useful for people already in a job, either for certification purposes or for ascertaining that competence is being maintained. In some work on assessment in the workplace (Wood *et al.* 1989) the contrast was made between more or less continuous (and unobtrusive) observation of real work performance in real time, and formalised work sample tests, sometimes called proficiency or skills tests, although skills tests is also used to refer to paper-and-pencil tests where people say what they would do instead of doing it.

It might be supposed that repeated observation of real work in real time would constitute almost perfect content-related evidence in the sense that there could hardly be a better match or point-to-point correspondence between job tasks and assessment tasks. Indeed the two become indivisible: if observed, each job task is an assessment task. The same, of course, is true of a skills test where the tasks have strong verisimilitude. The difference is that when done off-job (as is invariably the case) the skills test lacks the element of real work in real time with its attendant pressures.

That is the supposition but in practice the almost perfect point-to-point correspondence may not be achievable. The job analysis may be faulty or the assessors may be too partial, concentrating on some job tasks to the exclusion of others.

At issue, too, is the question of important tasks which occur rarely; it is said that in many jobs the important tasks **only** occur infrequently (Wigdor & Green 1986, p. 95). Often these tasks involve health and safety considerations. A good example occurs in the sea fishing industry where the demonstration of certain aspects of competence (which, however, are only needed in emergencies) has major safety implications (Miller *et al.* 1988, pp. 249–50). In fact, the sea fishing industry poses all sorts of difficulties for workplace assessment, not least the lack of an immediate supervisor to conduct observational, in situ assessments, although this can be overcome by using all crew members (the value of peer review has been greatly overlooked). In these circumstances assessment can only be done through a simulated or set piece performance of emergency stop procedures and questioning, preferably oral, regarding the situations when such procedures should be used (Miller *et al.*, p. 259).

When direct observation becomes impossible, it is necessary to turn to simulation, although even that was not an option in the sea fishing case. Work sample or skills tests offer the opportunity of programming tasks so that, unlike the assessment of real-time work performance, it is possible to assess a representative set of job activities in a reasonable amount of time. Although the observation settings are fairly stylised reproductions of real settings, the required responses can be very similar to actual on-the-job responses. Here is the Road Transport Industry Training Board (RTITB)'s description of what it does to create verisimilitude for its skills tests:

> The tests are administered in a workshop atmosphere, not only in so far as the equipment and general conditions, but to the extent that Radio 1 is played in the background. For example, a Parts person will be tested in an area set up like the service counter of a garage complete with microfiche reader, bin locations, cash register etc. (RTITB 1985, para. 10)

If the sampling of tasks is done judiciously, the content-related evidence coming from the work sample test suffers little by comparison with observation, which remains, in principle, the most authentic (that is valid) form of assessment. What should not be overlooked is that the degree of fidelity possible will vary from task to task, from job to job, and from instrument to instrument. Each task is delineated and isolated from the context of other tasks that normally surround it. This may be a more important drawback in some jobs than in others; for example it may distort the job performance of, say, paramedics more than that of car mechanics (Wigdor & Green, p. 105). A sophisticated approach to sampling job content would attempt to incorporate into the sampling procedure variations in importance, difficulty and frequency of tasks, using a probabilistic sampling model to produce representativeness (Green & Wigdor 1988, p. 15; also Wigdor & Green, pp. 45–7).

Trainability tests

Trainability tests are a subtype of work sample, that assess how well the applicant can **learn** a new skill. The instructor gives standardised instructions and a demonstration, then rates the trainee's efforts using a checklist. Robertson & Downs (1979) report good results for bricklaying, carpentry, welding, machine sewing, forklift truck driving, fitting, machining and even dentistry.

A similar technique, 'miniaturised training', shows individuals how to do something, gives them a chance to practise, then tests them (Siegel 1978). Siegel's validity data on small samples are unimpressive, but he finds the procedure popular with people – 'Gave me a chance to prove that I could do some things with my hands, not just my head' (see also Siegel 1983). Reilly & Manese (1979) used trainability tests to select staff for American Telegraph and Telephone's electronic switching system. Performance in seven self-paced lessons predicted time to complete training moderately well. Reilly & Manese presented no data on the validity of other tests; 'electronic switching' needs programming skills, so perhaps the Programmer Aptitude Test, which achieves a 'true' validity of 0·91 for training grades, would do as well or better, and take less time (Cook, p. 176).

People doing trainability tests can assess their own performance, even though they are not told the results. Downs found that applicants for machine sewing jobs selected themselves for the job. Scores on a sewing machine trainability test were not used to select, but high scorers took up sewing jobs, while low scorers generally did not (Downs 1983).

The minicourse approach is similar to miniaturised training and to trainability testing; in fact, Reilly & Israelski (1988) call them a specific example of the general class of trainability tests. In a minicourse a job candidate is given a standard sample of programmed training material relevant to the target position. Each minicourse unit or module is followed by a test designed to measure learning of the material. Although a typical minicourse has a six-hour time limit, some have had a limit of two hours and others have taken as long as three days (Reilly & Israelski). The results of a meta-analysis (Reilly & Israelski) indicate that validities for trainability tests are comparable with validities found for ability tests and work sample tests by Hunter & Hunter (1984).

In summary, work sample or hands-on tests (including trainability tests) have generally very good validities but are cumbersome and usually 'local'. To administer in a standardised fashion, they tend to be labour-intensive, time-consuming and relatively expensive. Also they are better suited to manual than to white-collar jobs. On the plus side, they are virtuous in the sense that 'fair employment' legislation favours tests that resemble the job as closely as possible, and indeed the work sample looks to be the least discriminating of any technique (Schmitt & Noe 1986).

Discussion

Hunter & Hunter (1984) produced two 'league tables' of assessment methods, one for selection and one for promotion. Naturally, selection is much more difficult to do than promotion where the employer is dealing with a more or less known quantity. Ability tests, work samples, peer ratings, job knowledge, all have decent validity coefficients so personnel managers can promote on the basis of cost, convenience, legal problems and so on.

Selection devices have to be chosen much more carefully. Taking validity as the overriding consideration, the Hunter & Hunter league table suggests that ability tests, biodata, trainability tests and work samples are the methods to be taken seriously, with references some way behind and interviews and the others (EQ, seniority, age) nowhere in sight, although there may be hope yet for interviews providing they are structured (Guion, 1989). As Cook observes (p. 241), ability tests are probably best, and are certainly the cheapest, so long as the employer does not get sued for using them. This ought not to happen. As chapter 14 reported, ability tests appear to be 'fair', at least in the narrow technical sense, in that they predict performance equally accurately for male and female, white and non-white.

If ability tests discover what the applicant **can** do, they are not so good at predicting what s/he **will** do. This implies that ability tests need to be supplemented by something else. Biodata is the obvious choice. Would a combination of ability test and biodata have greater predictive validity than either method alone? The Civil Service Commission is beginning to think so. Their work is particularly timely because up to now the big gap in our information, apart from how industry actually **uses** selection procedures, has been the validity of **combinations** of methods. For industry at large, the big gap in knowledge is likely to be any awareness at all of the respective validities of the various methods. Robertson & Makin found that the frequency of use of various techniques is in approximate inverse order to their known validity, although this inverse relationship is less strong with the major recruiters like the Civil Service Commission.

References

Arvey R. D., Miller H. E., Gould R. & Burch P. (1987) Interview validity for selecting sales clerks. *Personnel Psychology*, **40**, 1–12.

Associated Examining Board (1987) *Skillcheck*. Guildford: AEB.

Bethell-Fox C. E., Cureton R. N. & Taylor J. A. (1988) The effectiveness of biodata in pre-selection for the Appointments-in-Administration competition. *RRU Report No. 37*. London: Civil Service Commission.

Cascio W. F. & Phillips N. F. (1979) Performance testing: A rose among thorns? *Personnel Psychology*, **32**, 751–66.

Civil Service Commission (1987) *Annual Report for 1986*. Basingstoke: CSC.

Cook M. (1988) *Personnel Selection and Productivity*. Chichester: John Wiley.

Coussey M. & Whitmore J. (1987) *Jobs and Racial Equality*. London: British Institute of Management.

Downs S. (1983) *Testing Trainability*. Windsor: NFER-Nelson.
Edwards J. C., Johnson E. K. & Molidor J. B. (1990) The interview in the admission process. *Academic Medicine*, **65**, 167–77.
Elias P. & Blanchflower D. (1987) *Who Gets the Good Jobs? Parental Background, Education, Work History and Location as Factors in Early Career Formation*. University of Warwick: Institute for Employment Research.
Gordon M. E. & Fitzgibbons W. J. (1982) Empirical test of the validity of seniority as a factor in staffing decisions. *Journal of Applied Psychology*, **67**, 311–19.
Gordon M. E. & Kleiman L. S. (1976) The prediction of trainability using a work-sample test and an aptitude test: A direct comparison. *Personnel Psychology*, **29**, 243–53.
Green B. F. & Wigdor A. K. (eds.) (1988) *Measuring Job Competency*. Washington, DC: National Academy Press.
Guion R. M. (1989) Comments on personnel selection methods. In Smith M. & Robertson I. T. (eds.) *Advances in Selection and Assessment*. Chichester: John Wiley.
Hakel M. D. (1982) The employment interview. In Rowland K. M. & Ferris G. R. (eds.) *Personnel Management*. Boston, MA: Allyn & Bacon.
Harn T. J. & Thornton G. C. (1985) Recruiter counselling behaviours and applicant impressions. *Journal of Occupational Psychology*, **58**, 57–65.
Harrell M. S. *et al.* (1977). Predicting compensation among MBA graduates five and ten years after graduation. *Journal of Applied Psychology*, **62**, 636–40.
Harris M. M. (1989) Reconsidering the interview: A review of recent literature and suggestions for future research. *Personnel Psychology*, **42**, 691–726.
Hartigan J. A. & Wigdor A. K. (eds.) (1989) *Fairness in Employment Testing*. Washington, DC: National Academy Press.
Herriot P. (1988) Selection at a crossroads. *The Psychologist*, **1**, 388–92.
Herriot P. (1989) Selection as a social process. In Smith M. & Robertson I. T. (eds.) *Advances in Selection and Assessment*. Chichester: John Wiley.
Herrnstein R. (1973) *IQ in the Meritocracy*. London: Allen Lane.
Hunter J. E. (1986) Cognitive ability, cognitive aptitudes, job knowledge and job performance. *Journal of Vocational Behaviour*, **29**, 340–62.
Hunter J. E. & Hunter R. F. (1984) Validity and utility of alternative predictors of job performance. *Psychological Bulletin*, **96**, 72–98.
Jensen A. R. (1986) g: artifact or reality? *Journal of Vocational Behaviour*, **29**, 301–31.
Johnson C. E. (1986) Biographical sifting devices in Appointments-in-Administration. *RRU Report No. 29*. London: Civil Service Commission.
McClelland D. C. (1973) Testing for competence rather than for 'intelligence'. *American Psychologist*, **28**, 1–14.
McDaniel M. A., Schmidt F. L. & Hunter J. E. (1988) Job experience correlates of job performance. *Journal of Applied Psychology*, **73**, 327–30.
McEvoy G. M. & Cascio W. F. (1989) Cumulative evidence of the relationship between employee age and job performance. *Journal of Applied Psychology*, **74**, 11–17.
Meglino B. M. *et al.* (1988) Effects of realistic job previews: A comparison using an enhancement and a reduction preview. *Journal of Applied Psychology*, **73**, 259–66.

Meyer H. H. (1987) Predicting supervisory ratings versus promotional progress in test validation studies. *Journal of Applied Psychology*, **72**, 696–7.

Miller C. *et al.* (1988) *Credit where Credit's Due*. Glasgow: SCOTVEC.

Mitchell T. W. & Klimoski R. J. (1982) Is it rational to be empirical? A test of methods for scoring biographical data. *Journal of Applied Psychology*, **67**, 411–18.

Moore H. (1942) *Psychology for Business and Industry*. New York: McGraw-Hill.

Mosel J. N. & Goheen H. W. (1959) The validity of the Employment Recommendation Questionnaire. 3. Validity of different types of references. *Personnel Psychology*, **12**, 469–77.

Muchinsky P. M. & Tuttle M. L. (1979) Employee turnover: An empirical and methodological assessment. *Journal of Vocational Behaviour*, **14**, 43–77.

O'Leary B. S. (1980) *College Grade Point Average as an Indicator of Occupational Success*. Washington, DC: US Office of Personnel Management.

Pearlman K., Schmidt F. L. & Hunter J. E. (1980) Validity generalization results for tests used to predict job proficiency and training, success in clerical occupations. *Journal of Applied Psychology*, **65**, 373–406.

Recruitment Research Unit (1985) Science and Technology Division's pilot follow-up study of young graduate recruits. *RRU Report No. 26*. London: Civil Service Commission.

Reilly R. R. & Chao G. T. (1982) Validity and fairness of some alternative employee selection procedures. *Personnel Psychology*, **35**, 1–62.

Reilly R. R. & Israelski E. W. (1988) Development and validation of minicourses in the telecommunication industry. *Journal of Applied Psychology*, **73**, 721–6.

Reilly R. R. & Manese W. R. (1979) The validation of a minicourse for telephone company switching technicians. *Personnel Psychology*, **32**, 83–90.

Road Transport Industry Training Board (1985) External testing. Paper prepared for a seminar at the Technical Change Centre, 14 June, para. 20.

Robertson I. T. & Downs S. (1979) Learning and the prediction of performance: Development of trainability testing in the United Kingdom. *Journal of Applied Psychology*, **64**, 42–50.

Robertson I. T. & Makin F. J. (1986) Management selection in Britain: A survey and critique. *Journal of Occupational Psychology*, **59**, 45–57.

Robertson I. T. & Smith M. (1989) Personnel selection methods. In Smith M. & Robertson I. T. (eds.) *Advances in Selection and Assessment*. Chichester: John Wiley.

Samson G. E. *et al.* (1984) Academic and occupational performance: A quantitative synthesis. *American Educational Research Journal*, **21**, 311–22.

Schmidt F. L. *et al.* (1977) Job sample vs. paper-and-pencil test: Adverse impact and examinee attitudes. *Personnel Psychology*, **30**, 187–97.

Schmidt F. L. *et al.* (1988) Joint relation of experience and ability with job performance: A test of three hypotheses. *Journal of Applied Psychology*, **73**, 46–57.

Schmitt N. & Noe R. A. (1986) Personnel selection and equal employment opportunity. In Cooper C. L. & Robertson I. T. (eds.) *International Review of Industrial and Organizational Psychology*. Chichester: John Wiley.

Siegel A. I. (1978) Miniature job training and evaluation: A selection/classification device. *Human Factors*, **20**, 189–200.

Siegel A. I. (1983) The miniature job training and evaluation approach: Additional findings. *Personnel Psychology*, **36**, 41–56.

Super D. E. & Crites J. O. (1962) *Appraising Vocational Fitness by means of Psychological Tests*. New York: Harper Row.

Thorndike R. L. (1986) The role of general ability in prediction. *Journal of Vocational Behaviour*, **29**, 332–9.

Wanous J. P. (1989) Installing a realistic job preview: Ten tough choices. *Personnel Psychology*, **42**, 117–34.

Wiesner W. H. & Cronshaw S. F. (1988) A meta-analytic investigation of the impact of interview format and degree of structure on the validity of the employment interview. *Journal of Occupational Psychology*, **61**, 275–90.

Wigdor A. K. (1982) Psychological testing and the law of employment discrimination. In Wigdor A. K. & Garner W. R. (eds.) *Ability Testing: Uses, Consequences and Controversies, Part 2*. Washington, DC: National Academy Press.

Wigdor A. K. & Green B. F. (eds.) (1986) *Assessing the Performance of Enlisted Personnel*. Washington, DC: National Academy Press.

Wood R., Johnson C. E., Blinkhorn S. F., Anderson S. A. & Hall J. P. (1989) *Boning, Blanching and Backtacking: Assessing Performance in the Workplace*. Sheffield: Department of Employment/Training Agency.

Zedeck S., Tziner A. & Middlestadt S. E. (1983) Interviewer validity and reliability: An individual difference analysis. *Personnel Psychology*, **36**, 355–70.

19 Language testing

Of the two productive language skills, writing is dealt with in chapter 5. This chapter deals with speaking, the other productive skill, and the two receptive skills, reading and listening, although, to be exact, it is really about speaking and listening. Quite what the pecking order should be is a fascinating although ultimately unanswerable question. We know that listening is the very first language skill to develop, followed in order by speaking, reading and writing. For what it is worth, a survey of American academics found that reading was considered most important, at least in academic work, followed by listening, then writing, with speaking lagging some way behind. Perceptions of the importance of writing and speaking did, however, vary significantly from discipline to discipline (Powers 1986, p. 33). Where assessment is concerned, the pecking order has been different again. Expediency has produced a situation where the attention given to the four skills is in gross imbalance. Writing has been accorded primacy, reading has been taken largely for granted, and listening and speaking have been largely ignored. Only now is the assessment of competence *through* speech being addressed.

To observe the four-fold distinction is not to insist on separate assessment of each skill. A case can certainly be made out for thoroughly integrated testing procedures where the four modalities are deployed interdependently, as happens in practice, and no particular distinctions are made 'because a test of speaking only ... would surely be a test of a skill so meaningless as to be not worth testing, it is presumably necessary to accept that a meaningful, communicative test of speaking of *necessity* means testing a composite of related skills' (Sunderland, Yixing & Barr 1988, p. 31). The continued insistence on separate estimation can be seen as a product of the subskills mentality and the belief that any instrument can be made diagnostic (chapter 8) even if it has an overt selection function, such as ELTS. It ought to be possible to test the product of writing which has been gained as a result of listening. The Institute of Linguists, in its examinations in languages for international communication, claims to do just that. 'An important aspect of realism is **skill**

integration...This reality is reflected in the design of the examination tasks, which require candidates to carry out a chain of integrated activities leading to a final product. Adequate performance in all these activities is a prerequisite for task fulfilment.' (Institute of Linguists 1988, p. 2). The same conflict between separatism and holism is present in the assessment of practical science skills (chapter 15).

As a matter of fact, most research does reveal substantial correlations among measures of the four modalities (Powers 1984). There is a cognitive processing explanation for this. As Daneman, Carpenter & Just (1982) pointed out, except for visual decoding, both listening and reading appear to involve similar processes, which include speed of lexical access, efficiency in integrating information semantically and retention of information in working memory.

Evidence of the substantial correlations between listening and speaking and other more general verbal abilities comes from several sources, including studies of English as a second language. For example, Swinton & Powers (1980) reported average intercorrelations for six forms of the Test of English as a Foreign Language (TOEFL) as follows: 0·70 between listening comprehension and structure/written expression and 0·69 between listening comprehension and vocabulary/reading comprehension.

In exploring the development of a speaking test for foreign students, Clark & Swinton (1979) reported correlations of 0·58, 0·61, and 0·65 between a measure of oral proficiency (The Foreign Service Interview) and each of the three sections of the TOEFL (which does not contain an oral measure). Bachman & Palmer (1981) also reported high correlations for foreign students between various measures of speaking and reading. The correlations of five different methods of measuring reading with the corresponding methods of measuring speaking ranged from 0·46 to 0·69, with a median of 0·64.

Similarly, high correlations among verbal measures also have been reported for English-speaking students. For example, Devine (1967) summarised a number of studies that show correlations of 0·58 to 0·82 between measures of listening and measures of general or verbal intelligence.

The practical significance of separately measuring each skill is at issue. Swinton & Powers may have found clear evidence for a distinct listening comprehension factor but the task of distilling it out in an operational form has proved vexatious. Twenty-five years ago, Dixon (1964) referred to listening as the most neglected of the language arts and pointed to the lack of adequate tests of listening skills. Kelly's (1965) scepticism about the most widely used listening tests was accompanied by a call for more inventive measurement efforts. Later, Kelly (1966) argued that 'currently published listening tests are not valid measures of a unique skill...' (p. 455). He also complained that 'researchers to date have failed to produce any statistical verifications of listening test validity. In fact, evidence strongly suggests that currently published listening tests measure the same basic factors that are more reliably measured by established achievement tests not involving listening' (p. 458). Kelly concluded that 'A listening test that measures anything but verbal or general mental ability is hard, if not impossible, to find' (p. 450).

Larson *et al.* (1978) repeated essentially this same criticism of listening tests 13 years later, stating that 'None of the current listening tests seem to show adequate levels of validity, and we are not certain that these tests actually measure listening' (p. 57). This conclusion was reached after a careful review of some 90 tests of communication skills, 53 of which were designed for adults or college-level students. The authors also concluded that no one test provided a comprehensive evaluation of speaking *and* listening skills.

In dealing with this topic I have felt like a stranger gazing upon an unfamiliar scene, anxiously scanning the landscape for familiar features and activities. To my relief, I have seen much that is recognisable, although sometimes the emphasis is greater than I am used to. There **are** familiar psychometric issues which interweave and even sometimes coincide. Having surveyed the assessment of writing, I might have realised that getting my bearings would not be too difficult. It is argued that there is no simple, completely acceptable definition of listening, and no comprehensive theory of listening behaviour (Powers 1984, p. 3). Exactly the same has been said about writing (chapter 5). As for reading comprehension, the mental processing involved in that trait is apparently not known and understood (Shohamy 1984). It follows that reading comprehension in a second language is even more of a puzzle. Likewise, the little of what is known about listening comprehension in a second language is said to derive from research on native listeners (Powers 1984, p. 4).

What then of speaking? If there are no models of what constitutes good writing, there are certainly no models of what constitutes good speech. There is plenty of research to indicate that people do make judgements about a speaker's competence, integrity and social attractiveness on the basis of their accent. Maybin (1988, p. 12) suggests that pupils' willingness and ability to move into the tester's frame of reference may affect their assessment mark in terms of the speech style they adopt. All this is what sociolinguists tell us to expect. Variability of language use must be taken into account when devising assessment procedures (Spolsky 1985) and that holds as well for the other three skills.

As with assessment of science achievement, language testing gives the impression at first of being hermetically sealed from the mainstream of educational and psychological testing. In common with other testing tribes, there is the propensity to reinvent the wheel and then to draw back from the task of demonstrating that it is suitable for the new application. We all get excited when we encounter the Rasch model or item response theory (IRT) for the first time, but IRT did not commence with Woods & Baker (1985) as readers of *Language Testing* have been led to believe.

I take the two great issues to be:

validity vs. reliability;
direct vs. indirect methods of assessment.

These issues are connected reflexively. To lean towards direct methods is to enrich validity while threatening reliability; to favour indirect methods is a vote for reliability at the expense of validity. Together the two issues coalesce into one even greater issue:

authenticity vs. inauthenticity.

Both the great issues are treated with an intensity not experienced anywhere else in psychometric literature, so much so that any general appreciation of validity and reliability and their interplay could do worse than use language testing as an illuminative application.

There is another issue which has certainly attracted fierce partisanship and if I do not place it with the other two, it is because it appears, for the time being at any rate, to have subsided or to have been settled if not resolved through a dialectic. I refer to the issue:

general vs. specific abilities or subskills.

The name associated with the general ability position is that of Oller. Writing of the general language hypothesis, Spolsky (1986, p. 149) remarked that it 'has been no more firmly established (in spite of John Oller's best efforts) than has the related (and Oller would claim directly related) construct of general intelligence'. In fact, Oller has pulled back from an extreme *g* (language) position, but in practice this is immaterial. What should not be assumed is that because *g* (language) will not stand up, the many subskills position is validated. The operational difficulties of separating abilities and skills, and the prevalence of wishful thinking in this area, have been emphasised many times in this survey.

There is one more issue, already touched upon, which will have to be dealt with. It is the application of item response theory (IRT), especially Rasch, to language testing bearing in mind that IRT is, in fact, a misnomer. What is actually going on is item response modelling (IRM). The 'theory' is no more than a probabilistic statement of what may happen when a person encounters an item, and as such is indistinguishable from the model (Goldstein & Wood 1989).

The three phases of language testing

The identification by Spolsky (1978, 1985) of three phases of language testing has been helpful in thinking about this and other fields. The phases are:

1. **Prescientific or traditional phase**
   Examinations where measurement is based on the subjective judgement of one examiner alone (or perhaps a group).
2. **Psychometric–structuralist or modern phase**
   Characterised by efforts made to optimise objectivity and reliability but with little attention to validity. Knowledge of language generally broken up into small parts and measured by standardised, objective 'discrete-point' tests normally consisting of multiple choice items. These tests always test what is easiest to measure.
3. **Psycholinguistic–sociolinguistic or post-modern phase**
   Here the main concern is to secure not only objectivity and reliability, but also validity.

   Psycholinguistic = relationship between competence and performance.
   Sociolinguistic = importance of taking variability of language use into account.

The interesting thing about the definition of the prescientific phase is that it coincides with French's (1985) notion of what an examination is – an exercise in examiner judgement and not an objective measurement procedure (cf. chapter 10). Harrison (personal communication) suggests that it is even more true of phase 3, where more factors have to be judged (crucially, 'appropriacy').

Phase 2 would appear to be the phase we are mostly in, that is modern, and the one we are struggling to get out of. The APU's Oracy Surveys are held to exemplify the strain of thinking which subordinates substance to method:

> The APU's construction of tests perhaps also arises from a need to obtain oral texts which are more amenable to their methods of analysis. (Maybin 1988, p. 8)

> In order to develop tests to assess children's oracy the APU have had to construct an 'oracy' to test. (Maybin, p. 13)

Phase 3 sounds wonderful but dreadfully vague. We would all like to keep up validity and reliability, but as Andrew Harrison rather quaintly but exactly puts it, in the jar of jam the validity fruit and the reliability sugar are obscured by the opaque pot called communication (Harrison 1983). Legislating reliability and validity out of the way, as Morrow (1986) does, cuts no ice at all. Between-rater reliability is unproblematic, he argues. Criteria may be woolly yet 'perhaps because of all this, the qualitative description of a level of language performance which they embody seems to be meaningful to the large number of assessors who have now gone through the training programme; and to be handled by them with very few problems' (Morrow, p. 10). This attitude is the 'Assessors are good chaps and know what they are doing – trust them' school of assessment.

More down to earth, Shohamy found little agreement on the quality of oral performance either between-rater or within-rater (Shohamy & Reves 1985, p. 53). Chapter 5 contains comparable data on assessment of writing performance. The APU is criticised for treating the two productive modes as analogous (Maybin). What is certain is that they have shared methodological problems. Presumably we do not expect any better agreement for talking than writing performance, even if the possibilities for spurious consensus (what Coffman (personal communication) called brainwashing) are certainly present.

On validity, Morrow is scarcely less polemical. The only kinds of validity which matter are 'washback' (backwash) validity, which is something to do with whether a test has the effect intended in the classroom, and 'operational' validity, which is about the relationship between test performance and real work performance. He sees that this is akin to predictive validity but claims to see a 'crucial difference' when, in fact, criterion-related validity covers what he is referring to. Morrow observes that both kinds of validity are easier to expound than to investigate, leaving the impression that investigation and analysis are the last things he would wish to do, an attitude reminiscent of the German irrationalist school of the early nineteenth century – to dissect is to murder, and so on (Berlin 1981).

Authenticity

Morrow might have been one of those Shohamy & Reves (1985) had in mind when they noted that in the wave of enthusiasm towards the development of authentic language tests, two major problems have been overlooked:

1 the lack of attention to psychometric properties of authentic tests;
2 a naive belief that the so-called authentic tests are really authentic.

Someone like Morrow is transparent in his resistance to analysis; the worrying cases are the deceptive cases. It is claimed for the English

Language Testing Service (ELTS) that it achieves a compromise between the 'constructive interplay with unpredictable stimuli' and 'scientific measurement' by trying on the one hand to mirror real life in the oral interview, while on the other providing the interviewer with assessment scales based upon the taxonomy of skills to be rated (Carroll 1980, pp. 53–5). Indeed, Carroll indulges in triumphalism – 'Nowhere is the contrast between the old and the new approaches to language testing clearer than in the testing of speaking – or, more precisely, of oral interaction.' (Carroll & Hall 1985, p. 49). So Carroll & Hall have attempted to resolve the conflicting demands of authenticity and consistency. Now we have to ask what they have to say about the psychometric properties of the scales, that is their approach to a scientific measurement procedure. The answer is very little. They fail to approach two vital questions: firstly, how much consistency between raters is necessary to ensure that adequate reliability has been achieved? And secondly, how much consistency can we reasonably expect? (Cameron 1987)

On validity, too, the ELTS scales have been challenged. Fulcher (1987) manages to demonstrate (by reproducing a conversation) that the ELTS categories signally fail to capture 'real-life' communication. Four participants (three lecturers, one non-native and a medical practitioner) produced conversation which failed by some distance to meet the appropriate criteria embedded in the ELTS assessment scales. Fulcher concluded that a fixation with content validity, brought about by excessive allegiance to the Munby (1978) taxonomy of skills, has resulted in construct validity being ignored (the theory has been 'slipped under the door'). The scale, says Fulcher, is attempting to describe not what actually happens in communicative situations, but what communicative theorists think happens in communicative situations. If, as critics claim, the Munby taxonomy is merely a roll-call of desirable subskills, with strictly speculative status, then the ELTS is bound to be vulnerable to the kind of criticism Fulcher makes.

In indirect unauthentic language tests, the variations that exist in natural language use do not come across. Indirect tests screen these variations out. Assessment is therefore more stable and does not express the variability which exists in real conversation (Shohamy & Reves). If Carroll was not claiming to be a direct, authentic communicative tester, this description of an indirect test might be said to apply to ELTS. This only helps to make the point that there are relativities in the authenticity enterprise, and it does not do to be triumphalist.

The crux of the matter seems to be that any language test is, by its very nature, inauthentic. Only part of this difficulty can be overcome by authentic-seeming tasks (Spolsky 1985, p. 31). The inauthenticity arises because the test-taker is being asked to engage in abnormal language behaviour; not to answer a question giving information, but to display knowledge or skill. Searle (1969) observed that real questions ask for information, whereas examination questions call for performance. In her critique of the APU Oracy Surveys, Maybin has remarked (p. 10):

> However ingeniously the oracy tasks are constructed, the purpose of the assessor is always to test, and of the pupils to do what they think the tester wants – or maybe just to get through a morning.

Even when information is sought, the communication will be inauthentic if the student knows that the tester knows the answers already, or if the questions are of a kind that a total stranger would never dream of asking at a first encounter (like 'How old are you?', 'What does your father do?') As Ducroquet (1986, p. 47) observes (also Harrison 1983) none of these questions makes sense from a communicative point of view. Questions must never be asked that would never be asked in a real-life situation. Just because it is an examination does not give the tester the right to intrude upon a student's right of privacy. As for asking questions to which you already know the answer, this is even more true of essay questions.

The best that can be achieved, it would appear, is authentic **test language**, given that authentic real-life language is too hard to handle (Shohamy & Reves). Or, as Raatz (1985) puts it, there is authentic material which should be demanded at the very least, and there is authentic behaviour from test-takers, which is actually too much to ask for in the circumstances.

Direct vs. indirect tests

Clark's (1975) distinction between direct and indirect tests became the rationale for research studies which examined the relationship between direct and indirect measures. The aim of these studies was to determine if the more efficient indirect tests could be made valid surrogates for the less efficient, yet more valid, direct tests. With respect to assessment in general, the question has been whether multiple choice tests can replace free response tests.

The perils of relying too heavily on simple correlational analysis for getting answers to this question have been pointed out elsewhere (chapters 4 and 15). It is easy to forget that respectable correlations can arise because of factors which are secondary to the association being investigated. Only negative evidence for discriminant validity really counts. In fact, research studies which used the multitrait–multimethod validation procedure have found that the method of testing affects the assessment of the trait and therefore it cannot be claimed that direct and indirect tests are functionally equivalent, and that one can stand as surrogate for the other (Shohamy & Reves, p. 50).

Yet investigators continue to appeal to correlational analysis for settling claims, as I am afraid they always will. An Educational Testing Service (ETS) report on the new cloze–elide tests invoked factor analysis to back the claim that cloze–elide is a good indirect measure of English Language proficiency. It was one of the two predictors of teacher ratings of students' English proficiency (Manning 1987). So what? Did anyone check their maths scores?

Cloze seems to divide the language testing world as no other technique. Some, like Manning, think it a good indirect measure; some, like Lado (1986), think it a rather poor indirect measure; some, like Oller (1979), think it might even qualify as a direct measure in the sense that it taps pragmatic language use. On the face of it, cloze would appear to be unauthentic; as Harrison (1983, p. 78) says, 'Who wants to stay in a hotel so damp that parts of the notices on the wall are obscured by patches of mould?' Nor does recognising unnecessary superfluous words which have been inserted into the text (cloze–elide) strike one as unpredictable, interaction-based, contextualised, purposive, behaviour-based and all those other features of communicative testing. The luminary Lado, interestingly an early advocate of indirect measures, got really rather cross about cloze. In reporting that an 'overwhelming majority' of subjects in his study (87%) responded in clear negative terms concerning cloze, he felt that Carroll, Carton & Wild's (1959) conclusions regarding cloze still stood:

> the ability to restore texts is somewhat independent of competence in a language as it is ordinarily defined. That is to say, we observed many people who are perfectly competent and literate in a language but who do not show facility in a special task of guessing what a missing letter or word in a text might be.

As for the C-test, which appears to be a super-cloze test, and which its supporters claim overcomes the main objectives to scoring of cloze (Porter (1978) found that students' scores may vary markedly according to what is deleted) the advocacy for it has a definite whiff of special pleading (Grotjahn 1986). As long as it is a cloze test, there is no reason to suppose it has escaped from the charge of artificiality.

Nevo (1986) makes three telling points about surrogacy in the context of the new Test of Writing Effectiveness in TOEFL. He says that Stansfield (1986) gives the impression that the indirect measure of writing ability was an appropriate measure of writing ability; its only problem was that its clients do not like it. In fact, the request was for a measure that would be more valid, that is direct.

In concentrating on the reliability of the new measure, ETS, argues

Nevo, is once again making the mistake of sacrificing validity for high reliability, thus repeating the mistake it made when it used multiple choice to test writing ability.

Thirdly (and rather cynically) the absence of an external independent evaluation may give ETS the opportunity to conclude that its efforts were in vain since the cost of testing increased without a concomitant improvement in quality.

I remarked earlier that the validity vs. reliability and direct vs. indirect issues were more intensely experienced than anywhere else in the psychometric literature. A poignant example is the candid account by Hart, Lapkin & Swain (1987) of their attempt to design tests of communicative language proficiency (in French, for Anglophone immersion groups in Canada) by breaking with traditional test formats. Because authentic language tests do not have recognisable discrete and unsequenced items, an atomistic approach to testing language will not do. Instead, there are dependencies in operation and therefore no local stochastic independence. This rules out the Rasch model and other IRT models (Raatz 1985, p. 60). The problem with the Hart *et al.* attempt seems to have been that operationalisation of the dimensions of communicative competence essentially requires operationalising single skills, in other words, utilising discrete-point measures (p. 89). Furthermore, their failure, or lack of opportunity, to collect sufficient Francophone data, meant that they were stuck with immersion group norms and were unable to demonstrate the reliability and validity of their measures.

The application of item response theory

Given the lack of congruence between traditional testing formats and the real demands of communicative situations, it seems extraordinary that anyone should ever have thought that IRT could possibly have anything to offer language testing. Almost everyone seems agreed that dichotomously scored items will not do for authentic language testing. After all, if authentic material cannot be manipulated, then classical (or modern) item analysis is a waste of time since it cannot be followed up by improvements. But there are those who are not so easily put off. They believe that the advantages IRT offers (on paper) will be good for any branch of testing, and are therefore inclined to see criticism as nit-picking. Thus, Henning, Hudson & Turner (1985) are sanguine about the effect of local independence being violated. For them it is not a problem even for cloze tests which are strongly suspected of violation (p. 142). This is an *echt* 'true believer' article in the best Rasch modellers' tradition. It was too much for Pollitt (1987), himself a committed Rasch modeller. His review of Henning's (1987) book takes Henning to task for glossing too readily over objections to the use of IRT. Lately, Henning has been more circumspect. He admits that violations of item unidimensionality do produce distorted estimates of personal ability; likewise violations of person unidimensionality produce distorted estimates of item difficulty (Henning 1988).

If the atomistic approach will not do, what is wanted, says Raatz, is a holistic approach. He argues that these methods have been neglected (p. 62), but that is not strictly true. With the simple Rasch model ruled out, people have sought to apply the extended model for the graded scoring case, known by some as the Partial Credit model. This offers the possibility of rating longer stretches of talk. Methodologically, Adams, Griffin & Martin (1987) and Pollitt & Hutchinson (1987) have taken quite different approaches, the latter being really just the classic IRT approach where performance quality (ability) and question toughness (difficulty) are dealt with simultaneously. Neither, however, can escape the assumptions the Partial Credit model must meet (or at least not patently not meet). Each question must discriminate equally between the scores of zero and one; given those students who have reached one, all questions must discriminate equally between the scores of one and two; and so on. Readers can decide for themselves about the likelihood of this being met in practice, or being made to happen without jeopardising authenticity.

Assessment through speech

An area of enquiry which has barely been opened up is the assessment of competence **through** speech. There is a movement now to develop oral assessment in Mathematics, Science, History and so on, but there is a feeling that the Task Group on Assessment and Testing (TGAT) report (DES 1987) perhaps ran too far ahead of itself in giving the impression that the enterprise is relatively unproblematic. Given that the root question is 'Are you judging their **talk**, or their **science**?', that can hardly be so. It seems certain that at key stage 1 of national assessments the standard tasks will be framed in such a way that assessment through speech will be unavoidable. Depending on the directives issuing from the National Curriculum Council, teachers may find that they have to engage in assessment through speech in order to properly carry out the teacher-assessed component of national tests.

Discussion

Davies (1986, p. 58) asks a basic question. How can test items of the conventional kind employ the features of the communicative use of language, namely interaction-based, unpredictable, contextualised, purposive, authentic, behaviour-based, and so on? Finding no answer, he suggests that we may have to make the best of indirect tests which, sensibly devised, are not the spent force the champions of direct tests make them out to be. Tests, says Davies (p. 66), are both samples and measures; tasks, however interesting, which are not both samples and measures, are not tests. In his view, this means that language tests are more likely to be indirect than direct, and that communicative tests are not tests in his sense. What he thinks they could do is to help formulate a verbal description of learners without enabling us to derive scores. In that sense, they are akin to the ethnographic methods involving continuing observation of how people use language, which for sociolinguists represent the solution to direct testing.

Otherwise, it appears that attempts to move the validity–reliability trade-off in the direction of validity while curbing the reliability loss will depend on exploring the properties of one-off ideas for tests. An example is the so-called 'Reporting Test' of oral proficiency. Pairs of learners are given role cards and asked to hold a conversation. There is doubt as to whether this procedure is at all new, but an Israeli study (Shohamy, Reves & Bejarano 1986) was sufficiently encouraging (high between-rater reliability, positive attitudes among test-takers) for Sunderland, Yixing & Barr (1988) to mount a replication in Shanghai. The study went well but seems not to have been subjected to anything like a rigorous evaluation; besides which a version of the ELTS assessment scales was used. Even so, it was felt that there are features of the Reporting Test which make it particularly suitable for use in China. In authentic situations, like introducing products to people from all over the business world, the information gap can appropriately be bridged only by interactive reporting, not mere translation. Sunderland *et al.* make the point that the Reporting Test involves a collection of skills – memory, reading comprehension and reading skills (in this case Chinese), communicative skills and inevitably translation from the mother tongue to English. It is therefore by no means a test of speaking alone. As integrationists would say, 'speaking' tests must necessarily involve the integration of speaking with other skills.

References

Adams R. J., Griffin P. E. & Martin L. (1987) A latent trait method for measuring a dimension in second language proficiency. *Language Testing*, **4**, 9–27.

Bachman L. F. & Palmer A. S. (1981) The construct validity of the FSI oral interview. *Language Learning*, **31**, 67–86.

Berlin I. (1981) *Against the Current*. Oxford: Oxford University Press.

Cameron D. (1987) Review of Carroll B. J. & Hall P. *Write Your Own Language*

Tests, Pergamon Institute of English, 1985. *English Language Teaching Journal*, **41**, 149–51.

Carroll B. J. (1980) *Testing Communicative Performance*. Oxford: Pergamon Press.

Carroll B. J. & Hall P. (1985) *Write Your Own Language Tests*. Oxford: Pergamon Institute of English.

Carroll J. B., Carton A. S. & Wild C. (1959) An investigation of 'cloze' items in the measurement of achievement in foreign languages. College Entrance Examination Board Research and Development Reports. Laboratory for Research in Instruction, Graduate School of Education, Harvard University. (ERIC) Ed. 021–513.

Clark J. L. D. (1975) Theoretical and technical considerations in oral proficiency testing. In Jones R. L. & Spolsky B. (eds.) *Testing Language Proficiency*. Arlington, VA: Center for Applied Linguistics.

Clark J. L. D. & Swinton S. S. (1979) An exploration of speaking proficiency measures in the TOEFL context. *TOEFL Research Report No. 4*. Princeton, NJ: Educational Testing Service.

Daneman M., Carpenter P. A. & Just M. A. (1982) Cognitive processes and reading skills. In Hutson B. A. (ed.) *Advances in Reading/Language Research: A Research Annual* (vol. 1). Greenwich, CT: Jai Press.

Davies A. (1986) Indirect ESP testing: Old innovations. In Portal M. (ed.) *Innovations in Language Testing*. Windsor: NFER-Nelson.

Department of Education and Science (1987) TGAT report.

Devine T. G. (1967) Listening. *Review of Educational Research*, **37**, 152–8.

Dixon N. R. (1964) Listening: Most neglected of the language arts. *Elementary English*, **41**, 285–8.

Ducroquet L. (1986) Practical problems for communicative oral language testing. *British Journal of Language Teaching*, **24**, 147–51.

French S. (1985) The weighting of examination components. *The Statistician*, **34**, 265–80.

Fulcher G. (1987) Tests of oral performance: The need for data-based criteria. *English Language Teaching Journal*, **41**, 287–91.

Goldstein H. & Wood R. (1989) Five decades of item response modelling. *British Journal of Mathematical and Statistical Psychology*, **32**, 139–68.

Grotjahn R. (1986) Test validation and cognitive psychology: Some methodological considerations. *Language Testing*, **3**, 159–85.

Harrison A. W. (1983) Communicative testing: Jam tomorrow? In Hughes A. & Porter D. *Current Developments in Language Testing*. London: Academic Press.

Hart D., Lapkin S. & Swain M. (1987) Communicative language tests: Perks and perils. *Evaluation and Research in Education*, **1**, 83–94.

Henning G. (1987) *A Guide to Language Testing: Development–Evaluation–Research*. Rowley, MA: Newbury House.

Henning G. (1988) The influence of test and sample dimensionality on latent trait ability and item difficulty calibrations. *Language Testing*, **5**, 83–99.

Henning G., Hudson T. & Turner J. (1985) Item response theory and the assumption of unidimensionality for language tests. *Language Testing*, **2**, 155–63.

Institute of Linguists (1988) *Examinations in Languages for International Communication*. London: Institute of Linguists.

Kelly C. M. (1965) An investigation of the construct validity of two commercially published listening tests. *Speech Monographs*, **32**, 139–43.

Kelly C. M. (1966) Listening: Complex of activities – and a unitary skill? *Speech Monographs*, **34**, 455–65.

Lado R. (1986) Analysis of native speaker performance on a cloze test. *Language Testing*, **3**, 130–46.

Larson C., Backlund P., Redmond M. & Barbour A. (1978) *Assessing Functional Communication*. Urbana, IL: ERIC Clearinghouse on Reading and Communication Skills; and Falls Church, VA: Speech Communication Association.

Manning W. (1987) Development of cloze–elide tests of English as a Second Language. *TOEFL Research Report No. 23*. Princeton, NJ: Educational Testing Service.

Maybin J. (1988) A critical review of the DES Assessment of Performance Unit's Oracy Surveys. *English in Education*, **22**, 3–18.

Morrow K. (1986) The evaluation of tests of communicative performance. In Portal M. (ed.) *Innovations in Language Testing*. Windsor: NFER-Nelson.

Munby J. L. (1978) *Communicative Syllabus Design*. Cambridge: Cambridge University Press.

Nevo D. (1986) Comments on Stansfield: A history of the Test of Written English; the developmental year. *Language Testing*, **3**, 235–6.

Oller J. (1979) *Language Tests at School*. London: Longman.

Pollitt A. (1987) Review of Henning G. (1987) *A Guide to Language Testing: Development–Evaluation–Research*, Rowley, MA: Newbury House. *Language Testing*, **4**, 233–5.

Pollitt A. & Hutchinson C. (1987) Calibrating graded assessments: Rasch partial credit analysis of performance in writing. *Language Testing*, **4**, 72–92.

Porter D. (1978) Cloze procedure and equivalence. *Language Learning*, **12**, 333–41.

Powers D. E. (1984) Considerations for developing measures of speaking and listening. *ETS Research Report RR 84-18*. Princeton, NJ: Educational Testing Service.

Powers D. E. (1986) Academic demands relating to listening skills. *Language Testing*, **3**, 1–38.

Raatz U. (1985) Better theory for better tests? *Language Testing*, **2**, 60–75.

Searle J. (1969) *Speech Acts*. Cambridge: Cambridge University Press.

Shohamy E. (1984) Does the testing method make a difference? The case of reading comprehension. *Language Testing*, **1**, 147–70.

Shohamy E. & Reves T. (1985) Authentic language tests: Where from and where to? *Language Testing*, **2**, 48–59.

Shohamy E., Reves T. & Bejarano Y. (1986) Introducing a new comprehensive test of oral proficiency. *English Language Teaching Journal*, **40**, 212–20.

Spolsky B. (1978) Language testing: art or science? In Nickel G. (ed.) *Language Testing*. Stuttgart: Hochschuleverlag.

Spolsky B. (1985) What does it mean to know how to use a language? An essay on the theoretical basis of language testing. *Language Testing*, **2**, 180–91.

Spolsky B. (1986) A multiple choice for language testers. *Language Testing*, **3**, 147–58.

Stansfield C. (1986) A history of the Test of Written English: The developmental year. *Language Testing*, **3**, 224–34.

Sunderland J., Yixing Z. & Barr B. (1988) 'To be an explainer': A reporting test of oral proficiency. *English Language Teaching Journal*, **42**, 28–33.

Swinton S. S. & Powers D. E. (1980) Factor analysis of the TOEFL for several language groups. *TOEFL Research Report No. 6*. Princeton, NJ: Educational Testing Service.

Woods A. & Baker R. (1985) Item response theory. *Language Testing*, **2**, 119–40.

20 Innovation and the influence of research

Rather than suppose that persuasive research findings have necessarily precipitated change, it is more realistic to ask how influential they have been in bringing about innovations and in shaping them. That changes can occur quite innocently of research evidence is well known. When the decision to introduce GCSE was taken, it was still not known whether differentiated papers could be made to work technically so as to deliver equity to candidates. The indications were, if anything, negative, although perhaps the rather ragged state of the research portfolio after 14 years (1972–86) was more damning of the researchers than of the decision-makers.

The interesting thing about GCSE is that it was only after the decision was taken that serious, intensive research got under way, notably the Novel Examining at 16+ project at SEG. Perhaps it is only when a change is announced, preparations for it are made and awareness is raised, that serious research becomes possible. Those of us who tried to do research on 16+ examinations in the 1970s were frustrated by our inability to create any kind of verisimilitude (with the exception of the Welsh Board where the right structure already existed).

At any rate, the GCSE experience suggests that a function of research, perhaps the primary function at least in the context of examinations, is to provide a resource after the event; as a means of discovering how the change is being received, as an exercise in finding ways of helping people cope, in other words, making the change work, and beyond that as a strategy for legitimating the change itself. Research done prior to the change would then be viewed against the yardstick embodied in the question 'Is there anything we know which indicates strongly, perhaps irresistibly, that this innovation would be harmful?' Choosing to look negatively at research evidence is quite appropriate in any case, since we would rather have false negatives than false positives. In the case of a false positive where prior research almost certainly did bring about change, or at the very least shaped a climate of opinion – Bennett's work on teaching styles and open classrooms – misplaced optimism had to give way a few years later to, if not a recantation, then a much more cautious reading of the evidence (Aitkin, Bennett & Hesketh 1981).

To examine whether the history of innovation in British examinations bears out the 'act first, research afterwards' manner of proceeding, it is necessary to look at what I take to be the two greatest innovations of the past 30 years – the introduction of multiple choice testing and the introduction of school-based assessment. The other great innovation may be the one we are seeing now, that is graded assessment, but it is too early to tell, Christie's (1989) remarks notwithstanding.

At the end of the 1950s, multiple choice testing was well enough known in the context of the 11+. This use had been legitimated by the work of people like Ballard in the 1920s, and the development in the 1930s of psychological tests like Raven's Progressive Matrices. But multiple choice had not found its way into examinations. We have it from Nuttall (1974) that in 1963 there were very few objective tests in British public examinations; the JMB used an objective test in its General Studies examination at A level, but there were none at O level. In 1965, the London Board entered the field with objective tests set on the Nuffield Science syllabuses. Nuttall's opinion as to why this came about is interesting. The effect of the behavioural objectives movement (inaugurated by Bloom's *Taxonomy*) was to identify constituent parts of achievement which are ideally suited to objective testing and it was the Nuffield Science schemes that largely pioneered in this country detailed consideration of the aims and educational objectives of science courses. The connection is also seen quite clearly in the JMB's decision to adopt multiple choice for examining science subjects at A level (JMB 1970).

This is a plausible reconstruction. It says that multiple choice came in on the coat-tails of behavioural objectives. At that time the (American) research portfolio on multiple choice was quite extensive; after all the SAT had been running for nearly 40 years. All the questions College Board and ETS had asked themselves in the beginning, and over the subsequent years, must have been answered satisfactorily, or so it would have appeared. For the British examination boards to have said 'This will be harmful' would have been to fly in the face of the American experience. Besides, the computer technology which the Americans had developed was now becoming available. In particular, access to machines which would score answer sheets, which Lindquist had invented at the University of Iowa back in 1950 (Peterson 1983), was now possible.

There is a very real sense in which in Britain in 1965 the technology was primed for multiple choice. It is a pity that there has been so little exploitation of the computer in examining once automated scoring and data processing procedures had been implemented.

Multiple choice may have passed muster in 1963 but, where behavioural objectives were concerned, the research evidence for the authenticity of Bloom's *Taxonomy* was scanty or non-existent (chapter 1). Even the first attempt at validating the hierarchical structure (Kropp, Stoker & Bashaw 1966) had not yet appeared. Taking on the *Taxonomy* was a real act of faith, justified at the time (not unfairly) as a necessary move if teachers' and examiners' notions of what was to be taught and assessed were to be clarified and reconceptualised so as to benefit students.

So, multiple choice was introduced. London gradually extended it to other subjects, not without controversy, especially with respect to O level English Language, and other boards followed suit. The monograph by Vernon, published by the Schools Council as an Examinations Bulletin (Vernon 1964), no doubt helped to legitimate the technique. Subsequently, multiple choice has been the subject of research, albeit of a desultory nature. If it has achieved respectability it has been through the passage of time, rather than through any thorough investigations of its properties. By and large, it can be said that this particular innovation goes down as an example of 'act first, research afterwards', with the proviso that American experience with multiple choice, practical and research, and with computer applications, served as a kind of security collateral. Were the clock to be wound forward to today, that notion of collateral could not be supported. There is deep disenchantment with multiple choice, or rather with the extent to which standardised testing in schools using MCQ has been allowed to grow unchecked (Haney & Madaus 1989). The search is on for what is being called 'authentic' measurement (Neill & Medina 1989; McLean 1990), which in this case (but see chapter 19) seems to boil down to portfolios of students' work marked by their teachers. This latest call is coming fully 30 years or more since standardised tests were pressed as an alternative to teachers' grades. *Plus ça change*...

With school-based assessment no such collateral existed, American or otherwise; certainly not in America, as just explained. Given that school-based examining was meant to be something more than the prediction of examination results, there was no research to go on. The political decision to establish the CSE examination created overnight the phenomenon of school-based assessment. Here is a prime example of research being done afterwards, something which continues to this day. In this effort the Schools Council Examinations Bulletin series was again influential, as Nuttall notes, whether in raising consciousness, summarising research to date, reporting the results of experiments or in fostering generally a state of readiness for innovation, even if that innovation had already occurred. In fact, as we know, the state of readiness was ultimately for school-based assessment on the scale now seen in GCSE, which far exceeds anything operationalised in 1965 or even proposed.

Twenty-five years on, it has to be said, the research questions we would like answered about school-based assessment, remain on the table (chapter 6). They are the same as they always were. Are teachers assessing something complementary or supplementary to external examinations, or merely replicating it? Are they assessing ability (IQ) or achievement? Or, maybe, industry? What is the payoff from all the extra samplings of achievement they can make, compared to external examiners? If teachers award higher grades than those their students obtain in examinations, is this merely to be construed as leniency, or are there other interpretations which derive from the quality of teaching? What extraneous factors affect teachers as they make assessments, and how determining are they? And so on. If an extension of the 'act first, research afterwards' model is that the research be done quickly and incisively so as to fulfil the functions asked of it, that is monitoring, comforting and legitimating, then it is evident that school-based assessment falls far short.

Whether or not graded assessment turns out to be a major innovation, the manner in which it is being handled does not exactly conform with the 'act first, research afterwards' model. The strategy of introducing it on an experimental basis represents a sort of compromise in which research is done while acting – action research! As things stand, the external observer is more aware of graded assessment being propelled rather by rampant boosterism, of which Christie's remarks are typical (see also chapter 7), than by a following wind of supporting data.

The SSCC study is disappointing in many respects (see chapter 7) but it did perform the valuable service of flagging up what would need to be done to make graded assessment work as intended. In that respect, it should be seen as a necessary corrective to boosterism. Otherwise, the only glimmer of a counterperspective comes from Nuttall & Goldstein (1984) who discuss various technical problems certain to be encountered in graded assessment. They call for a different kind of research from 'the sort of detailed technical research of the type that has been done for 50 years on existing examination systems', although my view would be that we have not had enough of that (the good variety at any rate).

If it is clear that innovation is not driven by research, and that the reverse may frequently be true, there remain some pointed questions about innovation which beg to be explored. It cannot be enough to say that innovation is driven largely by something called political will, and that is that, making questions about whether innovation is necessary or desirable superfluous. As long as innovations continue to occur, it is important to understand how they happened, and whether they were actually necessary, if only to appreciate how marginal the part research evidence plays in the decision.

An orderly approach to the topic requires that there be some principles for deciding the necessity for change. Without going quite that far, Alderson (1986) produced what he called a set of 'guidelines for innovators', organised as a series of questions. He was writing in the context of language testing, but his questions, or most of them, are quite applicable to innovation in assessment and testing as a whole. In what follows I have used all but one of them. My responses to the questions are less firm answers as commentaries, using examples from British examining and testing, and also picking up remarks Alderson himself has made.

Are the changes that are claimed to be innovations actually new? Alderson may legitimately wonder whether there is anything new under the sun, but when multiple choice was introduced it was new; not new in the sense that no one had ever seen it before because it was used in 11+ and in psychological tests, but new in the sense of being based on a radically different assessment rationale from essay tests. Any judgement on newness must be conditioned by the state of progress in the particular sphere of application. When Alderson remarks that the history of language teaching is littered with ideas that have been rediscovered by subsequent generations and reintroduced in a new guise, usually without acknowledgement of the origins of the idea, it is possible to echo him to the hilt as someone who has suffered in that regard, but when I complain, as I do (chapter 8), of the propensity of science and medical educators to reinvent the multiple choice wheel, or of language testers who suddenly discover IRT (chapter 19), I have to accept that these are innovations for them. Likewise, for UCLES to introduce the Academic Aptitude Profiles hardly seems an innovation when TAA has gone before, (chapter 17), but it would be an innovation because TAA was never operational, and also because no examining board will have done anything like it (including the JMB with its General Studies test).

Alderson may have had in mind the innovation that appears new, but is not actually new because it has been lying around for some time waiting to be discovered or given an application. A good example is linear scaling of marks which is now being put forward by Cresswell & Good (chapters 6, 10 and 13) as the preferred method for dealing with differentiated paper marks and for moderating school assessments. This is a topic with a long history and the fact is that examining boards could, and should, have been scaling paper marks for years, whether by linear scaling or by some other method, as a matter of routine.

Does it matter whether the innovations are new, provided that they actually work? This is Alderson's second question, and the answer, as he says, is inevitably 'No'. This leads him to the major question, which he says remains unanswered: Do the innovations, be they old or new, actually work? And if they actually work, do they work better than what they replace? And if they do not work better, then why would one wish to introduce change?

These are complex questions, as Alderson acknowledges, unlikely to permit unequivocal answers. Alderson subdivides the major question into a series of questions, not all of which I am reproducing here:

1 Does the innovation predict better what it is supposed to predict?
2 Does the innovation have a better effect on the teaching or the learning, however we choose to measure or observe this?
3 Is the innovation more acceptable to experts (theorists and professionals in teaching and testing) and also to the 'lay public'?
4 Is the innovation more efficient – that is does it give the same or similar results with less effort, or with less time or money devoted to administration or scoring?
5 Does the innovation involve less training, fewer specialists to produce, administer, score and interpret?

(1) is a question which could be asked of the Academic Aptitude Profiles. Enthusiasts for graded assessment believe that, for it, the answer to (2) and to (3) is affirmative, although they may not have considered question (5). Question (4) they would discard as irrelevant. For multiple choice a clear answer to (2) has never materialised. Perhaps a 'better' effect has never been expected, rather the hope has been that the damage will not have proved too great. It is in the answer to (4) that it is, of course, most directly justified.

Applying the questions to school-based assessment throws up an interesting pattern of answers. (1) is not supposed to be answered but it nevertheless gets addressed. The answer to (2) is usually 'Yes' except that there have been complaints from learners (and teachers) about the extra work GCSE school-based assessment has brought with it. (3) has invariably attracted a 'Yes' from theorists, at least in principle, but not always from teachers and not always from the lay public. The answer to (4) is surely 'No', except that the object is not to produce the same result, although 'similar' might suffice. (5) is likewise a 'No', given that school-based assessment in the GCSE has created a veritable army of auxiliary examiners.

It was noted earlier that it is difficult, if not impossible, to properly vet an innovation and its likely effects before its introduction, at least when it is anything other than an armchair exercise, such as investigating linear scaling. It does seem that to find out whether innovations actually work or will work, you have to introduce them first, whether overnight, like differentiated papers, or in creeping fashion, like graded assessments.

Do we know that the instruments or techniques that we supposedly replaced by the innovation actually do not work adequately? What is the nature of the evidence? This is the other side of the coin. Unless it has only been introduced recently, it must be possible to know whether what is in place works adequately or not. And yet there are practices of many years' standing where we are still in the dark. Suppose another model of achievement came along to challenge Bloom's *Taxonomy* and its adaptations (and why should it not?); would we be in any position to evaluate whether the *Taxonomy* should be thrown out? Or, to take another example, is it known well enough how paper marking arrangements stand up in terms of keeping error to acceptable limits? I am afraid we often know as little about what we are replacing, or choose to leave alone, as about what we regard as innovations, and in that respect it is often not possible to get an answer to the question as posed.

Might there be a need for innovation even if what is being replaced does work? Is there, in short, a value in change for its own sake? Alderson asks whether change might actually revive the interest and enthusiasm of both teachers and students, regardless of the nature of other benefits deriving from the innovation. No doubt there have been examples of such change in the annals of examining, where subjects have been jazzed up or relaunched. Whether they have revived flagging energies is probably unknown.

The other side of the question is whether some tests or methods or practices are shuffled off before their time. In the course of a nice exposition of the life cycle of a test (3–5 years to become established, 5–8 years as acceptable, finally senescence in the shape of criticism that the test is exerting a restrictive influence on the teaching), Alderson cites as an example the JMB's Test in English (Overseas). Having been in existence (in 1986) for ten years, the feeling is abroad that it is time for a change. Yet, says Alderson, the Board lacks any evidence that such change is necessary and there are few indications from test performance, as opposed to changes in thinking in language teaching, that any change is needed.

The point is well taken. It would be a pity, however, if awareness of the possibility of premature retirement were to encourage the sort of conservative outlook summed up by 'Better the devil you know'.

Why do innovations come about? Who demands and causes them, and on what basis? Citing political will is no good. The answers are many and various. The idea for the subject 'Applicable Mathematics' which the London Board ran for a few years came up from a lobby belonging to the mathematics and statistics teaching profession. Incidentally, it is an example of an innovation which replaced nothing, and when it went, nothing came to replace it. 'Why do innovations not come about?' is an equally good question. If I had my way I would change the way papers are marked, which is essentially a cottage industry, to a system where markers are brought together to participate in a properly designed, modern marking procedure (see the latter part of chapter 5). That would be an innovation which I reckon would be an improvement on what happens now, and I could bring forward research evidence to back me up. In fact, it is as good a candidate for an immediate innovation as I can think of. Why does it not happen? Is it that the examining boards see no percentage in doing it, a reason which would, without being unduly cynical, apply to most prospective innovations? That makes even more fascinating why we see the innovations we do.

Leaving Alderson's questions behind, a quick fix on how much innovation has occurred in examination offerings over the 20 years up to the first year of GCSE can be gained by looking at the make-up of the same subject examination at ten-year intervals. I have done this for UCLES, using for reference the regulations for 1967, 1977 and 1987 (UCLES 1965, 1975, 1985). Thus, it is only a partial picture and I have no idea what it would be like for other GCE boards, though I imagine it would be much the same since the boards generally kept in step during this period.

There are two striking impressions. The first is that the number of papers has increased by one and that this has happened because of the introduction of multiple choice. Otherwise the total testing time has remained the same, or much the same. The second is that most change occurred between 1967 and 1977 with little apparently happening between 1977 and 1987. Perhaps the prospect of GCSE put a stop to innovation.

O level Chemistry in 1967 consisted of a written paper ($2\frac{1}{2}$ hours) and a practical test (timing not given but probably 2 hours). By 1977 the written paper had been split into a multiple choice paper (1 hour) and a theory paper ($1\frac{1}{2}$ hours), with a practical test (2 hours). Through to 1987 this provision remained constant. The same pattern occurs with Biology. In Physics there has been, on the face of it, no change at all. In 1967, two papers ($2\frac{1}{2}$ hours and 2 hours), and the same in 1987.

English Language O level also follows the same pattern. In 1967 it was two papers of $1\frac{1}{2}$ hours each; in 1977, three papers of 1, $1\frac{1}{2}$ and 1 hour; in 1987, unchanged. Economic and Public Affairs at O level is slightly different. In 1967 it was a single $2\frac{1}{2}$-hour paper divided into two sections. By 1977 the $2\frac{1}{2}$ hours had been split into $\frac{1}{2}$ hour for a short answer paper, and 2 hours for another paper. In 1987, the $\frac{1}{2}$ hour had been increased to 1 hour, a change but hardly an innovation.

At Advanced level the pattern in the sciences is similar with three papers going into four. In 1967 it was two papers (each $2\frac{1}{2}$ hours) with a 3-hour practical. In 1977 the two papers, and the five hours, had been redistributed into an essay paper ($2\frac{1}{2}$ hours), a short answer structured questions paper ($1\frac{1}{2}$ hours) and a multiple choice paper (1 hour). In addition, an individual studies paper based on a project had been added. In 1987, this offering still held good, except that a teacher-assessed practical option had been added. Whether the last counts as an innovation, given that Nuffield had gone before, is a moot point.

Obviously, this is a superficial external check and a thorough-going analysis would need to look at the contents and formats of the papers over the years. It would appear, however, that major innovations have been few, and indeed are the ones already mentioned – multiple choice (and the *Taxonomy* on whose back it rode), school-based assessment latterly, to which might be added structured questions and projects. A short answer to the question 'Why did examinations look the way they did in 1987?' would be 'Because multiple choice came along'. This is not to say that there should have been many more innovations, and some will think this list quite honourable. If a guiding principle for deciding on the composition of an examination is to assess candidates by as many different methods and modalities as possible, then the innovation most obviously absent is assessment of competence through speech but, as we know (chapter 19), that innovation must still be some way off.

The influence of research evidence on change, if it is there at all, is going to be present in small ways – in the choice of item types, in the wording of instructions (perhaps), in the wording of multiple choice items. If I take the contribution to date to be modest, it need not be so in future. A serious attempt at the research programme I have outlined at the end would be bound to have an impact even if the environment is not wholly supportive.

If I were pushed into coming up with a prescription for an idealised examination, it would look something like this:

assessment conceived in developmental terms so as to identify attainment at various levels of acquisition;
assessment of multiple modalities and by multiple methods;
clear instructions, with opportunity to clarify at outset;
adequate time limits;
imaginative modifications for the disabled;

specifications published and defended;
mark schemes published and defended;
marking methods described and defended;
reliabilities estimated;
subgroup differences reported and interpreted;
validation attempted;
scaling of marks before aggregation and grading;
more exploitation of computers;
reports written regularly on examinations or clusters of them.

The research programme I have drawn up from what I spotted as outstanding business while compiling the chapters speaks directly to the idealisation. Of all that needs to be done I regard as paramount the reconceptualisation of achievement in developmental terms, as outlined by Messick (1984) and Glaser (1986). The notion of achievement as knowledge in pieces, to borrow di Sessa's term (chapter 13), is something we inherited from Binet, and we ought to throw it away in favour of an integrated body of knowledge and understanding evolving over time.

In setting out the lines of work, I have used short descriptions which will have to be filled out by reference to the relevant chapters where, hopefully, the need to try has been substantiated. Obviously, each line of work could, and should, be translated into a costed research proposal, but that would be going beyond the bounds of this survey.

Chapter 1 Preparing specifications for achievement tests
Reconceptualisation of achievement in developmental terms
Validation work
Reproducibility experiments – same specification, different examinations?
System maintenance reports on how exams are meeting desiderata

Chapter 2 Selecting and ordering of questions and question choice
Understanding what makes an item difficult – complex or obscure?
Protecting equity where there is choice
Discarding choice

Chapter 3 Administrative issues
Improving rubrics and instructions
Provision for disabled
Proper timing
Training in test-taking
Open book exams
Use of electronic calculators

Chapter 4 Multiple choice testing
Instructions, simple but penetrative
Multiple matching items
Exercising control in item writing (following Gagné)
How partial knowledge is utilised as, for instance, through the answer-until-correct format

Chapter 5 Essay questions
Wording of questions
Validation of analytical marking and the multitrait conceptualisation
Designed experiments in real time for essay marking
Applicability of IRT models to scoring, (e.g. partial credit models)

Chapter 6 School-based assessment including Records of Achievement
Appropriateness of tasks as set by the teacher
Investigating teacher bias
Are teachers rating ability, or achievement, or industry?
Constructing clear criteria for self-assessment when compiling records of achievement
Effects of linear scaling (Good's preferred method) at the school level

Chapter 7 Criterion-referenced testing including graded assessment
How do grade-related criteria get translated into criterion-referenced examinations?
Graded assessment, in all its aspects

Chapter 8 Diagnostic assessment
Devising new kinds of instrument with developmental orientation
Error analysis
Subskill differentiation checks (profile authentication)
Follow-up materials for teachers

Chapter 9 Item analysis
Applicability and utility of item response modelling methods

Chapter 10 Scoring, weighting, combining and scaling
Evaluating the DAATE project
Linear vs. equipercentile scaling (the issue is far from being settled)
Scaling of differentiated papers
Weighting formulas – will Govindarajulu's do?

Chapter 11 Reliability
Generalisability studies, extended to school-based assessment
Reliability studies of the conventional kind

Chapter 12 Validity and validation

Construct validity studies (multitrait, multimethod)

Validation of the naming of skills

Chapter 13 Differentiation

Two-stage testing

Training examiners in how to get mark value equivalence from one paper to another

Training examiners to target skills

Equating papers

Grading modular arrangements

Chapter 14 Bias

Format or question mode, especially short-answer questions and school-based assessment

More generally, have any candidates been disadvantaged by format or mode?

Checks on paper contents with a view to picking up sexism, and racism

Aptitude test studies – gender, minorities, differential validities

Chapter 15 How practical work is assessed

How many students per group?

What kind of recording protocols?

Check assumptions about mastery of basic skills

Testing of observation

Validation of subskill differentiation; clear working definitions of the various skills

Chapter 16 Assessing individuals working collaboratively in groups

What reward formula to adopt?

Exploration of 1:1 interviewing

Peer assessment

Chapter 17 Aptitude testing

Continuing validation work on the model of SAT and LSAT

Individualised testing

Relationship between predictors and criteria and, especially, criterion reliability

Monitor functioning of item types

Chapter 18 Personnel selection and assessment

Structuring of interviews

Biodata instrument development

Work samples and trainability tests

Combination of methods

Joint relationship of ability and job experience to job performance

Chapter 19 Language testing
Test development to improve validity–reliability trade-off
Assessment of competence **through** speech

References

Aitkin M., Bennett S. N. & Hesketh J. (1981). Teaching styles and pupil progress: A reanalysis. *British Journal of Educational Psychology*, **51**, 170–86.

Alderson J. C. (1986) Innovations in language testing? In Portal M. (ed.) *Innovations in Language Testing*. Windsor: NFER-Nelson.

Christie T. (1989) Remarks quoted in: Assessment boom 'will end' GCSE exam. *Times Educational Supplement*, 3rd February, A4.

Glaser R. (1986) The integration of testing and instruction. In *The Redesign of Testing for the 21st Century: Proceedings of the 1985 ETS Invitational Conference*. Princeton, NJ: Educational Testing Service.

Haney W. & Madaus G. (1989) Searching for alternatives to standardized tests: Whys, whats and whithers. *Phi Delta Kappan*, **70**, 683–7.

Joint Matriculation Board (1970) Examining in Advanced level science subjects of the GCE. *JMB OP 30*. Manchester: JMB.

Kropp R. P., Stoker H. W. & Bashaw W. L. (1966) The validation of the taxonomy of educational objectives. *Journal of Experimental Education*, **34**, 69–76.

McLean L. D. (1990) Time to replace the classroom test with authentic measurement. *Alberta Journal of Educational Research*, **36**, 78–84.

Messick S. (1984) The psychology of educational measurement. *Journal of Educational Measurement*, **21**, 215–37.

Neill D. M. & Medina N. J. (1989) Standardized testing: Harmful to educational health. *Phi Delta Kappan*, **70**, 688–97.

Nuttall D. L. (1974) Multiple-choice objective tests – a re-appraisal. *Conference Report No. 11*. University of London University Entrance and School Examinations Council, 28–36.

Nuttall D. L. & Goldstein H. (1984) Profiles and graded tests: The technical issues. In Mortimore J. (ed.) *Profiles in Action*. London: Further Education Unit, DES.

Peterson J. J. (1983) *The Iowa Testing Programs: The First Fifty Years*. Iowa City, IA: University of Iowa Press.

UCLES (1965) *General Certificate of Education: Regulations for the Examination 1967*. Cambridge: UCLES.

UCLES (1975) *General Certificate of Education: Regulations for the Examination 1977*. Cambridge: UCLES.

UCLES (1985) *General Certificate of Education: Examination Regulations for 1987*. Cambridge: UCLES.

Vernon P. E. (1964) The Certificate of Secondary Education: An Introduction to Objective-type Examinations. *Examinations Bulletin No. 4*. London: Secondary Schools Examination Council.

Glossary

* British institution/ organisation/ group/ initiative/ qualification/ term

ACT	American College Testing program
A level*	Advanced level examination (the highest level school examination)
AEB*	Associated Examining Board
ANOVA	Analysis of variance
APU*	Assessment of Performance Unit (run by the DES)
CPRA*	Cambridge Partnership for Records of Achievement (run by UCLES)
CRE*	Commission for Racial Equality
CRT	Criterion-referenced testing
CSC*	Civil Service Commission
CSE*	Certificate of Secondary Education (replaced by GCSE in 1988)
CSSB*	Civil Service Selection Board
DAATE*	Decision Analytic Aids to Examining project
DAT	Differential Aptitude Test battery (published by The Psychological Corporation)
DES*	Department of Education and Science
DHSS*	Department of Health and Social Security
DIME*	Differentiation in MEG Examinations project (run by MEG)
DRP	Degrees of Reading Power test
ELTS*	English Language Testing Service (run by UCLES and the British Council)
EOQT*	Executive Officer Qualifying Test (run by CSC)
EQ*	Educational qualifications
ETS	Educational Testing Service
GACDT*	Graded Assessment in Control, Design and Technology
GAIM*	Graded Assessment in Mathematics
GAMLL*	Graded Assessment in Modern Language Learning
GASP*	Graded Assessment in Science Project

GCE*	General Certificate of Education
GCSE*	General Certificate of Secondary Education
GMA*	Graduate and Managerial Assessment (tests published by NFER-Nelson)
GOML*	Graded Objectives in Modern Languages
GPA	Grade-point average
GRE	Graduate Record of Education (tests run by ETS)
HMI*	Her Majesty's Inspectorate
IEA	International Study of Educational Achievement
IGCSE*	International General Certificate of Secondary Education (run by UCLES)
IQ	Intelligence quotient
IRM	Item response modelling
IRT	Item response theory
ITBS	Iowa Test of Basic Skills
JMB*	Joint Matriculation Board
KMP*	Kent Mathematics Project
LEA*	Local education authority
LEAG*	London and East Anglia Examining Group
LSAC	Law School Admission Council
LSAS	Law School Admission Services
LSAT	Law School Admissions Test
MBA	Master of Business Administration
MCQ	Multiple choice questions
MEG*	Midland Examining Group (UCLES is a member)
NCDS*	National Child Development Study
NCTE	National Council of Teachers in English
NFER*	National Foundation for Research in England and Wales
OCEA*	Oxford Certificate of Educational Achievement
O level*	Ordinary level examination (replaced by GCSE in 1988)
OE	Open-ended question
PRAISE*	Pilot Records of Achievement in Schools Evaluation
RANSC*	Records of Achievement National Steering Committee
RoA*	Record of Achievement
RRU*	Recruitment Research Unit (run by CSC)
RTITB*	Road Transport Industry Training Board
SAT	Scholastic Aptitude Test (run by ETS)
SEC*	Secondary Examinations Council, now SEAC
SEG*	Southern Examining Group
SES*	Socio-economic status
SMP*	School Mathematics Project
SSCC*	Secondary Schools Curriculum Council (replaced by SEC)

TAA*	Test of Academic Aptitude (defunct)
TDRU*	Test Development and Research Unit (defunct, was run jointly by UCLES, Oxford Delegacy of Local Examinations, and Oxford and Cambridge Schools Examination Board)
TGAT*	Task Group on Assessment and Testing (set up by DES)
TOEFL	Test of English as a Foreign Language (run by ETS)
UCLES*	University of Cambridge Local Examinations Syndicate
ULSEB*	University of London School Examinations Board
WJEC*	Welsh Joint Examinations Committee

Index